About the Author

Dana Facaros is a professional trave
lived in several countries, concentratii
with her husband Michael Pauls she I
on, amongst others, Italy, Spain, Fran
Greek Islands; her father comes from
now in its seventh edition, was first pu

C000301392

Acknowledgements

A big *efcháristo parapolí* to my ever-affable hosts extraordinaire and experts on the Greek condition, Michael and Brian; and many thanks to all the people on the various island tourist offices who lent a hand. Also a heartfelt round of applause to Kate for her diligent editing.

Please Help Us Keep This Guide Up to Date

We have done our best to ensure that the information in this guide is correct at the time of going to press. But places and facilities are constantly changing, and standards and prices fluctuate. We would be delighted to receive any comments concerning existing entries or omissions. Authors of the best letters will receive a copy of a Cadogan Guide of their choice.

Contents

The Islands   141–230

Language   231–39

Glossary of Terms   240

Index   241–48

Maps

The furthest archipelago from mainland Greece, the Dodecanese (ΔΩΔΕΚΑΝΗΣΑ), meaning 'twelve islands' (although there are actually 16 inhabited ones, and even that depends on how you count them), weren't added to Greece until 1948, although union only confirmed a sense of national identity, language, religion and traditions their inhabitants kept smouldering on the home fires for centuries. But their distance from the mainland and long separation from the mainstream of Greek history have dealt them a unique deck to play with—medieval knights, Ottoman Turks and 20th-century Italians, all of whom contributed to the distinct character

Introduction

and architecture of the Dodecanese. Add a sunny climate and long sandy beaches and the striking individualism of each island—including even one bright white Cycladic rock pile, Astypálaia—and the holiday possibilities on the Dodecanese are infinite, covering the gamut from the feverish high-calibre international resorts of Rhodes and Kos to the low-key, relaxed, very Greek pleasures of Lipsí, Chálki, Kárpathos or volcanic Níssyros. Striking Sými and Pátmos attract upmarket crowds; while Léros, Kálymnos and Tílos remain best-kept secrets of seasoned travellers. Kastellórizo has an end-of-the-world atmosphere that seems to draw more people every year; Kássos has a similar air but attracts nobody, if you're looking for a real getaway. Connections by ferry, hydrofoil and excursion boat are good between the islands, making it easy to get around and even to pop over to Turkey for a day or two.

Travel

1

Getting To and Around Greece and the Islands

The bible of travel to and around Greece is the *Greek Travel Pages*, updated monthly. Consult a copy at the National Tourist Organization or a travel agency specializing in Greece, or check out the website *www.ellada.com*.

By Air

'The air and sky are free,' Daedalus told son Icarus as he planned their ill-fated winged escape from Crete. They aren't free any more, but you can fly for less if you look around. As competition increases in Europe, don't automatically presume charter flights with their restrictions are your best buy; flying the Greek national carrier Olympic opens up very reasonable onward prices to island airports. Students or anyone under 26 will find the most bargains (*see* p.6). The good news is that you can fly 'open jaws' into one Greek airport and out of another. The bad news is that a Greek airport tax (£20 at the time of writing) is added on to some ticket prices.

Charter Flights

Charter flights to Athens, Rhodes and Kos are frequent in the summer from Europe, less frequent from North America and non-existent from Australasia. Europeans also have the luxury of charter flights direct to many islands (notably, from London Gatwick, Luton, Glasgow, Cardiff, Newcastle, Manchester, Belfast and Dublin). Check the travel sections in any of the major weekend papers, *Time Out*, or the *Evening Standard* for last-minute discounts on unsold seats, or ask for advice from your local travel agent or the specialists listed below. Most UK charters run from May to mid-October but some firms feature early specials in March and April depending on when Greek Easter falls, usually from London Gatwick and Manchester.

Charter tickets have fixed outward and return dates with often as not departure and arrival times in the wee hours. They are also governed by several restrictions. Tickets are valid for a minimum of three days and a maximum of six weeks and must be accompanied by an accommodation voucher stating the name and address of the hotel, villa or campsite; you don't really have to stay there. Although a formality, every so often there is a crackdown aimed at what the Greeks consider undesirables flouting the law. Because they subsidize airline landing fees they want to prevent charter flights being used as a cheap way to get to other countries, especially Turkey. If you come on a charter flight you may visit Turkey or any neighbouring country for the day, but don't stay overnight, at the very real risk of forfeiting your return ticket home. Travellers with stamps from previous holidays in Turkey will not be barred entry, but if you have Turkish Cypriot stamps check with the Passport Office before you go. Returning from Greece, make sure you confirm your return flight three days prior to departure.

Scheduled Flights from the UK and Ireland

Scheduled flights direct to Athens operate several times daily from London on **Olympic**, **British Airways** and **Virgin Atlantic**. East European companies like **Czech Airlines** also fly to Athens and can work out cheaper in season, but you may have to wait for hours for connections in Prague and supply your own drinks and peanuts. Apex and Superapex flights offer substantially reduced fares, with flights from London to Athens ranging from £190 low season to £280 high season. They must, however, be paid for instantly and are not refundable or flexible. Rates range from £212 return midweek in low season to £298 weekends in high.

Scheduled flights from Ireland to Athens on Olympic and Aer Lingus fly via Heathrow and tend to be considerably pricier than charters.

Olympic Airways	London ✆ (0171) 409 3400 Dublin ✆ (01) 608 0090
British Airways	London ✆ (0181) 897 4000 Belfast ✆ (0345) 222 111 Dublin ✆ (1 800) 626 747
easyJet	UK (0990) 292929
Aer Lingus	Belfast ✆ (01232) 314844 Dublin ✆ (01) 844 4777
Virgin Atlantic	UK ✆ (01293) 747747
Czech Airlines	London ✆ (0171) 409 3400

discounts and special deals

Alecos Tours, ✆ (0171) 267 2092. Olympic Airways consolidator.

Avro, ✆ (0181) 715 0000. Charter and scheduled flights to Athens and major islands from London Gatwick and Luton, Manchester, Glasgow, Cardiff, Newcastle and Birmingham.

Balkan Tours, ✆ (01232) 246 795. Charter flights direct from Belfast.

Delta Travel, ✆ (0161) 272 8455; ✆ (0151) 708 7955; ✆ (0121) 471 2282. Manchester-based agents for scheduled flights from Heathrow to Athens; and from Manchester and Birmingham for Athens; wide range of island charters.

Island Wandering, ✆ (01580) 860733. Reasonable schedules to Athens, island packages and 'open jaws' routes. Use Olympic Airways flights.

Joe Walsh Tours, ✆ (01) 676 3053. Budget fares from Dublin.

Eclipse Direct, ✆ (01293) 554400; (0161) 742 2277. Flights from Gatwick, Manchester and Birmingham.

Sunset Air Fares, ✆ (01204) 701 111. Bolton-based agent with charters to the islands.

Teleticket, ✆ (01293) 567 640. Good for excess charter seats from Gatwick to Athens: cheap but often excruciating early arrivals.

Trailfinders, one of the best for finding affordable flights. London ✆ (0171) 937 5400; Bristol ✆ (0117) 929 9000; Birmingham ✆ (0121) 236 1234; Manchester ✆ (0161) 839 6969; Glasgow ✆ (0141) 353 2224.

Scheduled Flights from North America

Olympic, **TWA** and **Delta** offer daily nonstop flights from New York to Athens in the summer; Olympic also flies direct to Athens from Atlanta, Boston and Chicago several times a week depending on the season, and offers connecting flights from Dallas, Detroit, Houston, Los Angeles, Miami, Philadelphia, San Francisco and Washington DC; from Canada Olympic flies direct to Athens from Toronto and Montreal, with connecting flights from Vancouver and Calgary. Usually cheaper **Tower Air** flies direct from New York to Athens two or three times a week. American economy fares (Apex and Superapex/Eurosavers, booked at least three weeks in advance) range from $760 return New York–Athens in low season to $1200 high season; Canadian economy fares to Athens from Toronto or Montreal range from $1020 low season to $1350 high season. When ringing around, take into consideration the large discount Olympic offers its international passengers on flights to the islands; at the time of writing, only $100 US will take you on to any domestic destination in Greece.

From many cities in the USA and Canada, European airlines such as **KLM** or **Czech Airlines** offer the best deals to Greece. If you have more time than money, get a cheap or standby flight to London and once there hunt up a cheap ticket to an island (*see* above) although this may be a headache in July or August.

Olympic Airways	USA ✆ (800) 838 3600
	in Canada: Montreal ✆ (514) 878 9691
	Toronto ✆ (416) 920 2452
Delta	USA ✆ (800) 241 414
Air Canada	Canada ✆ (800) 555 1212
	USA ✆ (800) 776 3000
KLM	USA ✆ (800) 374 7747
	Canada ✆ (800) 361 5330
Tower Air	USA ✆ (800) 34 TOWER
TWA	USA ✆ (800) 892 4141

Czech Airlines	USA ℡ (800) 223 2365
British Airways	USA ℡ (800) 247 9297
	Canada ℡ (800) 668 1055

discounts and special deals

New Frontiers, USA ℡ (800) 366 6387; Montreal ℡ (514) 526 8444.

Travel Avenue, USA ℡ (800) 333 3335.

Air Brokers International, USA ℡ (800) 883 3273. Discount agency.

Council Charter, USA ℡ (800) 223 7402. Charter specialists.

Homeric Tours, USA ℡ (800) 223 5570, ℻ 753 0319. Charter flights and custom tours.

Last Minute Travel Club, USA ℡ (800) 527 8646. Annual membership fee gets you cheap standby deals.

Encore Travel Club, USA ℡ (800) 444 9800. Scheduled flight discount club.

Scheduled Flights from Australasia

Olympic flies at least twice a week direct to Athens from Melbourne and Sydney, and if their fares aren't the cheapest, consider the discounts the Greek carrier offers international passengers on its domestic flights. Other carriers include Qantas, Singapore Airlines, Aeroflot, KLM, Thai Airways, British Airways and Gulf Air. Prices in low season (Nov–Mar) average around $2000, $2350 at other times. There are no direct flights from New Zealand, but Air New Zealand, Qantas, Singapore Airlines or Alitalia will get you there with only one stop en route. If you can pick up a bargain flight to London it may work out cheaper to take that and find a discount flight from there (*see* above).

Olympic Airlines	Sydney and Brisbane toll free ℡ (008) 221 663
	Melbourne ℡ (008) 9331448
	Adelaide ℡ (008) 331 448
	(no office in New Zealand).
Thai Airways	Australia ℡ (1 800) 422 02
	Auckland ℡ (09) 377 3886
British Airways	Sydney ℡ (02) 9258 3300
	Auckland ℡ (09) 356 8690
Singapore Airlines	Sydney ℡ (02) 9236 0144
	Auckland ℡ (09) 379 3209
KLM	Australia ℡ (1 800) 505 474
Aeroflot	Sydney ℡ (02) 9233 7911
Alitalia	Sydney ℡ (02) 9247 1308
	Auckland ℡ (09) 366 1855

Qantas	International reservations 131211
	Auckland ✆ (09) 357 8900
Air New Zealand	✆ (09) 303 5826
Gulf Air	Sydney ✆ (02) 9321 9199

discounts and special deals

Flight Centres, Sydney ✆ (02) 9241 2422; Melbourne ✆ (03) 650 2899; Auckland ✆ (09) 209 6171; Christchurch ✆ (03) 379 7145.

Brisbane Discount Travel, in Brisbane ✆ (07) 3229 9211.

UTAG Travel, Sydney, ✆ (02) 956 8399 and branches in other Australian cities.

Budget Travel, Auckland, toll free ✆ (0 800) 808 040.

From Africa

Olympic flies three times a week from Johannesburg by way of Nairobi to Athens; in Johannesburg ✆ (880) 4120, ✆ (880) 7075; Cape Town, ✆ (021) 230 260, ✆ 244 166; Nairobi, ✆ 219 532.

Student and Youth Travel

If you're under 26 or a full-time student under 32 with an **International Student Identity Card** to prove it, you're eligible for **student/youth charters**; these are exempt from the voucher system and are often sold as one-way tickets, enabling you to stay in Greece longer than is possible with a regular charter flight. Students under 26 are sometimes eligible for discounts on scheduled flights as well; especially with Olympic Airways who currently offer 25% discount to ISIC card holders on all connecting flights from Athens to the islands. Young people of Greek origin (age 10–15) may be eligible for Gold Card discounts (contact your country's Greek National Tourist Office). Specialists in youth and student travel include:

Campus Travel, 52 Grosvenor Gdns SW1W, London, ✆ (0171) 730 3402; with branches at most UK universities: Leeds ✆ (0113) 246 1155; Bradford ✆ (01274) 383261; Bristol ✆ (0117) 929 2494; Manchester ✆ (0161) 833 2046; Edinburgh ✆ (0131) 668 3303; Birmingham ✆ (0121) 414 1848; Oxford ✆ (01865) 242067; Cambridge ✆ (01223) 324283. Runs own youth charters to Athens in summer.

STA Travel, 86 Old Brompton Rd, London SW7 3LH or 117 Euston Road NW1 2SX, ✆ (0171) 361 6161; Bristol ✆ (0117) 929 4399; Leeds ✆ (0113) 244 9212; Manchester ✆ (0161) 834 0668; Oxford ✆ (01865) 792800; Cambridge ✆ (01223) 366966 and many other branches in the UK.
USA: New York City ✆ (212) 627 3111.
Outside New York ✆ (1 800) 777 0112.
Australia: Sydney ✆ (02) 9212 1255; elsewhere ✆ (1 800) 637 444.

USIT, Aston Quay, Dublin 2 ✆ (01) 679 8833; Cork ✆ (021) 270 900; Belfast ✆ (01232) 324 073; Galway ✆ (091) 565 177; Limerick ✆ (061) 415 064; Waterford ✆ (051) 72601. **Ireland**'s largest student travel agents.

Council Travel, 205 E. 42nd St, New York, NY 10017, ✆ (800) 743 1823. Major specialist in student and charter flights; branches all over the **US**. In the **UK**, 28 Poland St, London W1V 3DB, ✆ (0171) 437 7767.

Travel Cuts, 187 College St, Toronto, Ontario M5T 1P7, ✆ (416) 979 2406. **Canada**'s largest student travel specialists; branches in most provinces.

Children and Pregnancy

Free child places on package holidays and discount air fares for tiny travellers vary from company to company. Get a good travel agent, trawl through the brochures and read all the small print. The big package operators geared to family holidays like Thomson offer a wide range of child discounts and seasonal savers with in-resort amusements, kiddie clubs and baby-sitting as well as deals for children under 12 in hotels and teenagers up to 17 in self-catering accommodation. On some UK charter flights infants under two travel free on a full fare-paying adult's lap, while on others you may be charged £15–£20 for the baby, or 10% of the adult fare. Children from two to twelve cost between 25% and 65%, and over 12 you'll have to fork out full fare. On international Olympic flights you'll pay 67% of the adult fare for children aged two to twelve, 10% for infants under two, while under-12s go for half-fare on all domestic flights. Watch out for birthdays; if your toddler has crossed the magic two-year-old age barrier by the return journey you'll have to pay for another seat. Note that many airlines won't let single mothers travel with two infants, although you may get through the restriction by having one on your lap and one in a car seat; explain your position when you book in case they are adamant on the one child per adult rule or turn you away at the check-in.

If you're pregnant, think before you fly. Although Greek hospitals have improved in recent years, you should make sure your insurance covers repatriation. Most airlines will carry women up to 34 weeks of pregnancy—Olympic even later—but you will have to provide a doctor's certificate after 28 weeks to prove you are well enough to fly. Again check when you book.

Domestic Flights to the Islands

Flights from Athens to Kos, Rhodes, Kárpathos, Astypálaia, Léros and Kássos can be booked in advance through **Olympic**; as many planes are small, do this as far in advance as possible. Some only have 18 seats, and are good fun; they seem to just skim over the mountaintops (but note, they can't take off or land in high winds, and you could end up back where you started). Because planes are small, baggage allowances (15kg) tend to be enforced—unless you've bought your ticket abroad, when you're allowed all 23kg. Children under twelve go half-price. **Air Greece**, the sole domestic competitor to survive, has cheaper daily flights to Rhodes from Athens; in Athens, ✆ 325 5011 or ✆ 324 4457.

Olympic Airways also offer **island-to-island flights** in season, which precludes the need to go to Athens. Although these have a habit of changing from year to year, flights between Crete and Kárpathos/Rhodes; Rhodes and Santoríni/Mýkonos/Kastellórizo/Kárpathos; and Kárpathos and Kássos are well-established. It's also possible to get a schedule 'open jaws' ticket to Athens and on to any permutation of islands, but you have to return home from Athens.

Getting to and from Ellinikon Airport, Athens

Athens' Ellinikon Airport is divided into three terminals: East Terminal (used by some charters, all non-Olympic international airlines and Air Greece), West Terminal or Olympiki (used for all Olympic Airlines flights, both international and domestic), and the Charter Terminal; if you're on a charter double check to make sure you go to the right one. Express bus 091 connects all three terminals to central Athens, stopping in front of the Post Office in Sýntagma Square and from Stadíou Street by Omónia Square every 20 minutes between 5.21am and midnight and every hour at night from 1.12am to 4.12am. Fares are 160dr from 7am to 11.30pm, 200dr otherwise. From Karaiskaki Square in Piraeus express bus no.19 goes to the airport's three terminals every hour from 6am to midnight, and at 2.30am and 5am. The same buses will take you from terminal to terminal, or catch a taxi (under 1000dr). For more on taxis and getting around Athens, *see* pp.80–81.

There's a **left luggage** facility in the Olympic airport, and another at the international airport, down at the far end beyond the charters' hall.

essential airport numbers (✆ 01–)

East Terminal	✆ 969 4111
West Terminal	✆ 926 9111
Charter Terminal	✆ 997 2581

airlines in athens (✆ 01–)

Aeroflot	14 Xenofóndos, ✆ 322 0986, ✉ 323 6375
Air Canada	10 Óthonos, ✆ 322 3206, ✉ 323 1057
Air France	18 Vouliagmenis, Glyfáda, ✆ 960 1100, ✉ 960 1457; airport ✆ 969 9334
Air Greece	22 Filellínon, ✆ 324 4457, ✉ 324 4479; airport ✆ 960 0646
Air Zimbabwe	22 Filellínon, ✆ 324 5415, ✉ 324 5446

Alitalia	577 Vouliagmenis, Argyroupoulis, ✆ 995 9200, 🖶 995 9214; airport ✆ 961 3621
American Airlines	15 Panepistimiou, ✆ 331 1045
British Airways	10 Óthonos, ✆ 890 6666; airport ✆ 961 0402
Continental Airlines	25 Filellínon, ✆ 324 9300
Czech Airlines	15 Panepistímiou, ✆ 323 0174
Cyprus Airways	10 Filellínon, ✆ 324 7801, 🖶 324 4935; airport ✆ 961 0325
Delta	4 Óthonos, ✆ 331 1668, 🖶 325 0451; airport ✆ 964 8800
Iberia	8 Xenofóndos, ✆ 323 4523, 🖶 324 0655; airport ✆ 969 9813
KLM	22 Voúlis, ✆ 988 0177; airport ✆ 969 9733
Lufthansa	East Terminal, ✆ 369 2200, 🖶 363 6881
Malev	15 Papepistímiou, ✆ 324 1116
Olympic	96 Syngroú, among many branches; reservations ✆ 966 6666, 🖶 966 6111. Information ✆ 936 3363
Qantas	East Terminal, ✆ 969 9323
Sabena	41c Vouliagmenis, Glyfáda, ✆ 960 0021, 🖶 960 0219; airport ✆ 961 3903
SAS	East Terminal, ✆ 960 1003, 🖶 960 1306; airport ✆ 961 4201
Singapore Airlines	9 Xenofóndos, ✆ 323 9111, 🖶 325 4326; airport ✆ 961 2815
South African Airways	8 Merlin, ✆ 361 7278, 🖶 362 7433
Swissair	4 Óthonos, ✆ 323 5813, 🖶 322 5548; airport ✆ 961 0203
Thai Airlines	1 Sekeri St, ✆ 364 7610, 🖶 364 7680; airport ✆ 960 0607
TWA	8 Xenofóndos, ✆ 322 6451, 🖶 322 8973; airport ✆ 961 0012
United Airlines	5 Syngrou, ✆ 924 2645, 🖶 922 9268
Virgin Atlantic	8–10 Tzireon, Makrigianni, ✆ 924 9100, 🖶 924 9144; airport ✆ 960 1461

London–Athens

There are 3 daily trains from London to Athens, the *Athenai Express*, the *Acropolis Express* and the *Hellas Express*, all of which take about three days. And a hot, crowded, stuffy three days too. Check on trains from Britain to Greece with British Rail International, ✆ (0990) 848 848. The alternative and pleasant though slightly costlier route is to go through Italy, either to Ancona or further south to Brindisi, and take the ferry over to Corfu and Pátras.

Hardy souls who deny themselves a couchette or cabin should bring plenty of provisions, including water, and toilet paper. Wear the oldest and most comfortable clothes you own (and save yourself the trouble of washing them before you go).

London–Athens

Taking a coach from London to Thessaloníki or Athens is always possible for those who decide that a train trip is too expensive or simply too easy a route to travel. It isn't usually much cheaper than a standby flight, and takes four days instead of four hours, but it's a chance to see Munich, Belgrade and other fine bus terminals en route. **Eurolines**, 52 Grosvenor Gdns, Victoria, London SW1W 0AU, ✆ (0171) 730 8235, make the journey from London to Athens for around £218 return if you're over 26; there's a £12 saving if you're under 26. Departures from London are on Friday mornings in July, August and September only. **Olympic Bus Ltd**, 70 Brunswick Centre, London WC1 1AE, ✆ (0171) 837 9141, offers 2½-day journeys from London to Athens via Brussels and Italy for a mere £50 one-way, or £100 return, departing London on Friday evenings. In Greece, you'll find agencies selling bus tickets on the most obscure islands, as well as in Athens; **Filellínon Street** near Sýntagma Square is Athens' budget travellers' boulevard, so check there.

Domestic Buses

The domestic bus service in Greece is efficient and regular, and still a bargain, although there never seem to be enough buses on the islands in the summer, nor is it customary to queue. However, you will not be left behind if it is humanly possible for you to squeeze on. If you can wake up in time, you will find that buses are rarely crowded early in the morning.

The most common sea route to Greece is from Italy, with daily ferry services from Ancona and Brindisi, and frequently from Bari and Venice. Ancona to Pátras takes a day and a half; Brindisi ferries connect with the night train from Rome and arrive in Pátras the next morning. Passengers are usually allowed a free stopover in Corfu if it is not their ultimate destination before continuing to Igoumenítsa or Pátras, but make sure it is noted on your ticket. In the summer, reserve in advance, especially if you bring a car (most travel agents can do this for you). Students and young people can get a discount of up to 20%. Discounts of up to 30% on car prices are also offered when buying a return ticket. As a rule, the costlier the ferry, the faster it sails (Minoan, for instance, takes only 22 hours from Ancona to Patras). If you're in a big hurry, **Catamaran Ferry Lines** (86 Filonos St, 18546 Piraeus, ✆ 429 3903, 🖷 452 3624) link Brindisi with Corfu and Igoumenítsa in under 4 hours.

Italy–Greece Ferries

The fares listed below are approximate 1998 prices in drachmae for an airline-type seat, one way, in low/high season; there are even cheaper deck class tickets, while cabins are considerably dearer. As a general rule, cars under 4.25m cost a few thousand drachmae more than the low season seat prices listed overleaf; double that price for taking a car in high season. **Hellenic Mediterranean** is the first to get its itineraries on the Internet, in English at *www.hml.it/indexen.htm*.

Ports	Seat Prices	Company
Ancona (or Venice)–Corfu–Pátras & Brindisi–Corfu–Igoumenítsa	11,500/23,400dr 8000/14,000dr	Strinzis Lines 26 Aktí Possidónos, Piraeus ✆ 422 5000, 🖷 422 5265
Ancona–Pátras & Trieste–Corfu–Igoumenítsa–Pátras	14,200/25,800dr 16,500/27,500dr	ANEK Lines 54 Amalías, Athens ✆ 323 3481, 🖷 323 4137
Ancona–Pátras (20 hrs)	18,800/24,800dr	Superfast Ferries 157 Alkyonidon,Voúla, Athens ✆ 969 1100, 🖷 969 1190
Ancona–Igoumenítsa–Corfu–Pátras & Brindisi–Corfu–Igoumenítsa	17,000/27,200dr 9000/16,000dr Athens	Minoan Lines 2 Vass. Konstantinoú,
& Venice–Igoumenítsa–Corfu–Kefalonía–Patras	price on application	✆ 689 8340, 🖷 689 8344

Ancona–Igoumenítsa–Pátras & Bari–Igoumenítsa–Ancona–Heráklion (Crete) in July/Aug	14,000/19,500dr 10,000/16,000dr	Marlines 38 Aktí Possidónos, Piraeus ☎ 411 0777, 📠 411 7780
Brindisi–Corfu–Igoumenítsa–Pátras & Brindisi–Kefaloniá–Páxi–Zákynthos–Pátras	6400/17,500dr price on application	Hellenic Mediterranean Lines, PO Box 80057, Piraeus ☎ 422 5341, 📠 422 5317
Bari–Igoumenítsa–Pátras	11,500/17,400dr	Ventouris Ferries 5 Nikodímou, Athens ☎ 324 0071
Brindisi–Corfu–Igoumenítsa	7000/13,400dr	Fragline 5a Réthymnou, Athens ☎ 821 1285, 📠 821 3095
Brindisi–Corfu–Igoumenítsa–Pátras	11,900/15,800dr	Adriatica 85 Aktí Miaoúli, Piraeus, ☎ 429 0487, 📠 429 0490

Ferries to the Islands

Comfort on Greek ferries has improved by leaps and bounds in recent years, especially the long-haul ferries: shops, video rooms, air-conditioning, disco bars, slot machines and small swimming pools are added attractions to the old pleasures of lazily watching passing islands, feeling the sea breeze (or tempest, if the wind kicks up), looking out for dolphins during the day or shooting stars at night. Most island ferries have three classes: the first or 'distinguished' class, with a plush lounge and private cabins (these often cost as much as flying); the second class, often with its own lounge as well, but smaller, porthole-less cabins, segregated by sex, not recommended for claustrophobes; and third or tourist class, which typically offers access to a large room full of airline-type seats and the deck and the snack bar area. As a rule the Greeks stay inside and the tourists stay out—on warm summer nights in particular this can be the most pleasant alternative, especially if you have a sleeping bag. Drinking water is never very good on the boats, but all sell bottled water, beer, coffee and soft drinks (for about twice as much as on shore). Biscuits and cigarettes complete the fare on the smaller boats, while the larger ones offer sandwiches, self-service dining or full meals (usually adequate and fairly priced) served in a dining room.

Athens' port Piraeus is the busiest in Greece, the main launchpad for the Dodecanese; *see* the map on p.99 for points of departure. The National Tourist Office publishes a free weekly list of sailings, both abroad and to the islands; for serious island hoppers, ask for their free booklet, *Greek Travel Routes: Domestic Sea Schedules*. At the same time, be aware that any number of factors (weather, health emergencies and unforeseen repairs) can throw timetables out of the window, so if you have to catch a flight home allow for the eccentricities of the system and leave a day early to be safe. For the latest information on departures and arrivals, ring the relevant port authorities (*limenarchíon*). Numbers are listed for each island. For mainland departures ring:

Piraeus Port Authority ✆ (01) 422 6000 (for ferry schedules); if busy try ✆ 412 3533

Before purchasing a ticket, check timetables in competing agencies—ticket prices will always be the same, but note that some ferries are faster than others, and others can take half a day stopping at tiny island ports. On smaller islands, agents moonlight as bartenders or grocers and may only have a handwritten sign next to the door advertising their ship's departures.

Always keep your ticket with you on a Greek ship, in case of a 'ticket control', a comedy routine necessitated by the fact that the crew doesn't always check tickets when passengers board. Instead, after one or two pleas on the ship's loudspeaker system for passengers without tickets to purchase them forthwith, you suddenly find all the doors on the boat locked or guarded by bored but obdurate sailors, while bands of officers rove about the boat checking tickets. Invariably mix-ups occur: children are separated from their parents, others have gone to the WC, someone has left a ticket with someone on the other side of the immovable sailor, crowds pile up at the doors and stowaways are marched to the purser's office.

Prices are still reasonable for passengers but rather dear for cars. All ships and hydrofoils are privately owned, and although the Greek government controls prices some will charge more for the same journey, depending on the facilities offered, speed, etc. In most cases children under the age of 4 travel free, and between 4 and 10 for half-fare. Buying a ticket on board will cost 20% more. In the summer, especially in August, buy tickets well in advance if you have a car or want a cabin. Refunds are given only if the ship never arrives.

Hydrofoils and Catamarans

There are several fleets of hydrofoils, several catamarans, and the occasional 'sea jet' thumping over the Greek seas, and new lines are added every year. Most services run throughout the year but are considerably less frequent between November and May. As a rule hydrofoils travel at least twice as fast as ferries and are twice as expensive. In the peak season they are often fully booked, so buy tickets as early as you can. In a choppy sea a trip may leave you saddle-sore, and beware, if the weather is very bad, they won't leave port.

Ferry and Hydrofoil Times and Prices from the Mainland

A list of some of the more popular scheduled mainland–island connections follows. Duration of each boat trip and approximate 1998 prices are given in drachmae but are subject to change without notice. Each port has its own port taxes (the paper bits the agent staples on your ticket) but these are minimal—from 50 to 300drs. You can roughly calculate the car prices on the ferries by multiplying the third class fares by five.

Piraeus to	1st Class (dr)	2nd Class (dr)	3rd Class (dr)	hours
Astypálaia	13–17,000	7–9000	6010	13
Chálki	16,000	13,500	8500	17
Kálymnos	17,000	9000	6200	13
Kárpathos	15,270	13,500	6800	18
Kássos	15,270	13,500	6800	18
Kos	20,000	9500	6500	15
Léros	17,000	8500	6000	11
Níssyros	21,370	9940	6810	17
Pátmos	17,000	9000	6000	10
Rhodes	21,300	12–16,000	7800	18
Sými	20,370	10–15,000	6400	17
Tílos	10,360	7940	6210	24

Tourist Excursion Boats

These are generally slick and clean, and have become quite numerous in recent years. They are usually more expensive than the regular ferries or steamers, but often have schedules that allow visitors to make day trips to nearby islands (though you can also take them one way), and are very convenient, having largely taken the place of the little caique operators, many of whom now specialize in excursions to remote beaches.

Boats to Turkey

Whatever axes are currently being ground between Greece and Turkey, a kind of *pax tourista* has fallen over the mutually profitable exchange of visitors from the Greek islands to the Turkish mainland. Ferries run daily year-round between Rhodes and Marmaris (3½hrs); between Kos and Bodrum (1½hrs); in season excursion boats also sail over from most of the smaller Dodecanese as well. Prices, once outrageous, are now more reasonable, although there is a mysterious array of taxes on both sides (sometimes less if you only make a day excursion). Often Turkish shops around the ports will take drachmae, but the Greeks will not take Turkish lira—and the exchange rate between the two is pretty dreadful. Also, **beware the charter restriction**: if you spend a night in Turkey the Greek authorities might well invoke the law and refuse you passage home on your flight.

By Car

Driving from London to Athens (and taking the ferry from Italy to Greece) at a normal pace takes around 3½ days. Don't even consider driving down unless you are planning to spend a few weeks on one or two islands, and if that's the case the smaller the better, both for squeezing the car on to the ferry, and for negotiating the sometimes very narrow village roads. Alternatively there are countless rent-a-car firms on the islands; most are family-run, and fairly reliable (asking around a bit will usually reveal who the stinkers are). If an island has a lot of unpaved roads and not a lot of competition, prices tend to be higher; at the time of writing, hiring a small car varies between 10 and 15,000dr a day in the summer, and open-air Jeeps at least a third more. Most require that you be at least 21, some 25. Read the small print of your contract with care (look out for mileage limits, etc.) and don't be surprised if you have to leave your driving licence as security. In the off season, negotiate. Arriving at a car hire agent's with a handful of brochures from the competition has been known to strengthen one's bargaining position. Fuel at the time of writing is around 230dr a litre; unleaded (*amólivdi*) a wee bit less.

An **International Driving Licence** is not required from EU citizens. Other nationals can obtain an international licence at home, or at one of the Automobile Club offices in Greece (ELPA), by presenting a national driving licence, passport and photograph. The minimum age is 18.

The Motor Insurance Bureau at 10 Xenofóntos Street, Athens, ✆ (01) 323 6733, can tell you which Greek insurance company represents your own, or provide you with additional cover for Greece.

The **Greek Automobile Club** (ELPA) operates a breakdown service within 60km (40 miles) of Athens: dial ✆ 104. If you belong to an automobile club at home, breakdown service is free anywhere.

Customs formalities for bringing in a car are very easy and usually take very little time. You are allowed a year of free use of the car in Greece, and after that can apply for a four-month extension. North Americans and Australians are allowed two years. If you leave Greece without your car you must have it withdrawn from circulation by a customs authority. ELPA has a list of lawyers who can offer free legal advice on car problems. They also have a 24-hour number for information useful to foreign motorists; call ✆ 174, and speak English.

While driving in the centre of Athens may be a hair-raising experience, the rest of Greece is fairly easy and pleasant. There are few cars on most roads, even in summer, and most signs, when you're lucky enough to find one, have their Latin equivalents. Traffic regulations and signalling comply with standard practice on the European Continent (i.e. driving on the right). Crossroads, tipsy tourists, Greeks arguing and gesticulating behind the wheel, and low visibility in the mountains are probably the greatest hazards. Where there are no right-of-way signs at a crossroads, give priority to traffic coming from the right, and always beep your horn on blind corners. If you're exploring you may want to take a spare container of petrol along, as stations can be scarce on the ground (especially on the islands) and only open shop hours. There is a speed limit of 50km per hour (30mph) in inhabited areas.

By Motorbike and Moped

Motorbikes and even more popular mopeds are ideal for the islands in the summer. It almost never rains, and what could be more pleasant than a gentle thyme-scented breeze freshening your journey? Scooters (the Greeks call them *papákia*, 'little ducks', supposedly for the noise they make) are both more economical and more practical than cars. They can fit into almost any boat and travel paths where cars fear to tread. Rentals are not expensive and include third party insurance coverage in most cases. You will have to have a valid driving licence (for Americans, this means an international one) For larger motorbikes (anything over 75cc) you may be asked to show a motorcycle driver's licence. The downsides: many of the bikes are poorly maintained, many of the roads are poorly maintained and everyone takes too many risks: hospital beds in Greece fill up each summer with casualties, both foreign and Greek (check your insurance to see if you're covered). Most islands have laws about operating motorbikes after midnight (the 'little ducks', often stripped of their mufflers, tend to howl like a flock of Daffys and Donalds on amphetamines) but they are enforced as often as the helmet requirement. Actually, no: you do see Greeks wearing helmets, but only on their elbows, which, judging by the way they drive their machines, must be where they keep their brains. Literally hundreds of people, nearly all young, are killed every year in Greece. Be careful.

By Bicycle

Cycling has not caught on in mountainous Greece, either as a sport or as a means of transport, though you can usually hire an old bike in most major resorts. Trains and planes carry bicycles for a small fee, and Greek boats generally take them along for nothing.

Greek taxi drivers have recently convinced the government to pass a law forbidding other Greeks from picking up hitchhikers. As with the aforementioned helmet-wearing law, this is regarded as optional, but it is true that you may find hitching slow going; perhaps because of the law, motorized holiday makers now seem to stop and offer more rides than the locals. The Greek double standard produces the following percentages for hopeful hitchhikers:

Single woman: 99% of cars will stop. You hardly have to stick out your thumb.
Two women: 75% of cars will find room for you.
Woman and man: 50%; more if the woman is pretty.
Single man: 25% if you are well dressed with little luggage; less otherwise.
Two men: start walking.

Entry Formalities

All **European Union** members can stay indefinitely. The only reason you would need special permission to stay would be for working or if complicated banking procedures were involved requiring proof of residence; contact the Aliens Bureau, 173 Leof. Alexandrás, 11522 Athens, ✆ 646 8103. The formalities for **non-EU tourists** entering Greece are very simple. American, Australian and Canadian citizens can stay for up to three months in Greece on presentation of a valid passport. South Africans are permitted two months. If you want to stay longer, take your passport to the Aliens Bureau or your local police station 20 days before your time in Greece expires, and be prepared to prove you can support yourself with bank statements and the like. If you overstay your three months, be prepared to pay a fine of 22,200dr.

Specialist Holidays

A complete list is available from the **National Tourist Organization of Greece** (*see* p.41).

in the UK

British Museum Tours, 46 Bloomsbury St, London WC1B 3QQ, ✆ (0171) 323 8895. Different archaeological guided tours every year.

Cox & Kings, Gordon House, 10 Greencoat Lane, London SW1P 1PH, ✆ (0171) 873 5000; ✆ 630 6038; e-mail *Cox.Kings@coxkings.sprint.com*. Botanic holidays on Rhodes.

Filoxenia, Sourdock Hill, Barkisland, Halifax, West Yorkshire HX4 0AG, ✆ (01422) 371796, ✆ 310340. Cookery on Léros.

Greco-File, ✆ (01422) 375999. Expert advice on where to go, flights and 'couture' holidays to unusual islands for the discerning traveller.

Laskarina Holidays, St Mary's Gate, Wirksworth, Matlock, Derbyshire DE4 4DQ, ✆ (01629) 824 884, ✉ 822 205. Painting on Sými, Rhodes, Kastellórizo, Lípsi and Chálki.

Norfolk and Suffolk Wildlife Trust Holidays, Dudwick House, Buxton, Norwich NR10 5HX, ✆ (01603) 278296. Join members of the Norfolk and Suffolk Wildlife Trust on botany and birdwatching trips to Rhodes.

Peregrine Holidays, 40–41 South Parade, Summertown, Oxford OX2 7JP, ✆ (01865) 511642. Wildlife and walking tours.

Ramblers Holidays, Box 43, Welwyn Garden City, Hertfordshire AL8 6PQ, ✆ (01707) 331133. Walking tours on Pátmos.

Symi International Art School, c/o Aruini Irini Constandinidi, 23 Glenkerry House, Burcham St, London E14 0SL, ✆ (0171) 515 6157. Photography courses on Sými.

Solos Holidays Ltd, 41 Watford Way, London NW4 3JH, ✆ (0181) 951 2800. Singles group holidays in four-star hotels in Rhodes for independent people in the 30–49 and 50–69 age brackets. Also spring and autumn rambling breaks in Rhodes.

Sovereign Small World, Astral Tower, Betts Way, Crawley, West Sussex RH10 2GX, ✆ (01293) 599966. Villa parties for single travellers in traditional houses on Sými and Kálymnos. Also Caique Cruising for singles afloat. Like a villa party on the ocean wave with excellent food and drink and a chance to meet people and see the islands.

Swan Hellenic Ltd, 77 New Oxford St, London WC1A 1PP, ✆ (0171) 800 2200. Cultural, archaeological and art history tours and cruises.

Travel Companions, 110 High Mount, Station Rd, London NW4 3ST, ✆ (0181) 202 8478. Vera Coppard can match you up with a kindred spirit, for a £40 fee, if you don't want to travel alone.

in the USA/Canada

Aegean Visions, 26 6th St, Suite 260, Stamford, CT 06905, ✆ (203) 667 2524, toll free ✆ (800) GREECE97, ✉ 969 0799. Scuba-diving, hiking, archaeological, alternative living.

Aegean Workshops, 148 Old Black Point Rd, Niantic, CT 06357, ✆ (860) 739 0378. Harry J. Danos, a university art teacher, offers water-colour, drawing and design workshops of 15 to 21 days on Pátmos.

Avenir Adventures, 1790 Bonanza Drm Suite 207, Park City, UT 84060, ✆ (800) 367 3230. Expeditions by land and sea for small groups.

Central Holiday Tours, Inc., 206 Central Ave, Jersey City, NJ 07307, ☏ (201) 798 5777, toll free ☏ (800) 935 5000, ✆ 963 0966. Tours in ancient history and archaeology, 'In the Steps of St Paul', mythology and theatre.

Cloud Tours, 645 5th Ave, New York, NY 10022, ☏ (212) 753 6104, toll free ☏ (800) 223 7880, ✆ 980 6941. Scuba-diving, biking, honeymoon tours, women's groups, religious history tours and many others.

IST Cultural Tours, 225 W. 34th St, Suite 913, New York, NY 10122, ☏ (212) 563 1202, toll free ☏ (800) 833 2111, ✆ 594 6953. Customized tours including yacht cruises and lectures on archaeology.

Our Family Abroad, 40 W. 57th St, Suite 430, New York, NY 10019, ☏ (212) 459 1800, toll free ☏ (800) 999 5500, ✆ 581 3756. Gay and lesbian tours.

Peddlers Destination & Adventures International, 8489 Crescent Dr, Los Angeles, CA 90046, ☏ (213) 659 7267, ☏ (800) 695 4599, ✆ (213) 650 6902. Island cycling tours.

The Greek Island Connection, 418 E. 14th Street, Suite 3, New York, NY 10009, ☏ (212) 674 4072, toll free ☏ (800) 241 2417, ✆ 674 4582. Archaeology, cooking, hiking, biking, gay and lesbian, religion.

Disabled Travellers

Many of the Greek islands, with their ubiquitous steps and absence of suitable transport, would put severe constraints on visitors in chairs, and ferry and hydrofoil access is difficult. Major islands such as Rhodes and many smaller ones that receive lots of visitors (such as Kos) have hotels with facilities—the Greek National Tourist Office has a list.

In the UK, several of the big package holiday companies like **Thomsons** have some suitable tours. Contact **RADAR**, 12 City Forum, 250 City Rd, London EC1V 8AS, ☏ (0171) 250 4119, or **Tripscope**, ☏ (0181) 994 9294, for advice and referrals.

In the USA similar service is provided by the **Travel Information Service**, Moss Rehabilitation Hospital, 1200 W. Tabor Rd, Philadelphia, PA 19141, ☏ (215) 456 9600, and the **Society for the Advancement of Travel for the Handicapped**, 347 5th Ave, Suite 610, New York, NY 10016, ☏ (212) 447-SATH, ✆ 725 8253. **New Directions**, 5276 Hollister Ave, Suite 207, Santa Barbara, CA 93111, ☏ (805) 967 2841, ✆ 964 7344. In Canada, the **Jewish Rehabilitation Hospital**, 3205 Place Alton Goldbloom, Montreal PQ H7V 1R2, is a good source of travel info. In Greece, contact **The Panhellenic Association for the Blind**, 31 Veranzérou St, 10432 Athens, ☏ (01) 522 8333, ✆ 522 2112, or **Association Hermes**, Patriárchou 13, Grigouiou E, 16542 Argyroúpolis, ☏ (01) 996 1887.

Are we sailing straight, or is the shore crooked?

old Greek proverb

One of the great thrills of sailing the Greek waters is the variety of places to visit in a relatively short time, with the bonus that nowhere in Greece is far from safe shelter or harbours with good facilities for yachtsmen. There is little shallow water, except close to the shoreline, few currents and no tides or fog. The 100,000 miles of coastline and a collection of islands and islets numbering three thousand provide a virtually inexhaustible supply of secluded coves and empty beaches, even at the height of the tourist season. The Greek National Tourist Organization has initiated a programme of rapid expansion in the face of mounting competition from Turkey and Spain; facilities are being improved and new marinas are being constructed throughout the country.

Individual island maps show main yacht supply stations and ports of entry and exit. Greek weather guarantees near-perfect sailing conditions. The only real problem you'll encounter are the strong winds in parts of the country at certain times of the year, notably April to October, when most yachtsmen are at sea. The Aegean Sea is affected by a northwest wind in the south and a northeasterly in the north, and when the *meltémi* blows in August and September it can reach force eight, testing all your skills at the helm. The Turkish coast has light, variable breezes, which are rudely interrupted by the forceful *meltémi*.

Average wind speeds (in knots) during the months April to October

Area	April	May	Jun	Jul	Aug	Sept	Oct
Kos–Rhodes	WNW	WNW	NW	NW	NW	NW	WNW
(Kos)	13.6	13.0	13.0	13.6	13.6	13.0	11.4
E. Cretan	NW	NW	NW	NW	NW	NW	NW
(Sitía)	6.6	5.0	7.0	8.6	8.2	6.6	5.0
Sámos Sea	NW	NW	NW	NW	NW	NW	NW
(Sámos)	9.4	7.8	9.4	11.0	10.2	8.6	7.0
W. Karpathion	W	W	W	W	W	W	W
(Kárpathos)	6.6	6.2	8.6	10.6	9.4	8.2	6.2

If you wish to skipper a yacht anywhere within the Greek seas, consult the *Compile Index Chart of Greek Seas*, otherwise known as *XEE*, published by the Hellenic Navy Hydrographic Service. Basically it is a map of Greece divided into red squares, each with an index number, from which you can select the

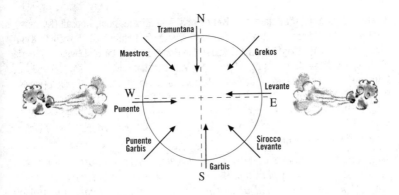

appropriate charts and order them accordingly For non-Greeks, you can buy what is known as *XEE 64*, a booklet of abbreviations explaining the signs on the charts, with text in English and Greek.

For the Dodecanese and Asia Minor you'll need the Pilot D book, which covers geographical data, possible dangers, and the present state of transportation and communication. All ports, marinas, and visible inland features are mentioned, including where to obtain fresh water and fuel. The Hydrographic Service constantly updates the books and sends additional booklets to authorized sellers and to all port authorities, where you may consult them. The nautical charts are updated using the latest, most sophisticated methods, and follow standardized dimensions. They are on a 1:100,000 scale for bigger areas and 1:75,000 for ports. Heights and depths are given in metres with functional conversion tables for feet and fathoms.

Further information is provided in booklets called *Notes to Mariners*, published monthly and available for consultation at port authorities. These give information on any alterations to naval charts you have purchased for your voyage. Besides all this there is the Navtex service. A special department of the Hydrographic Service keeps you informed about the weather or any special warnings for the day through telex, or Navtex. The text is in Greek and English, and there are four re-transmission coastal stations covering the Greek seas. Weather forecasts for yachtsmen are broadcast at intervals throughout the day on VHF Channel 16 (in Greek and English); security warnings are also broadcast on this channel, e.g. dangerous wrecks, lights not in operation, etc.

The following is a list of **bunkering ports and supply stations** in Greece where fuelling facilities and other provisions may be obtained:

Adámas (Mílos)*, Aegina, Ag. Nikólaos (Kéa), Ag. Nikólaos (Crete)*, Alexandroúpolis*, Álimos Marína, Argostóli (Kefaloniá)*, Chíos*, Corfu Port*, Ermoúpolis (Sýros)*, Flísvos Marína, Goúvia Marína*, Gýthion*, **Chalkís***, Chaniá

(Crete)*, Hýdra, Itéa*, Kalamáta*, **Kálymnos**, Kamáres (Sífnos), Kapsáli (Kýthera), **Kastellórizo**, Kástro (Ándros), Katákolo*, Katápola (Amorgós), Kavála*, Kými (Évia), Korínthos*, **Kos***, **Lákki** (**Léros**), Lávrion*, Lefkás, Liméni (Máni), Linariá (Skýros), Mýrina (Límnos)*, Mytilíni*, Monemvásia, Mýkonos*, Náfpaktos, Náfplion*, Náxos, Néa Róda, Paléa Epidávros, Paleokastrítsa, Párga, Parikía (Páros), **Pigádia** (**Kárpathos**), Pílos*, Póros, Pórto Koufó, Pórto Ráfti, Préveza*, **Rhodes** (**Mandráki**)*, **Skála** (**Pátmos**)*, Skiáthos*, Skópelos, Spétses, Thessaloníki Marína*, Thessaloníki Port*, Tínos, Váthi (Ithaca)*, Vólos*, Vouliagméni Marína, Zákynthos*, Zéa Marína.

* indicates official ports of entry and exit, where there are port, customs and health authorities, as well as immigration and currency control services. Others are: Égion, Gerakini (Chalkidikí), Glyfáda, Igoumenítsa, Herákleon, Kimássi (Évia), Pátras, Pérama, Pithagórion and Vathí (Samos), Dáfni (Agion Óros), Elefsína, Fíra (Santoríni), Ivira (Agion Óros), Kalí Liménes (Crete), Drépanon (Achaía) and Stilí (Lamia).

Yachts entering Greek waters must fly the code flag 'Q' until cleared by entry port authorities. Upon arrival the port authority (*limenarchíon*) issues all yachts with a transit log which entitles the yacht and crew to unlimited travel in Greek waters. It also allows crew members to buy fuel, alcohol and cigarettes duty free. It must be kept on board and produced when required, and returned to the customs authorities on leaving Greece at one of the exit ports. Permission is normally given for a stay of six months, but this can be extended. Small motor, sail or rowing boats do not require a '*carnet de passage*', and are allowed into Greece duty free for four months. They are entered in your passport and deleted on exit. For more information apply to the Greek National Tourist Organisation, 4 Conduit Street, London W1R 0DJ, ✆ (0171) 734 5997, who produce a useful leaflet, *Sailing the Greek Seas*.

Anyone taking a yacht by road is strongly advised to obtain boat registration documentation from the DVLA, Swansea SA99 1BX, ✆ (01792) 772134. The Royal Yachting Association, R.Y.A. House, Romsey Road, Eastleigh, Hampshire SO5 4YA, ✆ (01703) 627400, is a useful source of yachting information.

Yacht Charter

Chartering yachts is very popular these days, and, as the promotional literature says, can be cheaper than staying in a hotel (if you have enough friends or family to share expenses). Between the various firms there are over a thousand vessels currently available in all sizes, with or without a crew (though without a crew—bareboat charter—both the charterer and another member of the party must show proof of seamanship: a sailing certificate or letter of recommendation from a recognized yacht or sailing club). There are various options: motor yachts (without sails), motor sailers (primarily powered by motor, auxiliary sail power) and sailing yachts (with auxiliary motor power). The Greek National Tourist Organisation has a list of Greek charter firms, or contact **The Hellenic Professional Yacht Owners Association**, Zéa Marína A818 536, Piraeus, ☎ 452 6335, ✆ 452 6335 and 428 0465, and **Greek Yacht Brokers and Consultants Association**, 11 Poseidonos Av, Alimos, ✆ (01) 985 0122; 105 57 Athens, ✆ 323 0330. In the UK, the **Yacht Charter Association**, 60 Silverdale, New Milton, Hampshire BH25 7DE, ✆ (01425) 619004, supplies a list of its recognized yacht charter operators and offers advice on chartering overseas.

Flotilla and Sailing Holidays

If you want to float among the islands on the wine-dark sea but don't own your own yacht, or lack the experience to charter one, a flotilla holiday may be just the answer. A growing number of flotilla companies offer one- or two-week sailing holidays, some of which will take on instructing even the most inexperienced sailors (usually beginning with a week based on land). High season prices for a fortnight's holiday range from £550 per person to £9000 per head, on a four-person yacht. The yachts have 4–8 berths (there are shared boats available for couples and singles) and sail in flotillas, usually from six to a dozen yachts, supervised by a lead boat, with experienced skipper, engineer and social hostess. Plenty of free time built in. On the Internet check out *aegeansailing.simplenet.com*.

operators

Agemennon Yachts, 213B Karaiskaki St., 26222 Pátras, Greece ✆/☎ (61) 344009. Yacht charters.

BUOYS Cruising Club, 8 Chase Side, Enfield, Middlesex EN2 6NF, England ✆ (0181) 367 8462. Charters from Athens.

Euroyacht, 22 Akti Themistokleous, 18536 Piraeus, Greece ✆ (01) 428 1920, ☎ (01) 428 1926. Bareboat or crewed sail or motor boats, and flotilla sailing.

Ghiolman Yachts, 7 Filellínon St, Athens, ✆ 323 3696. Besides yachts, can supply mobile phones, helicopters, planes, and even put private islands at your disposal.

Grecian Holidays, 75 The Donway West, Don Mills, Ontario M3C 2E9, Canada ✆ (800) 268 6786, ☎ (416) 510 1509

Greek Island Cruise Centre, 4321 Lakemoor Dr, Wilmington, NC, 28405, USA ✆ (800) 341 3030. Yacht charters.

Interpac Yachts, 1050 Anchorage Lane, San Diego, CA, 92106 USA toll free ✆ (888) 99 YACHT. Crewed power or sail yacht charters.

The Moorings, 188 Northdown Rd, Cliftonville, Kent CT9 2QN, England
✆ (01843) 227140. Offers charters from Rhodes, Kos and Athens.

McCulloch Marine, 32 Fairfield Rd, London E3 2QB, England ✆ (0181) 983
1487. Offers charters from Athens.

Odysseus Yachting Holidays, 33 Grand Parade, Brighton BN2 2QA, England
✆ (01273) 695094. Flotilla holidays.

Sovereign Sailing, 120 St George's Rd, Brighton, E. Sussex BN2 1E, England
✆ (01273) 626284. Flotilla holidays.

Sunsail, The Port House, Port Solent, Portsmouth PO6 4TH, England ✆ (01705)
210345, for dinghies, flotillas, tuitional sailing and watersports.

Valef, 22 Aktí Themistokléous, Piraeus, Greece ✆ (01) 428 1920, ✉ 428 1926 (in
the USA: 7254 Fir Rd, PO Box 391, Ambler, Pa 19002 ✆ (800) 223 3845;
in Canada: Islands in the Sun Cruises, 10441 124 St, Edmonton, Alberta
T5N 1R7, ✆ toll free (800) 661 7958. *http//ValefYachts.com*). One of
the largest and most reputable firms, with more than 300 crewed yachts,
accommodating 4 to 50 people from $300 to $8000 a day.

Windstar Cruises, Standard House, 15-16 Bonhill St, London EC2P 2EA,
England ✆ (0171) 628 7711. Yacht charters.

World Expeditions Ltd, 7 North Rd, Maidenhead, Berkshire SL6 1TL, England
✆ (01628) 74174. Yacht charters.

Womanship, Learn to Sail Cruises For and By Women, USA ✆ (800) 324 9295.
North American company specializing in women-only flotilla holidays in
the Greek islands.

Yacht Agency Rhodes, 1 Vyronos & Canada, PO Box 393, 85100 Rhodes, Greece
✆ (241) 22927, ✉ (241) 23393. Yacht charters.

Practical A–Z

Climate, Measures and Time

Greece enjoys hot, dry, clear and bright Mediterranean summers, cooled by winds, of which the *meltémi* from the northeast is the most notorious and most likely to upset Aegean sailing schedules. Winters are mild, and in general the wet season begins at the end of October or beginning of November when it can rain 'tables and chairs' as the Greeks say. It begins to feel springlike in February, especially in Rhodes, when the first wildflowers appear.

Average Daily Temperatures, Rainy Days and Sunny Hours

	Athens		Temp (air)		Rhodes Temp (water)		Rainy days	Sunny hours
	F°	C°	F°	C°	F°	C°	(per month)	(per day)
Jan	48	11	56	14	54	13	5	7
Feb	49	11	56	14	54	13	5	6
Mar	54	12	58	15	58	14	7	8
April	60	16	66	19	60	17	7	9
May	68	20	70	21	64	19	2	11
June	76	25	78	26	74	23	0	11
July	82	28	80	27	76	26	0	12
Aug	82	28	82	28	76	26	0	12
Sept	76	25	78	26	76	25	2	12
Oct	66	19	70	22	71	22	6	10
Nov	58	15	62	17	60	16	7	8
Dec	52	12	59	16	58	15	7	8

Two uniquely Greek measurements you may encounter are the strémma, a Greek land measurement (1 strémma = ¼ acre), and the oká, an old-fashioned weight standard, divided into 400 drams (1 oká = 3lb; 35 drams = ¼lb, 140 drams = 1lb).

'God gave watches to the Europeans and time to the Greeks', they say. If you need more precision, Greek time is Eastern European, two hours ahead of Greenwich Mean Time, seven hours ahead of Eastern Standard Time in North America.

Embassies and Consulates

Australia: 37 D. Soútsou, 115 21 Athens, ✆ 644 7303, 🖷 644 3633.
Canada: 4 I. Gennadíou, 115 21 Athens, ✆ 725 4011, 🖷 725 3994.
Ireland: 7 Vass. Konstantínou, 106 74 Athens, ✆ 723 2771, 🖷 724 0217.
New Zealand: 24 Xenia, 115 28 Athens ✆ 771 0112.

Netherlands: 5–7 Vas. Konstantínou, Athens, ✆ 723 9701.
South Africa: 60 Kifissías, 151 25 Maroússi ✆ 680 6459, 📠 689 5320.
United Kingdom: 1 Ploutárchou St, 106 75 Athens, ✆ 723 6211,
📠 724 1872. Also *see* Rhodes, p.112.
USA: 91 Vassilías Sofías, 115 21 Athens, ✆ 721 2951, 📠 645 6282.

Events and Cultural Attractions

Besides the big religious and national holidays, the Dodecanese offer other events
in the summer. Each island has a section on its own particular feast days (all listed
in the text); below is a list of more ambitious annual events. Dates squirm around a
lot; ring the National Tourist Organization a month or two before the event to pin
them down.

April

Lenten carnival just before Easter.

Niptíras Ceremony, Maudy Thursday re-enactment of the washing of the
Disciples' feet, Pátmos.

Iprogós Festival, sponge diver's week, Kálymnos.

June

Scandinavian midsummer festivities (20–21) in Rhodes town.

June–September

Athens Festival. International culture. Modern and ancient theatre, jazz,
classical music and dance, often with visiting British companies, in the
stunning setting of the Herodus Atticus Odeon beneath the Acropolis. Also
a wide range of performances at the Lycabettus Theatre, Likavitós Hill,
including the **International Jazz and Blues Festival** in late June.

Epídavros Festival in the Peloponnese. Ancient Greek drama under the
stars in the authentic setting, so take a cushion to sit on. Special buses from
Athens. Festivals Box Office 4 Stadíou Street, Athens, in the arcade,
✆ 322 1459.

June–August

Hippocratia, Kos. Music in the castle.

Sými Festival, big name cultural events, dance, music and theatre, workshops, etc.

July

International Festival of Music, Rhodes.

Dáphní Wine Festival near Athens.

August

Koukania, Astypálaia, with sports and traditional games; also feasts with traditional music on 15 August.

Alintia Regatta, sailing races the first ten days of August, Léros.

Wine Festivals, Rhodes, with music and celebrities. Also at Léros.

Dance festivals at **Kallithiés, Maritsa** and **Embónas** (all on Rhodes).

August–October

Rhodes Festival with a wide programme of arts activities.

Food and Drink

> *Life's fundamental principle is the satisfaction of the needs and wants of the stomach. All important and trivial matters depend on this principle and cannot be differentiated from it.*

Epicurus, 3rd century BC

Epicurus may have given his name to gourmets, but in reality his philosophy was an economical one that advocated maximizing the simple pleasures of life: rather than continually seeking novelty and delight in ever more extreme sensations, Epicurus suggests, make a plate of bread and olives taste sublime by fasting for a couple of days. In that way modern Greeks are all epicureans: centuries of occupation and extreme poverty have taught them to relish food more than cuisine, and they eat with great zest and conviviality. Meals are not about scaling gastronomic heights, but a daily reminder to the Greeks of who they are and what their country has to offer—fish from the seas, lamb from the valleys, fresh herbs and honey from the mountains, wild young greens from the hills, olives, fruits and nuts from the groves. The method of cooking these things is often quite simple; Turkish and Italian influences remain strong, just as they do in the language. What's more, recent studies show that Greek food not only tastes good, but is remarkably good for you too.

For all that, Greece has acquired a poor reputation for food. In the 1970s the relatively few restaurants that existed were overrun, especially on the islands. Standards fell as they tried to cope with the influx of people; standards fell even lower when making as much money as possible in a few short months became the overriding consideration. Neither did the first generation of taverna owners in the tourist age see any reason to improve; the masses, mostly travelling on a shoestring, seemed content with cheap village salads, reheated moussaká, kebabs, taramosaláta and more kebabs, often served in a kind of caricature of Greekiness (plastic grapes and Zorba, Zorba, Zorba). Others, like the hotel owner in Páxos who dished out tinned brussels sprouts with everything, struggled haplessly to please middle-aged customers from the pale north who swore that they couldn't abide garlic or even olive oil, which in Greece is close to nectar (guide books used to train their readers to say WHORE-is LA-thi, parakaLO, 'without oil, please').

While too many tourist tavernas still grind out greasy grub, advertised with plastic idiot photos of food sun-blasted over the years into greenish plates of flaking scabs (no wonder that they have to hire obnoxious touts who drag in clients from the street!), their days seem to be numbered, as diners have come to know and expect better. The new generation of taverna owners are making a concerted effort to offer real Greek cooking, reviving recipes handed down from mother to daughter, recipes very much based on what's in season: vegetables like butter beans, green beans and okra in rich tomato and olive oil sauces; *briáms* of aubergines and courgettes; beetroot with hot garlic *skordaliá* dip; stuffed, lightly battered courgette flowers; prawns in filo parcels; octopus *stifádo*; beef stew with baby onions; lamb grazed on mountain herbs baked with fresh dill, yoghurt and lemon; ragout of snails; and whitebait so fresh they're almost wriggling. A simple sun-ripened Greek tomato in August, sprinkled with fresh oregano and anointed with olive oil from the family grove, is enough to jump start the old taste buds. Just try to reproduce the same sensation back home.

One criticism levelled at Greek food is that it's served cold. It usually is, and that's because Greeks believe tepid food is better for the digestion than hot in the summer (once you get used to it, you realize that many dishes are actually tastier once they're left to cool in their own juices). The pace of life is different as well. There's no rush. Lunches begin late and stretch long into the afternoon and dinners into the small hours. While we tend to shovel down quick dinners in front of the TV, the gregarious Greeks eat to enjoy, to relax, to talk. A night out with friends in a taverna is the best entertainment going.

vegetarians

Of all the people in the European Union, the Greeks now eat the most meat per capita, but they also eat most cheese, more than even the French, and follow only the Italians in eating pasta. Basically they just eat a lot, which means there are plenty of dishes for vegetarians, a wide range of pulses and *latherá* (fresh vegetable main courses cooked with olive oil, invented for the many Orthodox fasts) and salads from artichokes to aubergines as well as okra, beetroot leaves, spinach-style greens with lemon and in some places *cápari*, pickled caper plant, which looks like prunings from a rose bush but tastes delicious. There are delicate cheese and spinach pies in flaky filo pastry, and pasta dishes and pizzas up to Italian standards, thanks to the influx of those pickiest of all diners; stuffed peppers and tomatoes; deep-fried courgettes; *dolmádes*, sometimes using cabbage leaves instead of vines; and *oftés patátes*, potatoes roasted in their jackets.

If you're a vegetarian or used to buying pre-packed, sanitized meat, it's worth pointing out that in many parts of Greece, especially the remoter islands, food comes on the hoof, on the wing or in the net. It's not uncommon to see a kid or sheep despatched near a taverna by day and then turn up on the menu at night. Bunnies hopping round the village also hop into the pot, the family pig turns into sausages, free-range chickens end up being barbecued and after a while the washing line of drying octopus becomes part of the scenery.

Eating Out

So how can you find a good place to eat? As always, follow the locals. Greek families aren't going to throw away hard-earned cash on tourist food. If you're hungry for something a cut above taverna fare, keep an eye open for restaurants that have made an effort to revive traditional Greek décor, austere but colourful with hand-painted signs, painted chairs, weaving and so on; their owners usually prove to be just as serious about reviving traditional recipes in the kitchen.

Greek eating places are divided into five categories. **Tavernas** and *estiatória* (restaurants) are found everywhere and the differences between them are a bit blurred. But you'll generally find the *estiatório* has a wider menu and is a bit more upmarket. Tavernas are more like family-run bistros and can range from shacks on the beach to barn-like affairs called *Kéntrikos* that provide music in the evening. There may not be a menu as such. The waiter will reel off what's on or even invite you to have a look for yourself. Homemade English translations may leave you more baffled than ever (*see* p.73); the **menu decoder** on p.237 may help.

A typical Greek meal begins with bread and a range of starters that everyone shares: taramosaláta, *tzatzíki* (cucumbers and yoghurt), prawns, feta cheese, little cheese or spinach pies, *saganáki* (fried cheese sprinkled with lemon), greens in olive oil and lemon sauces, green beans, okra or butter beans in sauce or fried courgettes and aubergines. These are followed by a shared salad and potatoes, and a main course that you eat on your own—fish, a pasta, an oven dish ('Ready dishes', moussaká, stuffed vegetables, etc.) or else meat (lamb, pork, beef or kid), either stewed, baked in a casserole (*stifádo, kokinistó* and veal *youvétsi* with tear-drop pasta are typical) or freshly grilled (*tis óras*, 'the On Times')—chops (*brizóles*), lamb cutlets (*paidhákia*), kebabs (*souvláki*), meatballs (*keftédes* or *sousoukákia*), sausages (*lukániko*), or chicken (*koutópolou*, usually free-range). Greeks eat very little duck; if offered 'Quacker', you'll get rolled oats. Desserts are rare outside tourist places, although you may find some fresh watermelon or yogurt; Greeks make lovely sweets, puddings, cakes and ice creams (just look at the displays in any *zacharoplasteío* or pastry shop) but tend to eat them in the late afternoon with a coffee after the siesta, or in the early evening, hours before dinner.

At the seaside you'll find the fish tavernas, **psarotavérnes**, specializing in all kinds of seafood from freshly fried calamari, shrimps and giant prawns, to red mullet, swordfish, bream and sardines. Ironically, fish is expensive, because of depletion of stocks in the Med, but you can find cheapies like fresh whitebait (*marídes*), cuttle-fish stew (*soupiá*), small shrimps (*garídes*), sometimes cooked in feta cheese; and fish soups like *psarósoupa* or spicy *kakavia*, a meal in themselves with hunks of fresh bread and a bottle of wine. When eating fish soup it's customary to remove the fish, put it on a plate, drink the broth then tuck into the fish. Note that each type of fish has its own price, and portions are priced by weight.

If you're a red-blooded meat eater then head for the nearest **hasapotavérna**, which is a grill room attached to a local butcher's shop. Not that common, they offer fresh meat of all kinds, kebabs, home-made sausages and sometimes delicious stews, usually served by the butcher's assistant in a bloodstained apron for added carnivorous effect. The **psistariá** is another version of the theme specializing in chicken, lamb, pork or *kokorétsi*, a kind of lamb's offal doner. You may even find a **mageiria**, simple, old-fashioned pots simmering on the stove, home-cooking places, often only open for lunch. Other kinds of eateries in Greece need no intro-duction: the pizzeria (often spelled *pitsaria*) and, in big towns and major resorts, American fast fooderies, along with Goody's, the main Greek clone, and mom-and-pop attempts at the same.

A pitcher or bottle of tap water comes with each meal, and most Greeks order wine or beer. Note that when dining with Greeks it's customary to pour wine for each other—always guests first—and drink constant toasts, glasses chinking—*steen yámass*, good health to us, *steen yássou* or *yássas*, good health to you or, in Crete, *Avíva* or *Áspro Páto*—bottoms up. By all means clink glasses, but on no account bring your glass down on another person's (unless your intentions for the evening are entirely dishonourable). If a man does it to your glass, it's best to say '*yámass*' and act dumb, unless you want to take him up on it.

Eating out in Greece has always been something of a movable feast. Because of the intense heat in summer Greek families tend to eat late lunch at home, followed by their siesta or *mesiméri*. Then it's back to work, and around 8 or 9pm, it's time for the evening *vólta* or stroll to see and be seen, catch up on the news and decide where to go. Greeks eat late, rarely before 10pm, and meals can go on into the small hours. The children are there (they too nap in the afternoon) and are more than welcome—babies are rocked, toddlers crawl under the table and the older children get up to goodness knows what. Dinner is often boisterous, punctuated with fiery discussions, maybe bursts of song or dance. The more company the mer-rier, and the more likely your meal to turn into a spontaneous cabaret that no tour operator's organized 'Greek Night' can match. You may even get your table whipped away from under you in a dancer's jaws. *Kalí órexi! Bon appetit!*

A **Greek menu**, *katálogos*, usually has two-tier prices, with and without tax; you pay the highest. **Prices** are fixed according to category, although there can be seasonal fluctuations when they jump, especially at Easter and in August. If you suspect you're being ripped off, the system makes it easier to complain. If you eat with the Greeks there's no Western nit-picking over who's had what. You share the food, drink, company and the bill, *to logariasmó*, although hosts will seldom let foreign guests part with a drachma. A new law designed to catch tax evaders insists that you take a receipt (*apóthexi*); the police make periodical checks.

An average taverna meal—if you don't order a major fish—usually runs at around 2500–3000dr a head with generous carafes of house wine (*see* below). Prices at sophisticated restaurants or blatantly touristy places tend to be a bit higher, and places on remote islands can be just as costly because of extra transport prices. Quite a few places now offer set price meals with a glass of wine (often for under 2000dr), some for two people; some are better than others. In the 'Eating Out' sections of this book, any price given is per person with house wine.

kafeneíons and cafés

Every one-mule village will have at least one **kafeneíon**, a social institution where men (and increasingly women, although they're still outnumbered) gather to discuss the latest news, read the papers, nap in hard wood chairs, play cards or backgammon and incidentally drink coffee. Some men seem to live in them. They are so essential to Greek identity that in at least one instance, on Skópelos, when real estate interests threatened the last old *kafeneíon* with extinction, the town hall opened one for its citizens. The bill of fare features Greek coffee (*café hellinikó*), which is the same stuff as Turkish coffee, prepared to order in 40 different ways, although *glykó* (sweet), *métrio* (medium) and *skéto* (no sugar) are the basic orders. It is always served with a glass of water. '*Nes*' aka Nescafé with condensed Dutch milk has by popular tourist demand become available everywhere, though Greeks prefer their instant coffee whipped and iced (*frappé*)—and it's lovely on a hot day. Tea will be a pot of hot water and a bag. Soft drinks, *tsikoúdia* (rakí), brandy and ouzo round out the old-style *kafeneíon* fare.

Newer cafés (those with the cushy soft plastic chairs under awnings) usually open much earlier and close much later than *kafeneíons*. They are good places to find various kinds of breakfast, from simple to complete English, with rashers, baked beans and eggs, and attempts at cappuccinos. They also serve mineral water (try the sparkling ΙΟΛΗ), ice-cream concoctions, milkshakes, fruit juices, cocktails, pastries, and thick Greek yoghurt (cow, sheep or goat's milk) and honey. They are also a traditional place to stop for a late-night Metaxá; the more stars on the label (from three to seven) the smoother and the higher the price.

Nearly every island has at least one trendy music bar, usually playing the latest hit records and serving fancy cocktails as well as standard drinks. These establishments come to life at cocktail hour then again around midnight, when everyone has spent the day on the beach and the earlier part of the evening in a taverna. Bars used to close at dawn, although in 1994 the Greek government decreed a 2am weekday closing, claiming that the nation was nodding off at work after a night on the tiles. In general bars are not cheap, sometimes outrageously dear by Greek standards, and it can be disconcerting to realize that you have paid the same for your Harvey Wallbanger as you paid for your entire meal half an hour before in the taverna next door. Cocktails have now risen to beyond the 1000dr mark in many bars, but before you complain remember that the measures are triples by British standards. If in doubt stick to beer (Greece has a new brand to try, Mythos) ouzo, *suma* (like ouzo, but often sweeter—each island makes its own) wine and Metaxá (Metaxá and Coke, if you can stomach it, is generally about half the price of a rum and Coke). One unfortunate practice on the islands is the doctoring of bottles, whereby some bar owners use cheaper versions of spirits to refill brand-name bottles.

Just when it seemed time to write the obituary on a grand old Greek institution, the **ouzeríe**, it has come back with a vengeance. The national aperitif, ouzo—the *rakí* drunk by the Byzantines and Venetians, inexplicably renamed ouzo in the 18th century from the Latin *usere*, 'usable'—is clear and anise-flavoured, and served in small glasses or a *karafáki* holding about three or four doses which many drinkers dilute and cloud with water. It is cheap and famous for making its imbibers optimistic. As the Greeks look askance at drunkenness—as they did in ancient times, when they cut their wine with water and honey—ouzo is tradition-ally served with a little plate of snacks called *mezédes* which can range from grilled octopus, nuts, olives, chunks of cheese and tomatoes to elaborate seafood platters; for an assortment, ask for a *pikilía* (usually translated as '*seafood various*'). Similar to *ouzeríes* are **mezedopoieíons**, specializing in these Greek tapas, where you can build up an entire meal, sometimes from a hundred choices on the menu, and wash them down with wine or beer.

Wine

The country's best-known wine, **retsína**, has a very distinctive taste of pine resin. In ancient times, when the Greeks stored their wine in clay amphorae sealed air-tight with resin, the disintegration of the resin helped prevent oxidation in the wine and lent it its distinctive flavour. It is an acquired taste, and many people can be put off by the pungent odour and sharp taste of some bottled varieties. Modern retsínas show increasingly restrained use of resin; all retsínas are best appreciated well chilled. Draught retsína (*retsína varelísio*) can be found only on some islands, but in Athens it is the accepted, delicious accompaniment to the meal. Retsína is admirably suited to Greek food, and after a while you may find non-resinated wines a rather bland alternative. Traditionally it comes to the table in chilled copper-anodized jugs, by the kilo (about a litre), or *mesó kiló* (half) or *tétarto* (250ml) and served in small tumblers. Etiquette requires that they are never filled to the brim or drained empty; you keep topping up your companions' glasses, as best you can.

Ordinary red and white **house wines** are often locally produced bargains—ask for *krasí varelísio* (barrelled wine) or *krasí chíma* (loose wine). These wines are nearly always better than fine, though you may be unlucky; if you're suspicious, order a *tétarto kiló*. Greece also produces an ample selection of medium-priced red and white wines in bottles. They tend to be highly regionalized, each island and village offering their own varieties made from indigenous grapes; forget the tyranny of Cabernet Sauvignon and Chardonnay. All the principal wine companies—Boutari, Achaia-Clauss, Carras, Tsantali—have made strides to improve the quality in the past decade, investing heavily in new equipment and foreign expertise, and it shows; even that humblest of bottles (and Greece's best-seller) **Deméstika** has become very acceptable of late, and bears little resemblance to the rough stuff that earned it some unflattering sound-alike nicknames. Look out for the nobler labels: Boutari Náoussa is an old-style, slightly astringent red, while Boutari's Grande Réserve is their best red; Lac des Roches is their most popular white on the islands. Peloponnesiakos from Achaia-Clauss is an easy-drinking, light white wine which is popular at the moment anywhere within exportable distance of the Peloponnese. From Carras, Château Carras is a Bordeaux-style red wine made from the Cabernet Sauvignon and Merlot grapes; if you're lucky you might find Carras Limnio, one of Greece's most distinctive red wines. Boutari's Santoríni is their finest island white, while in Rhodes CAIR supplies Greece with its sparkling *méthode traditionelle* white, Caïr. Emery produces some good whites including Villare. The most noble red wines come from Nemea, and are superb with roast lamb.

In recent years small bottle-producers have become very fashionable with the wine-drinking elite. Some of these are superb; others deserve obscurity. But for the most part you are unlikely to come across them in the average taverna. If you're a wine buff, it's worth seeking them out from local recommendations in wine shops (*kávas*) and high-class restaurants.

Health

At the bare minimum there is at least one doctor (*iatrós*) on every island with more than a couple of hundred people, whose office hours are 9 to 1 and 5 to 7. On bigger islands there are hospitals, open all day, and outpatient clinics, open in the mornings. EU citizens are entitled to free medical care; British travellers are often urged to carry a Form E111, available from DSS offices (apply well in advance on a form CM1 from post offices), which will admit them to the most basic IKA (Greek NHS) hospitals for treatment; this doesn't cover medicines or nursing care. In any case, the E111 seems to be looked on with total disregard outside Athens; expect to pay up front, and get receipts so you can be reimbursed back home. As private doctors and hospital stays can be very expensive you should take out travel insurance. Make sure your holiday insurance has adequate repatriation cover; Greek hospitals have improved by leaps and bounds, but as it's still common for families to supply food and help with the nursing you may feel neglected. Non-Europeans should check their own health policies to see if they're covered while abroad.

Greek general practitioners' fees are usually reasonable. Most doctors pride themselves on their English, as do the pharmacists (found in the *farmakeío*), whose advice on minor ailments is good, although their medicine is not particularly cheap. If you forgot to bring your own condoms, they are widely available from *farmakeío* and kiosks, with lusty brand names such as 'Squirrel' or 'Rabbit'. If you can't see them on display ask for *kapótes* (condoms). You can also get the Pill (*chápi anti-siliptikó*), morning-after Pill and HRT over the pharmacy counter without a prescription. Be sure to take your old packet to show them the brand you use.

For some reason Greeks buy more medicines than anyone else in Europe (is it hypochondria? the old hoarding instinct?) but you shouldn't have to. The sun is the most likely cause of grief, so be careful, hatted and sunscreened. If you find the olive oil too much, Coca Cola or retsína will help cut it. Fresh parsley is good for stomach upsets. *See* pp.62–3 for possibly unkind wildlife. If anything else goes wrong, do what the islanders have done for centuries: pee on it.

Money

The word for **bank** in Greek is *trápeza*, derived from the word *trapézi*, or table, used back in the days of money-changers. On all the islands with more than goats and a few shepherds there is some sort of banking establishment, or, increasingly, at least an automatic teller. If there's no bank travel agents, tourist offices or post offices will change cash, traveller's cheques and Eurocheques. If you plan to spend time on a remote island it is safest to bring enough drachmae with you. Beware that small but popular islands often have only one bank, where exchanging money can take forever: beat the crowds by going at 8am, when the banks open (normal banking hours are 8–2, 8–1.30 Fri). The number of 24-hour **automatic cash-tellers** on the islands grows every year: some accept one kind of credit card and not another (VISA is perhaps the most widely accepted). You can also use these to withdraw cash at banks. Major hotels, luxury shops and resort restaurants take cards (look for the little signs) but smaller hotels and tavernas certainly won't.

Traveller's cheques are always useful even though commission rates are less for cash. The major brands (Thomas Cook and American Express) are accepted in all banks and post offices; take your passport as ID, and shop around to get the best commission rates.

Running out? Athens and Piraeus, with offices of many British and American banks, are the easiest places to have money sent by cash transfer from someone at home—though it may take a few days. **American Express** may be helpful here; their office in Athens is 2 Ermou Street, right by Sýntagma Square, ℂ 324 4975, and there are branches on Mýkonos, Rhodes and Santoríni.

The Greek drachma (abbreviated dr, in Greek δρχ) comes in coins of 100, 50, 20, 10, and 5 drachmae and in notes of 100, 500, 1000, 5000 and 10,000 drachmae.

Museums and Archaeological Sites and Opening Hours

Significant archaeological sites and museums have regular admission hours. Nearly all are closed on Mondays, and open other weekdays from 8 or 9 to around 2, although more important sites now tend to stay open later, until 4 or 5pm. Hours tend to be shorter in the winter. On the other hand, churches are often open only in late afternoon (from 6 to 7pm), when they're being cleaned. Students with valid ID often get a discount on admission fees. These are usually between 400 and 1000dr; more expensive ones are listed as such in the text.

National Holidays

Note that most businesses and shops close down for the afternoon before and the morning after a religious holiday. If a national holiday falls on a Sunday, the following Monday is observed. The Orthodox Easter is generally a week or so after the Roman Easter.

1 January	New Year's Day	*Protochroniá*; also *Ag. Vassílios* (Greek Father Christmas)
6 January	Epiphany	*Ta Fóta/ Theofánia*
February–March	'Clean Monday'	*Katharí Deftéra*
	(precedes Shrove Tuesday, and follows a three-week carnival)	
25 March	Annunciation/ Greek Independence Day	*Evangelismós*
late March–April	Good Friday	*Megáli Paraskeví*
	Easter Sunday	*Páscha*
	Easter Monday	*Theftéra tou Páscha*
1 May	Labour Day	*Protomayá*
40 days after Easter	Pentecost (Whit Monday)	*Pentikostí*

15 August	Assumption of the Virgin	*Koímisis tis Theotókou*
28 October	'*Ochí*' Day (in celebration of Metaxás' 'no' to Mussolini)	
25 December	Christmas	*Christoúyena*
26 December	Gathering of the Virgin	*Sináxi Theotókou*

In Greece, Easter is the equivalent in significance of Christmas and New Year in northern climes, the time when far-flung relatives return to see their families back home; it's a good time of year to visit for the atmosphere, feasts and fireworks.

After Easter and May 1, spring (*ánixi*—the opening) has offically come, and the tourist season begins. Festival dates for saints' days listed in the text vary over a period of several given days, or even weeks, owing to the Greek liturgical calendar's calculations for Easter; check these locally. It's also worth remembering that the main partying often happens the night *before* the saint's day.

Packing

Even in the height of summer, evenings can be chilly in Greece, especially when the *meltémi* wind is blowing. Always bring at least one warm sweater and a pair of long trousers, and sturdy and comfortable shoes if you mean to do any walking—trainers (sneakers) are usually good enough. Plastic swimming shoes are handy for rocky beaches, often the haunt of those little black pincushions, sea urchins; you can easily buy them near any beach if you don't want to carry them around with you. Greeks are inveterate night people: bring ear plugs if you don't want to hear them scootering home under your hotel window at 4am.

If you travel in August without any reservations, consider bringing a sleeping bag, just in case your destination is all full up. Serious sleeping-baggers should also bring a Karrimat or similar insulating layer to cushion them from the gravelly Greek ground. Torches come in very handy for moonless nights, caves and rural villages. Note that the **electric current** in Greece is mainly 220 volts, 50Hz; plugs are continental two-pin. Buy an adaptor in the UK before you leave, as they are rare in Greece; North Americans will need adaptors and transformers.

On the pharmaceutical side, bring extras of any prescription drug you need, just in case—other items, such as seasickness remedies, sunscreen, insect repellent, women's sanitary towels and sometimes tampons, tablets for stomach upsets and aspirin are widely available in pharmacies and even kiosks, but on remote islands you'll need to seek out the *farmakeío*; if there's no pharmacy, you've had it.

Soap, washing powder, a clothes line, a knife for picnics and especially a towel are essential budget traveller's gear. A photo of the family and home is always appreciated by new Greek friends.

Photography

Greece lends herself freely to photography, but a fee is charged at archaeological sites and museums. For a movie camera of any kind, including camcorders, you are encouraged to buy a ticket for the camera; with a tripod you pay per photograph at sites, but cameras (especially tripod-mounted ones) are not allowed in museums, for no particular reason other than the museum's maintaining a monopoly on its own (usually very dull) picture stock. 35mm film, both print and slide, can be found in many island shops, though it tends to be expensive and the range of film speeds limited. Disposable and underwater cameras are on sale in larger holiday resorts. Large islands even have one-hour developing services.

The light in the summer is often stronger than it seems and is the most common cause of ruined photographs; opting for slow film or filters will help. Greeks usually love to have their pictures taken and, although it's more polite to ask first, you should just go ahead and take the photo if you don't want them to strike a pose. You should avoid taking pictures (well, who would want to anyway?) of the aircraft, military installations and barracks, communications systems on mountain tops and military look-out posts. If you have an expensive camera, it never hurts to insure it. Above all, never leave it alone. Although Greeks themselves very rarely steal anything, other tourists are not so honest.

Post Offices

Signs for post offices (*tachidromío*) as well as post-boxes (*grammatokivótio*) are bright yellow and easy to find. Post offices (which are also useful for changing money) are open from Monday to Saturday 7.30am to 8pm; on small islands they may shut for lunch. Stamps (*grammatósima*) can also be bought at kiosks and in some tourist shops, although they may charge a small commission. Be warned that postcards can take up to three weeks to arrive at their destinations, while anything in an envelope will usually get there in a week or so, depending on the route. If you're in a hurry, pay extra for an express service. To send a package, always go to an island's main post office. If you do not have an address, mail can be sent to you poste restante to any post office in Greece, and picked up with proof of identity (you'll find the postal codes for all the islands in the text, which will get your letters there faster). After one month all unretrieved letters are returned to sender. In small villages, particularly on the islands, mail is not delivered to the house but to the village centre, either a *kafeneíon* or bakery.

Shopping

Official shopping hours in Greece are: Mon and Wed 9–5, Tues, Thurs and Fri 10–7, Sat 8.30–3.30 and Sun closed; in practice, tourist-orientated shops stay open as late as 1am in season. Leather goods, gold and jewellery, traditional handcrafts, embroideries and weavings, onyx, ceramics, alabaster, herbs and spices and tacky knick-knacks are favourite purchases; also check the text for island specialities. Duty-free Rhodes has some of the biggest bargains.

Non-EU citizens tempted by Greek jewellery, carpets, perfumes and other big ticket items can perhaps justify their indulgences by having the sales tax (VAT) reimbursed—this is 18% of the purchase price (or 13%, on Aegean islands). Make sure the shop has a TAX FREE FOR TOURISTS sticker in the window, spend at least 40,000dr inside, and pick up a tax-free shopping cheque for your purchases. When you leave Greece, you must show your purchases and get the customs official to stamp your cheques (allow an extra hour for this, especially at the airport), and cash them in at the refund point as you leave. If you are flying out of another EU country, hold onto the cheques, get them stamped again by the other EU country's customs and use their refund point. You can also post your tax free cheques back to Greece for refund (10 Nikis St, 10563 Athens, ✆ (01) 325 4995, ✆ (01) 322 4701) but they skim off 20% of the amount on commission.

Sports

watersports

Average Sea Temperatures

Jan	Feb	Mar	April	May	June	July	Aug	Sept	Oct	Nov	Dec
59°F	59°F	59°F	61°F	64°F	72°F	75°F	77°F	75°F	72°F	64°F	63°F
15°C	15°C	15°C	16°C	18°C	22°C	24°C	25°C	24°C	22°C	18°C	17°C

Greece was made for watersports, and by law all the beaches, no matter how private they might look, are public. All but a fraction meet European guidelines for water cleanliness, although a few could stand to have less litter on the sand. Beaches near built-up areas often have umbrellas and sunbed concessions and snack bars, and if there's a breeze you'll probably find a windsurfer to rent at affordable prices (favourite windy spots are Rhodes and Kárpathos). Bigger beaches have paragliding and jet skis, and waterskiing is available on most islands and large hotel complexes; on Kos you can bungee jump over the sea. The Ministry of Tourism has just allocated huge sums to build up marinas on the islands, which may improve chances of finding a small sail or motor boat to hire by the day; at the time of writing they are relatively few.

Nudism is forbidden by law, but tolerated in numerous designated or out-of-the-way areas. Topless sunbathing is legal on the majority of popular beaches as long as they're not smack in the middle of a village; exercise discretion. Even young Greek women are shedding their tops, but nearly always on someone else's island.

Scuba diving, once strictly banned to keep divers from snatching antiquities and to protect Greece's much-harassed marine life, is permitted between dawn and sunset in specially defined coastal areas; local diving excursions will take you there. The areas in the Dodecanese are **Kos/Kálymnos** (Vlichádia bay) and **Rhodes** (at Kallithéa). For information contact the Hellenic Federation of Underwater Activities, West Air Terminal Post Office, 16604 Elliniko, ✆ (01) 981 9961.

land sports

Walking is the favourite activity on every island with their superb natural scenery, gorges, wildflowers and wide open spaces; *see* special interest holidays, p.17, for guided walking tours. Increasingly locals are arranging treks, and little, often locally produced, maps and guides are a big help for finding the most interesting country paths. Never set out without a hat and water; island shops have begun to sell handy water-bottle shoulder slings. **Tennis** is very popular in Athens, with numerous clubs from Glyfáda to Kifissiá, and at all major resort hotels (many are lit up at night so you can beat the heat); often non-residents are allowed to play in the off season. **Golf courses** are rare, although on Rhodes you can swing away at the **Afandou Golf Club**, 19km from Rhodes town, ✆ (0241) 51 255, which has 18 holes, par 70, equipment hire and shop, lounges, changing rooms and a restaurant. Fees are from 3000dr per round, or 16,000dr for seven rounds in one week. Many small stables offer horse-riding on the islands. For precise details, call the **Riding Club of Greece**, Parádissos, ✆ 682 6128.

Telephones

The new improved Organismós Telefikoinonía Elládos, OTE, has replaced most of its old phone offices with new card phones, although many on the islands, for some reason, are set up for basketball players only. If you can reach the buttons, you can dial abroad direct (dial 00 before the country code). Cards for 100 units are 1500dr. For a decent long-distance chat you may need more, although the 500 unit (6500dr) and the 1000 unit (11,500dr) *telekártas* are hard to find outside big resort areas. As a last resort, find a telephone *me métriki* (with a meter), which are often more costly and usually located in kiosks (*períptera*), *kafeneíons*, some travel agents, hotels and shops. As a general rule, calls are cheaper between 3 and 5pm and after 9pm, but this may change. **Telegrams** can be sent from one of the surviving OTE offices in big cities or from the post office. When **phoning Greece** from overseas, the county code is 30 and drop the first '0' of the local area code.

Toilets

Greek plumbing has improved dramatically in the past few years and in the newer hotels you can flush everything away as merrily as you do at home, at least as often as your conscience lets you on arid islands strapped for water. Tavernas, *kafeneíons* and sweet shops almost always have facilities (it's good manners to buy something), and there are often public pay toilets in strategic areas of the towns.

In older pensions and tavernas, the plumbing often makes up in inventiveness for what it lacks in efficiency. Do not tempt fate by disobeying the little notices—'the papers they please to throw in the basket'—or it's bound to lead to trouble (a popular new sticker has Poseidon himself bursting out of the toilet bowl and pricking an offender with his trident). Old *kafeneíons* and bus stations tend to have only a ceramic hole squatter. Always have paper of some sort handy.

If you stay in a private room or pension you may have to have the electric water heater turned on for about 20 minutes before you take a shower. In most smaller pensions water is heated by a solar panel on the roof, so the best time to take a shower is in the late afternoon or early evening (before other residents use up the finite supply of hot water). In larger hotels there is often hot water in the mornings and evenings, but not in the afternoons. Actually 'cold' showers in the summer aren't all that bad, because the tap water itself is generally lukewarm, especially after noon. A good many showers are of the hand-held variety, which is potentially dangerous (especially if you have kids) because Greeks don't believe in shower curtains and one thoughtless moment means your towel or toilet paper is soaked.

Greek tap water is perfectly safe to drink, but on some islands it tastes less than delicious. On the other hand, inexpensive plastic bottles of spring water are widely available (and responsible for for untold pollution, taking up half the available room in landfill sites). On dry islands, remember to ask what time the water is turned off.

Tourist Information

If the National Tourist Organization of Greece (in Greek the initials are **EOT**) can't answer your questions about Greece, at least they can refer you to someone who can. You can find out basic information and look at pictures of the various islands on the Internet, at *www.vacation.net.gr.*

Australia and New Zealand

51 Pitt St, Sydney, NSW 2000, ℂ (02) 9241 1663/4, ✆ 9235 2174.

Canada

1300 Bay St, Toronto, Ontario, M5R 3K8, ℂ (416) 968 2220, ✆ 968 6533.
1233 De La Montagne, Montreal, Quebec, H3G 1Z2 ℂ (514) 871 1535, ✆ 871 1498.

Great Britain and Ireland

4 Conduit St, London W1R 0DJ, ℂ (0171) 734 5997 or 499 4976, ✆ 287 1369.

Netherlands

Leidsestraat 13, NS 1017 Amsterdam, © (20) 625 4212/3/4, © 620 7031.

USA

Head Office: Olympic Tower, 645 5th Ave, 5th Floor, New York NY 10022, © (212) 421 5777, © 826 6940, *gnto@orama.com*

168 N. Michigan Ave, Chicago, Illinois 60601, © (312) 782 1084, © 782 1091.

611 West 6th St, Suite 2198, LA, Calif. 90017, © (213) 626 6696, © 489 9744.

in Greece

The most popular islands have EOT offices, while the others often have some form of local tourist office; if not, most have tourist police (usually located in an office in the regular police station, although nine times out of ten they're the only people on the island who don't speak any foreign language). If nothing else, they have listings of rooms on the island.

Legal Assistance for Tourists is available free, but in July and Aug only: in Athens at 43–45 Valtetsiou St, © (01) 330 0673, © 330 1137.

Travelling with Children

Greece is a great country for children, who are not barely tolerated, but generally enjoyed and encouraged. Depending on their age, they go free or receive discounts on ships and buses. However, if they're babies don't count on island pharmacies stocking your brand of milk powder or baby foods—they may have some, but it's safest to bring your own supply. Disposable nappies, especially Pampers, are widely available, even on small islands.

Travelling with a tot is like having a special passport. Greeks adore them and spoil them rotten, so don't be surprised if your infant is passed round like a parcel. Greek children usually have an afternoon nap (as do their parents) so it's quite normal for Greeks to eat *en famille* until the small hours. Finding a babysitter is rarely a problem: some of the larger hotels even offer special supervised kiddie campgrounds and activity areas for some real time off.

Superstitions are still given more credit than you might expect; you'll see babies with amulets pinned to their clothes or wearing blue beads to ward off the evil eye before their baptism. Beware of commenting on a Greek child's intelligence, beauty or whatever, as this may call down the jealous interest of the old gods and some of the nastier saints. The response in the old days was to spit in the admired child's face, but these days, superstitious grannies are usually content with a ritual 'phtew-phtew-phtew' dry spit, to protect the child from harm.

Hotels

All hotels in Greece are classed into six categories: Luxury, A, B, C, D and E. This grading system bears little relationship to the quality of service, charm, views, etc., but has everything to do with how the building is constructed, size of bedrooms, lifts, and so on; i.e. if the hotel has a marble-clad bathroom it gets a higher rating. **Pensions**, most without restaurants, are a confusing subdivision in Greek hotel classifications, especially as many call themselves hotels. They are family-run and more modest (an A class pension is roughly equivalent to a C or D class hotel and is priced accordingly). A few islands still have their government-built hotels from the 1960s, the *Xenias*, many of which resemble barracks, the fashion in those junta-ruled days. On the Internet *www.greekhotel.com* lists, with musical accompaniment, 8000 hotels and villas in Greece, with forms for more information about prices, availability and booking.

prices

Prices are set and strictly controlled by the tourist police. Off season (i.e. mid-September–mid-July) you can generally get a discount, sometimes as much as 40%. Other charges include an 8% government tax, a 4.5% community bed tax, a 12% stamp tax, an optional 10% surcharge for stays of only one or two days, an air-conditioning surcharge, as well as a 20% surcharge for an extra bed. All these prices are listed on the door of every room and authorized and checked at regular intervals. If your hotelier fails to abide by the posted prices, or if you have any other reason to believe all is not on the level, take your complaint to the tourist police.

1999 Approximate Hotel Rates (drachma) for High Season (mid-July–mid-Sept)

	L	A	B	C	D
Single with bath	20–70,000	15–40,000	15–23,000	9–20,000	4–7000
Double with bath	30–200,000	25–50,000	20–35,000	11–28,000	6–14,000

Prices for E hotels are about 20% less than D rates.
Out of season rates are often 30–40% lower.

During the summer, hotels with restaurants may require guests to take their meals in the hotel, either full pension or half pension, and there is no refund for an uneaten dinner. Twelve noon is the official check-out time, although on the islands it is usually geared to the arrival of the next boat. Most Luxury and class A, if not B, hotels situated far from the town or port supply buses or cars to pick up guests. Hotels down to class B all have private en suite bathrooms. In C most do, as do most Ds; E will have a shower down the hall. In these hotels don't always expect to find a towel or soap, although the bedding is clean.

In the 'Where to Stay' sections of this book, accommodation is listed according to the following price categories:

luxury	29,000 to astronomical
expensive	12,000–30,000
moderate	6000–13,000
inexpensive	4000–7000

Prices quoted in the book are approximate and for **double rooms**.

booking a hotel

The importance of reserving a room in advance, especially during July and August, cannot be over-emphasized. Reservations can be made through the individual hotel, through travel agents, through the Hellenic Chamber of Hotels by writing, at least two months in advance, to 24 Stadíou St, 105 61 Athens, @ (01) 322 5449, or in person in Athens, at the Hotels Desk in the National Bank of Greece building, 2 Karageorgi Servias, © 323 7193, open Mon–Thurs 8.30–2, Fri 8.30–1.30, and Sat 9–12.30.

Rooms and Studios

These are for the most part cheaper than hotels and sometimes more pleasant. Although you can still find a few rooms (ΔOMATIA, *domátia*) in private houses, on the whole rooms to rent are found off a family's living quarters, sometimes upstairs or in a separate annexe; an increasing number have en suite baths.

One advantage rooms hold over hotels is that nearly all will provide a place to handwash your clothes and a line to hang them on. Another is the widespread availability of basic kitchen facilities (sink, table and chairs, at least a couple of gas rings, fridge, utensils and dishes) which immediately turns a room into a **studio**; these obviously cost a bit more, but out of season the difference is often negligible. Depending on facilities, a double room in high season will cost between 4000 and 8000dr with bath, a studio from 6,000 to 12,000. Until June and after August prices are always negotiable. Owners will nearly always drop the price per day the longer you stay.

Prices also depend a lot on how much competition exists between owners on each island. On some it's good-natured dog eat dog (you can, for instance, get a very good deal on Santoríni, because the locals have overbuilt); when you step off the ferry you will be courted with all kinds of interesting proposals, photos of the rooms and even guidebook reviews of their establishments. On others, room and hotel owners have co-operated to organize accommodation booths by the port to sort out customers; if the room is not within walking distance, they'll collect you in a car or minivan. If you still can't find a room most travel agencies will be able to dig one up (although these always cost more).

Youth Hostels

Some of these are official and require a membership card from the Association of Youth Hostels, or alternatively an International Membership Card (about 2600dr) from the Greek Association of Youth Hostels, 4 Dragatsaníou Street, Athens, ☏ 323 4107; other hostels are informal, have no irksome regulations, and admit anyone.

Most charge extra for a shower, sometimes for sheets. Expect to pay 2000dr a night, depending on the quality of facilities and services offered. The official ones have a curfew, which in Greece means you miss the fun.

Camping Out

The climate of summertime Greece is perfect for sleeping out of doors, especially close to the sea, where the breeze keeps the the worst of the mosquitoes at bay. Unauthorized camping is illegal (the law was enacted to displace gypsy camps, and is still used for this purpose) although each village enforces the ban as it sees fit. Some couldn't care less if you put up a tent at the edge of their beach; in others the police may pull up your tent pegs and fine you. All you can do is ask around to see what other tourists or friendly locals advise. Naturally, the more remote the beach, the less likely you are to be disturbed.

Most islands have at least one privately operated camping ground, though most have only minimal facilities. Islands with no campsites at all usually have a beach where free camping is tolerated. If the police are in some places lackadaisical about enforcing the camping regulations, they come down hard on anyone lighting any kind of fire in a forest, and may very well put you in jail for two months; every year fires damage huge swathes of land.

Camping prices are not fixed by law but these are approximate prices per day:

Adult	1200dr
Child (4–12)	600dr
Caravan	1800dr
Small tent	700dr
Large tent	1400dr
Car	650dr
Sleeping bag	350dr

On most islands it is possible to rent cottages or villas, generally for a week or more at a time. Villas can often be reserved from abroad: contact a travel agent or the National Tourist Organisation (EOT) for names and addresses of rental agents, or see the list below. In the off season villas may be found on the spot with a little enquiry, which, depending on the facilities, can work out quite reasonably per person. Generally the longer you stay, the more economical it becomes. If you book from abroad, packages generally include flights, transfers by coach, ferry, hydrofoil or domestic planes.

in the UK

Best of Greece, 23–24 Margaret St, London W1N 8LE, ✆ (0171) 331 7070. Luxury villas.

Direct Greece, Oxford House, 182 Upper Richmond Rd, Putney, London SW15 2SH, ✆ (0181) 785 4000. Particularly good for Líndos on Rhodes with a wealth of traditional Lindian houses. Jenny May is the uncrowned queen of Líndos. Also villas and flats on Chálki plus low season specials. The reps are extremely helpful and knowledgeable and most have lived in Greece for a long time.

Elysian Holidays, 14 Tower St, Rye, East Sussex TN31 7AT, ✆ (01791) 225482. Specialists in restored houses in pretty spots.

Filoxenia Ltd, Sourdock Hill, Barkisland, Halifax, West Yorkshire HX4 0AG, ✆ (01422) 371796, ✆ 310340. Haute couture holidays to Athens and a select range of islands. Suzi Stembridge and family have scoured Greece for unusual holiday places and pass on their favourites to fellow Grecophiles. Houses, villas, tavernas, pensions, fly-drive. Also **Opus 23** for travellers with disabilities.

Greek Sun Holidays, 1 Bank St, Sevenoaks, Kent TN13 1UW, ✆ (01732) 740317. Helpful and family-run, offering Athens and a range of unusual islands like Kárpathos. Tailor-made holidays and two-centre breaks.

Island Wandering, 51A London Rd, Hurst Green, Sussex TN19 7QP, ✆ (01580) 860733, ✆ 860282. Island-hopping without tears, with hotels or studios on the Dodecanese, pre-booked before you go or with a wandering voucher system.

Kosmar Villa Holidays plc, 358 Bowes Rd, Arnos Grove, London N11 1AN, ✆ (0181) 368 6833. Self-catering villas, studios and apartments on Rhodes, Sými and Kos. Two-centre holidays, flights from Glasgow and Newcastle and family savers.

Laskarina Holidays, St Mary's Gate, Wirksworth, Derbyshire, ✆ (01629) 822203/4 and 824881, ✇ 822 205. Named after the heroine of Spétses, Laskarina has the largest independent programme in Greece, specializing in the lesser-known islands of the Dodecanese, sometimes featuring restored traditional accommodation selected by directors Kate and Ian Murdoch. The Murdochs were made citizens of Sými for services rendered and Kate Murdoch shares honorary citizenship of Chálki, the former UNESCO island of Peace and Friendship, with Lady Thatcher. Two-centre holidays, out of season long stays available.

Manos Holidays, 168–172 Old St, London EC1V 9BP, ✆ (0171) 216 8000. Good value holidays to the major resorts and lesser-known islands, island-hopping and two-centres. Ideal for children, low season specials and singles deals.

in the USA/Canada

Amphitrion Holidays, 1206 21st St, NWm Suite 100A, Washington DC 20036, ✆ (800) 424 2471, ✇ (202) 872 8210. Houses, villas and apartments.

Apollo Tours, 1051 N. Waukegan Rd, Clenview, IL 60025, ✆ (800) 228 4367, ✇ (847) 724 3277. Upmarket villas and apartments.

CTI Carriers, 65 Overlea Blvd, Suite 201, Toronto, Ontario M4H 1P1, ✆ (800) 363 8181, ✇ 429 7159. One of the biggest Canadian operators with villas.

European Escapes, LLC, 483 2nd Avenue, San Francisco, CA 94118, toll free ✆ (888) EUROLUX, ✇ (415) 386 0477, *members.aol.com/euroluxury.* Luxury villas.

Greek Island Connection, 889 9th Ave, New York, NY 10019, ✆ (212) 581 4784, ✇ 581 5890. Customized seaside villas and condos.

Omega Tours, 3220 West Broadway, Vancouver, British Columbia, ✆ (800) 663 2669, ✇ (604) 738 7101. Villas and apartments.

Triaena Tours, 850 7th Ave, Suite 605, New York, NY, 10019, ✆ (800) 223 1273, ✇ (212) 582 8815. Long-established operator.

Zeus Tours, 209 W. 40th St, New York, NY 10018, ✆ (800) 447 5667, ✇ (212) 764 7912, *www.zeustours.com.*

for artists

The **Athenian School of Fine Arts** has an annexe at Rhodes, providing inexpensive accommodation for foreign artists (for up to 20 days in the summer and 30 in the winter) as well as studios, etc. One requirement is a recommendation from the Greek embassy in the artist's home country. Contact the School of Fine Arts, 42 Patission St, Athens, ✆ (01) 361 6930 for further information.

Women Travellers

Greece is a choice destination for women travellers but going it alone can be viewed as an oddity. Be prepared for a fusillade of questions. Greeks tend to do everything in groups or pairs and can't understand people who want to go solo. The good news for women, however, is the dying out of that old pest, the *kamáki* (harpoon). These 'harpoons'—Romeos in tight trousers and gold jewellery who used to roar about on motorbikes, hang out in the bars and cafés, strut about jangling their keys, hunting in pairs or packs—would try to 'spear' as many women as possible, notching up points for different nationalities. A few professional *kamákia* still haunt piano bars in the big resorts, gathering as many hearts, gold chains and parting gifts as they can; they winter all over the world with members of their harem.

Thank young Greek women for the decline in *kamáki* swagger. Watching the example set by foreign tourists as well as the torrid soaps and dross that dominate Greek TV, they have decided they've had enough of 'traditional values'. Gone are the days when families used the evening promenade or *vólta* as a bridal market for their carefully sheltered unmarried daughters; now the girls hold jobs, go out drinking with their friends and move in with their lovers. They laughed at the old *kamákia* so much that ridicule, like bug spray, has killed them dead.

Working

Casual summer jobs on the islands, legal for EU citizens, on the black for others, tend to be bar or restaurant work in a resort (although with the influx of impecunious Albanians low-paying jobs are becoming harder to find) or alternatively as a travel rep/greeter/co-ordinator with island travel offices that deal with holiday companies. Expect wages to pay your expenses but that's about it. One of the seven English/American schools in Athens always seems to be in need of qualified teachers, or if you have a university degree or TEFL (teaching English as a foreign language) qualification you may find a job teaching English in a *frontistírion* or private language school (although this is getting to be harder with new laws that give Greeks or people of Greek origins priority). You can get around this by giving private lessons on your own, with a bit of advertising; the market for learning English seems wide open, and if you're any good you can make quite a decent living. The *Athens News*, the country's English daily, and *The Hellenic Times*, a rather nationalistic weekly paper, often have classified advertisements for domestic, tutorial, and secretarial jobs. Working legally requires an often unpleasant descent into Greek bureaucracy (the local police will tell you what you must do); if you mean to stay over three months, *see* p.17.

History, Art and Architecture

More than any other group of islands, the Dodecanese have been affected, for better or worse, by their distance from the Greek mainland and their proximity to Asia Minor—specifically, the southwest coast known in ancient times as Caria. At the same time, as anyone who visits several of the islands soon realizes, their very island nature has allowed them to mould strong, individual characters, in spite of having to put up with more than their fair share of invaders. Although the notion that these twelve islands plus a few others formed any kind of geographical or political entity is surprisingly recent (the term Dodecanese only dates from 1908) they broadly share a common past. Rhodes and Kos, the two richest, most fertile and populous islands, hog history's stage, but occasionally the smaller islands get to put in their two cents.

History

Good Old Days: Formation of the Dorian Hexapolis (2000–500 BC)

The Dodecanese flourished early on, populated by the elusive Carians from the nearby coast of Asia Minor; late Neolithic and early Bronze Age settlements have been found on Kos, Tílos, Rhodes and Kálymnos. Some time around 2000 BC the islands were either subjugated by, or became allies of, the seafaring Minoans, a connection reflected in myth. When Minoan Crete fell (c. 1450BC) the Mycenaeans took over as elsewhere in Greece. Ancient versions of islands' names figure in the Homeric list of kingdoms that contributed ships to the Trojan war (c. 1190 BC).

In the various invasions that followed the fall of Troy and plunged the Greek world into its first Dark Age, Aeolians, Ionians and Dorians swept through Greece, the islands and the Asia Minor coast. The result, at first, was happiest in Ionia, along the middle coast of Asia Minor and nearby islands, where only a few centuries would pass before the first philosophers and mathematicians began to change the way the world thinks. The Dorians, who occupied the southern Peloponnese—most notably Sparta—plus Crete, the southern Cyclades, the peninsulae of the Carian coast, and the Dodecanese (with the exception of Pátmos and Léros), had less of a philosophical bent, but were no slackers in political organization. Some time around 1000 BC, in reaction to the first Ionian confederation, they formed a powerful political, economic and religious union, a proto-EU known as the Dorian Hexapolis, which included three cities on Rhodes (Líndos, Kámiros and Iálysos), Kos, Halikarnassos (modern Bodrum) and Cnidos (near modern Datça) in Caria.

Located on the main trade routes between east and west, the Hexapolis quickly boomed and in the 8th century BC began establishing colonies and trading counters as far away as Naples, Costa Brava in Spain, and Egypt. Commercial relations with the Phoenicians in the late 8th century helped revive the art of writing, lost since Mycenaean Linear B fell by the wayside in the Dark Ages. Inscriptions found on the Dodecanese were among the earliest examples of the new Greek alphabet, derived from the Phoenicians. Cultural development followed apace; Líndos in particular had the good fortune in the 7th century BC to be ruled by Cleoboulos, a contemporary of the great Solon and like him one of the Seven Sages of Greece.

Persians and Greeks (500–332 BC)

Proximity to the east brought not only the advantage of trade and cultural relations, but also invasions. The Dodecanese managed to repel the first Persian invasion in 490 BC, but in 480 BC the Persians obliged the islanders to contribute ships to their fleet in their great invasion against Greece. Once the Persians were defeated at Salamis, the Dodecanese joined the famous maritime league at Délos as a hedge against further attacks. Although Athens used the league to dominate the smaller islands, the Dodocanese used the advantage of distance to maintain a greater degree of autonomy, and they produced a dazzling array of artists, scientists and intellectuals—including Hippocrates, the father of medicine.

In spite of sharing a common Dorian ancestry with the Spartans, the Dodecanese remained loyal to Athens during the Peloponnesian War (431 BC). Far away from the centre of the conflict, they saw little action—a naval battle at Sými and the sneaky destruction of Kos' old capital by the Spartans. Like the majority of Athens' allies, they changed sides after the disastrous Athenian defeat at Syracuse. The main event of this period was the unique decision in 408 BC of the three city states of Líndos, Kámiros and Ialysós on Rhodes to join forces, found a whole new city from scratch and move most of their populations there. The new site had five good harbours, an advantage that was to make the new city a major force in the eastern Mediterranean. With the exception of Líndos, the mother cities today are mere archaeological sites, while Rhodes city has never looked back.

An early hiccup, however, occurred in 355 BC when Rhodes and several other islands were seized by Mausolus of Halikarnassos, satrap of Caria and ally of the king of Persia. His heir (and builder of the Mausoleum, one of the wonders of the ancient world) Queen Artemisia ordered Rhodes to succour her ally Tyre, the then trading capital of the Levant, against the armies of Alexander the Great. It was like standing in front of a racing locomotive; Alexander punished Rhodes and Kos in particular by sending Macedonian garrisons to occupy them. Although they moped, Alexander promoted their trade at the expense of Athens, and when he founded Alexandria he based its political organization on that of Rhodes' new city.

A Hellenistic Golden Age, Romans, & Byzantines (332 BC–AD 1082)

In the power plays following the death of Alexander, the Dodecanese sent the Macedonian garrisons packing, determined to maintain their neutrality. It proved impossible. When one of Alexander's generals, Antigonos, demanded that Rhodes join his army against his rival general, Ptolemy of Egypt, Rhodes refused, bringing down upon her head one of the greatest sieges in antiquity (304–305 BC), by Antigonos' son Dimitrios 'the Besieger', the conqueror of Cyprus and Salamis. This time, however, Dimitrios failed to live up to his nickname, and after a year and a battle of wits as well as weapons (*see* p.108) he lifted the siege. Rhodes erected its proud Colossus to celebrate its bold defiance.

For the next century and a half Rhodes became the main shipping transit centre of the Mediterranean; goods sent between Palestine, Phoenicia, the Black Sea, Italy, mainland Greece and Egypt all passed through her ports. Her banks loaned money to Greek cities, and her coins have been found throughout the Mediterranean world. She owed her success not only to the decline of Egypt in the 3rd century BC but to the sound administration of her fleet, both military and commercial—our modern law of the sea is a direct descendant of the maritime code of Rhodes. Kos, too, was beginning a golden age, not only from the success of its famous Asklepeion, linked to the august name of Hippocrates, but also from the renown of a school of poetry founded by Theocritus. It had especially close links to the Ptolemies as well, who sent their sons to Kos for their education. In later years it was rumoured that Cleopatra stashed some of her treasure on the island.

In 220 BC Rhodes reached the height of its military power when it defeated Byzantium, when that city attempted to impose a tax on grain leaving the Black Sea. She assisted Rome in the defeat of Philip V of Macedon in 197 BC and was given the Cycladic islands in return; she gained the Carian coast after helping Rome defeat Antiochus the Great of Syria. Kos, too, prospered with the advent of the Big Noise from Italy, finding in Rome a ready market for its lascivious transparent silks and other luxury goods, and the Romans granted the island a special autonomous status for the sake of the Asklepeion; it seems to have been made something of a luxury resort. Astypálaia, for its part, became Rome's base in the fight against pirates in the south Aegean.

The Aegean was rarely peaceful, and in 164 BC Rhodes made the mistake of backing the wrong horse (Persius) against Rome's favourite, and was punished by the loss of Caria and much of its trade. The island recovered her former status after joining Rome in its fight against a more serious threat, Mithridates of Pontus (88 BC), and once again the money poured in; the school of Rhetoric (founded in 330 BC) drew the cream of Roman society, and her scientists and astronomers came up with the first computer (*see* p.119). Rhodes was a great supporter of Julius Caesar and his great-nephew and successor, the future Augustus, and this earned it a terrible pillaging in 43 BC at the hands of Cassius, who went out of his way to devastate or sell off the island's bread and butter—her fleet. Although Augustus promoted Rhodes to the status of Allied City for having backed the right horse, the island never recovered, even though Diocletian made it capital of the Roman province of the islands in the late 3rd century AD.

The Dodecanese converted to Christianity early on. St Paul called in at Líndos and in AD 95 Rome sent a certain John into exile to Pátmos, where he converted the inhabitants and got his own back by penning the *Book of Revelations* (*see* p.63). The Metropolitan, or Cathedral of Rhodes, in the 4th century held sway in an archdiocese that included most of the Greek islands. The next few centuries saw all the islands turn away from Rome towards Constantinople. In the 7th century many were occupied by the Saracens before the Byzantine emperors rallied to chase them away.

Western Europeans Move In and Won't Go Away (1082–1522)

The Dodecanese got a preview of coming events in 1082, when Byzantine Emperor Alexius Comnenus granted the Venetians free trading rights in the Byzantine empire as well as specific rights in the ports of Rhodes. Venice had helped Alexius defeat the Normans in the Adriatic, and was competing with all the other Italian mercantile republics (Amalfi, Pisa and Genoa) for trade in the eastern Mediterranean. In 1095 the islands came in contact with another aspect of the Latin West, when the Crusaders stopping en route to the Holy Land introduced their aggressive brand of Christianity. After capturing and losing Jerusalem, the Crusaders' bit of pillaging and piracy on the side climaxed in the Fourth Crusade (1204) and the capture of Constantinople, egged on by Venice, who supplied their ships. In the subsequent division of spoils the Venetians claimed nearly all the Greek islands, but in the Dodecanese managed to occupy only the more northerly islands—Pátmos, Astypálaia, Léros and Kálymnos—while their arch-rivals, the Genoese, seized the more southerly.

In 1291 the tables turned when Jerusalem fell to the Ottomans, the rising power in the east. This disrupted, among other things, the work of the Knights of St John, or the Knights Hospitallers, an exclusive order made up of the second and third sons of Western Europe's aristocracy, who took vows of chastity, poverty and obedience and operated a hospital in Jerusalem for pilgrims. Forced to abandon Jerusalem, the Knights, who were never as poor as their vows suggested, eventually purchased the Dodecanese from the Genoese pirate-admiral Vinioli. The Greeks who lived on the islands begged to differ and the Knights had to spend several years conquering their purchase before moving in.

They set up headquarters on Rhodes, built a new hospital and fortified the big island and most of the smaller ones against the Ottomans. They communicated by means of carrier pigeons and smoke signals, while raiding the coast in swift vessels made on Sými, letting Christian pirates pass through their territory unmolested, but hijacking ships carrying Muslim pilgrims and in general behaving just like pirates themselves, even daring to raid the most important ports in the Middle East. In 1522 Sultan Suleiman the Magnificent had had enough of the pests and attacked Rhodes with an enormous army. All the men of the Dodecanese rallied to its defence, but after a long bitter siege the Knights were betrayed by a disgruntled German and forced to surrender (*see* pp.69 and 110).

Turks and Italians

The Ottomans were exceedingly fond of their new islands, and to sweeten the pill of occupation Suleiman granted them special privileges that most of the Dodecanese maintained until the early 20th century. Still, Turkish occupation wasn't exactly a bed of roses. Many of the churches were converted into mosques, although over time the pashas relaxed some of their policies towards the Christians and allowed missionaries, both Orthodox and Catholic, to return. On the smaller islands their main concern was collecting taxes, and they had correspondingly small, if any, permanent Turkish populations. Merchant captains prospered in otherwise rocky places—Sými, Kastellórizo, Kássos, Kárpathos and Líndos—as sailing and trading were never Ottoman strong points. Because the Turks respected the Imperial Charter of the Monastery of St John, Pátmos enjoyed a good deal of autonomy; the monks operated a fleet of galleys, and kept the torch of Orthodox learning alight. In the 18th century they were openly running a theological school.

When the Greek War of Independence broke out in 1821 the sea captains of Sými and Kássos at once sent ships to aid the Greeks. Sými lost many of its privileges for its pro-independence activities, inhabitants of Rhodes who dared to rally to the cry of 'Freedom or Death!' got the latter, while Kássos, in 1824, was singled out for one of the worst atrocities in a war that had no lack of them, when the Ottomans' Egyptian allies devastated the little island and massacred the population.

In 1912, during the Balkan War, Italy opportunistically took 'temporary possession' of the islands and made Léros, with its huge sheltered harbour, an important base, while Kárpathos became the launch pad for Italian activities in Egypt. This occupation was made 'permanent' by the second Treaty of Lausanne, after Greece was discredited by its terrible débâcle in Asia Minor in 1922. Mussolini, the great wannabe imperialist, poured money into his new colonies, sponsoring massive public works (each island has at least one of his public buildings), new roads, reforestation, archaeological excavations and historical reconstructions. While Turkish rule had been depressing, negligent and sometimes brutal, the Fascists, in spite of their lavish expenditure, were even worse in the eyes of the islanders, outlawing their Orthodox religion and Greek language, to the extent that even today you can occasionally find older people on the Dodecanese who are more comfortable speaking Italian. The women of Kálymnos in particular put up stiff resistance to the Italianization programme, not only painting all of their houses Greek blue and white in protest, but marching and rioting in the streets.

With Italy's surrender in 1943 Churchill sent in the British troops to withstand German occupation, but lacked sufficient numbers to do the job, as was unhappily proved in the Battle of Léros. During their tenure, the Germans reduced the once-important Jewish populations on Rhodes and Kos to virtually nil. In May 1945, after their defeat, the British returned to fill in the subsequent vacuum; many islanders claim to this day that Churchill meant the British occupation to be as 'temporary' as the Italian. But whatever was going on in Churchill's brain, a treaty was duly signed in March 1948, uniting the Dodecanese with Greece. Unfortunately the story isn't quite over: the union with Greece has yet to be recognized by Turkey, which never signed the Treaty of Lausanne and claims the Dodecanese were never Italy's to concede after the war. This has created a climate of mistrust and tense incidents such as the quarrel that almost led to an armed conflict over two rock piles near Kálymnos, Ímia/Kardak, in 1996. On a more positive note, since the demise of nationalist prime minister Andreas Papandreou visits between the islands and Turkey have notably increased, not only by tourists but by Greeks and Turks, and on a local scale relations seem to be more cordial than they have been in the recent past.

Art and Architecture

Although the Dodecanese, in particular Rhodes and Kos, were once famous for their richness, Roman pillaging, invasions and earthquakes have put paid to nearly everything made in Classical times or earlier.

Mycenaean–Classical (2000–400 BC)

The earliest finds on the islands from the 2nd millennium BC suggest a close relationship with Crete and the Mycenaean civilization on the mainland. Although no palaces have ever been found on any of the Dodecanese, the tombs of the period produced weapons and jewellery in Minoan-Mycenaean styles, though the pottery, of a unique peach colour adorned with reliefs of marine and floral designs, appears to be of local manufacture. Other Minoan-style tombs were found near Kos town, and rock-cut Mycenaean tombs can still be seen on Kálymnos (at Pigádia).

After the fall of Troy, invasions and the subsequent Dark Age, the whole Aegean went back to the artistic blackboard and slowly learned to draw again in the Geometric and Orientalizing Periods (1100–700 BC). The ancient Rhodian cities of Líndos, Kámiros and Ialysós have all yielded rich pottery finds, including fine pieces decorated with animals and leaf patterns; other ceramic exports from this period came from Corinth, Cyprus and the Near East. Votive offerings of Phoenician origin from the 10th century BC were discovered in the temple of Athena on the Acropolis of Líndos. By the 7th century Rhodes was one of Greece's most talented producers of black-figure pottery.

The creation of the city of Rhodes, designed by the foremost architect and planner of the day, Hippodamos of Miletus, in 408 BC, which pooled together the talent and populations of Líndos, Kámiros and Ialysós, resulted in a wealthy city that developed its own school of art, attracting painters and sculptors from Greece and Caria whose names were lauded in antiquity, although disappointingly little has survived.

Hellenistic and Roman (380 BC–AD 400)

The great inspiration for Rhodes' golden age of art was the presence of Lysippos, court sculptor to Alexander the Great, who spent a period working on Rhodes. Lysippos and his followers were part of the great Hellenistic movement that was influenced by the art of eastern lands conquered and Hellenized by Alexander. Hellenistic art, especially sculpture, left behind the cool, aloof perfection of the Classical era for a more emotional, Baroque approach, all windswept drapery, violence and passion. The Rhodes school was at its height: Chares produced his celebrated Colossus, extreme in its own way, while Agesander, Polydorus and Athenodorus sculpted the famous writhing *Laocoön* from the 1st century BC (now in the Vatican museum), and the Aphrodites (including Durrell's *Marine Venus*) in the **Rhodes** museum. Apelles, the greatest painter in Alexander's day although his work only survives in mosaic copies, was a native of Kos. What remains of the Temple of Athena at Líndos is Hellenistic, especially the ship's prow carved in the rock.

The architectural record has survived somewhat better on **Kos**, thanks in part to the numerous earthquakes that buried it in antiquity. Houses became decidedly more plush, decorated with lavish mosaics; many of these, both Hellenistic and Roman, have been excavated in Kos town (only to be carted off on Mussolini's orders to decorate his reconstruction of the Palace of the Grand Masters in Rhodes town). The oldest houses found on Kos are contemporary with the famous Asklepeion, built after the death of Hippocrates in 353 BC. Excavated and partly reconstructed, the Asklepeion remains an impressive sight and produced many of the fine Hellenistic statues now in the island's archaeology museum.

The Pax Romana not only ended the rivalries between the Greek city-states but pretty much dried up the sources of their inspiration, although sculptors, architects and other talents found a ready market for their skills in Rome, cranking out fair copies of Classic and Hellenistic masterpieces. Rhodes and Kos, granted all kinds of privileges by the Romans, were exceptions. The reconstructed Casa Romana in **Kos** town offers a good example of the scale on which a well-to-do Roman lived, while the city's public facilities easily compare to ours today, with their heated pools at the baths and a covered running track to protect athletes from sun and rain. Rhodes, before Cassius' destructions, was even more splendid. Much was rebuilt after Cassius, but next to nothing has survived quarrying by the Knights.

Byzantine and Latin (400–1522)

The art and architecture of the Byzantines began to show its stylistic distinction under the reign of Justinian (527–565). The immediate post-Justinian period saw a golden age in the splendour of Hagia Sofia in Istanbul and the churches of Ravenna in Italy. On the islands, however, the early Byzantine period is recalled only in the remains of simple three-naved basilicas with geometric mosaic floors on **Kárpathos**, **Kálymnos**, **Kos** and **Rhodes**.

After the austere art purge of the Iconoclasm, the old Roman basilica plan was jettisoned in favour of a central Greek cross crowned by a dome, elongated in front by a vestibule (narthex) and outer porch (exonarthex) and at the back by a choir and three apses. The age of the Comnenus emperors (12th–14th centuries) produced some fine painting: the 12th-century frescoes and manuscripts at the Monastery of St John on **Pátmos**, home to the finest Byzantine art in the Dodecanese. Other places to look are **Tílos** (Ag. Panteleímon) and **Rhodes** (at Líndos, Monólithos, Asklipío, Archángelos, Mount Filérimos and Iálysos). **Sými** has a fine set of 18th-century churches, most importantly the Monastery of Taxiárchis Michael Panormítis.

The Venetians left impressive fortresses on **Astypálaia** and **Léros**, and the Knights of St John left castles and fortifications on just about all the other islands. The walls of **Rhodes** town and the streets within, lined with the Knights' Inns, public buildings and reconstructed Palace of the Grand Master, as well as the former Jewish and Turkish quarters, has recently been declared part of the World's Artistic Patrimony by UNESCO.

Turks, Italians and Modern Times (1522–the Present)

The Turks left few important monuments in Greece, and much of what they did build was wrecked or neglected to death by the Greeks after independence. Because the Dodecanese only became Greek in 1948, they haven't had a chance to fall over in **Rhodes** town and **Kos**, both of which have some of the best surviving mosques, hammams, houses, libraries and other public buildings on Greek soil. A couple are still used by the islands' small Turkish minorities. Of late, some of the buildings have even been restored, notably the Turkish baths in Rhodes town (still used as such) and in Kos town, now beautifully converted into a restaurant.

The independent-minded islands and towns with their own fleets, notably **Sými**, **Pátmos** and especially **Líndos**, are full of impressive mansions built during Turkish rule by sea captains and ship owners, many a cross between early 19th-century neoclassicism and native traditional and Turkish styles. Nearly all have been beautifully restored; work has at last begun even on the ruined old captains' houses of **Kastellórizo,** which suffered the worst vicissitudes of all, especially in the last war.

The Italians did a surprising amount of building during their 30-year tenure. Nearly every principal port in the Dodecanese has an Italian harbour master's palazzo, down at heel but often painted in gaudy pastel colours like Zorba's girlfriend Boubalina. And like Boubalina they have a sense of style and add a bit of Art Deco pizzazz in the Aegean, although like the Turkish mosques the Greeks who have long memories are content to let them slowly fall to bits. The dilapidated port town of Lakkí on **Léros** stands out as a surreal memorial to their disappointed dreams and schemes. On **Rhodes** the Italians, believing themselves the heirs of the Italian branch of the Knights of St John, fastidiously restored the walls and medieval inns and rebuilt the Palace of the Grand Masters, as well as adding a number of public buildings in the new town, all based on Italian models. Most of the more recent structures in the Dodecanese are generic Mediterranean, although the newest hotels usually make at least superficial references to traditional styles—not of the Dodecanese as much as that of the sugar cube architecture of the Cyclades.

Topics

The Father of Medicine

Not a few ancient Greeks could claim descent from the gods and heroes, and Hippocrates was no exception. Born on Kos in 460 BC, in the year of the 20th Olympiad, his mother was Phainareti, 20th descendant from Herakles, and his father was a doctor named Gnosidikos Asklepiades Herkleides, 18th descendant of Asklepios, the god of healing. Hippocrates took after his father, but had little time for the divine side of his family: while not rejecting the gods, his great revolution was to dismiss the idea that human diseases resulted from their wrath.

The medicine Hippocrates fathered was an art and a science, based on the systematic examination of the patient: the review, the audition, and the clinical description of pathological situations. He believed in natural causes, but not in the materialistic way of modern medicine; the patient's mental attitudes and beliefs were as important to his diagnosis as the more obvious symptoms. Psychosomatic remedies—a calm environment, good air and water and relaxation, and the power of suggestion—were an essential part of the cure.

Hippocrates lived in the Golden Age of philosophy, at the same time as Plato, Empedocles and Democritus, all of whom attempted to explain the universe and the nature of man. But again Hippocrates was different. He had little time for what he labelled the 'unproven hypotheses' of the philosophers: according to him, one could learn the truth only through the study and observation of nature and people, of the healthy and diseased. Yet at the same time he saw in humanity something extra that did not exist elsewhere in nature; medicine was a religion in itself and Hippocrates added the moral and spiritual code that formed the basis of his celebrated Oath:

1. I swear by Apollo Physician, by Asklepios, by Hygeia and Panacea and by all the gods and goddesses, making them as my witnesses, that I will carry out, according to my ability and judgement, this oath and this indenture.

2. To hold my teacher in this art equal to my parents; to make him partner in my livelihood; when he is in need of money to share mine with him, to consider his family as my own brothers, and to teach them his art, if they want to learn it, without fee or indenture.

3. To impart instruction, written, oral and practical, to my own sons, the sons of my teacher, and to indentured pupils who have taken the physician's oath, but to nobody else.

4. I will use treatment to help the sick according to my ability and judgement, but never with a view to injure or doing wrong.

5. Never will I administer a poison to anybody when asked to do so, nor will I suggest such a course. Similarly, I will not give a woman a pessary to cause abortion.

6. But I will keep pure and holy both my life and my art.

7. I will not use the knife, not even verily, on sufferers from gall stone, but I will place to such as are craftsmen therein.

8. Into whatsoever house I enter, I will enter to help the sick, and I abstain from all intentional wrongdoing and harm, especially from abusing the bodies of man or woman, bond or free.

9. And whatsoever I shall see or hear in the course of my profession, as well as outside my profession in my intercourse with men, if it be what should not be published abroad, I will never divulge, holding such things to be holy secrets.

10. Now if I carry out this oath, and break it not, may I gain forever reputation among all men for my life and for my art; but if I transgress it and forswear myself, may the opposite befall me.

Besides the oath, Hippocrates and his school compiled a collection of 70 works, the Hippocratic corpus, taking what was valid from the ancients and adding their own observations; until the 18th century these works remained the classic medical text. Some of Hippocrates' most precocious work dealt with the brain: he differed from others in the 5th century in saying that the brain, and not the heart, was the thinking organ: 'From the brain only arise our pleasures, joys, laughter and tears. Through it, in particular, we think, see, hear and distinguish the ugly from the beautiful, the bad from the good, the pleasant from the unpleasant... To consciousness the brain is messenger.' His later writings on epilepsy inspired Wilder Penfield's comments in *The Mystery of the Mind*:

> *His discussion constitutes the finest treatise on the brain and the mind that was to appear in medical literature until well after the discovery of electricity... Some of the notes that Hippocrates made after examining his patients were copied and recopied through the centuries. They are models of brevity and insight. Epileptic patients of a certain type, not infrequently, re-live some previous experience in which they see, perhaps, and hear what they have seen and heard at an earlier time in their lives. Realizing, as Hippocrates did, that 'epilepsy comes from the brain when it is not normal', he must have guessed the truth—that the engram of experience is a structured record within the brain.*

The Environment: Endangered Animals and Plain Old Pests

When Western Europe was busy discovering the beauties of nature in the Romantic era, Greece was fighting for survival; when the rest of the west was gaining its current environmental awareness in the 1960s and 70s, the Greeks were throwing up helter-skelter resorts on their beaches, making Athens the citadel of sprawl it is today, merrily chucking plastic bags of garbage in the sea and killing off the monk seals because they ate too many fish.

Ever so slowly, the average Greek is waking up to the fact that nature can only take so much before she turns on her persecutors. A small but dedicated band of ecologists has been sounding the alarm for decades, but most Greeks only saw their country as something to exploit: if the law forbids building on forested land, the Greek solution was—and sadly, still is—to burn the forest. But now these past excesses are beginning to hurt, not just the environment but where it counts for everyone, in the pocketbook.

Tourism has been responsible for much of the damage, but also for many of the changes in attitude. The great influx of people is in part responsible for the severe depletion of fishing stocks. Laws limiting industrial fishing and dynamiting are constantly flouted—demand for fish has drained the Aegean's key resource by nearly 60% in recent years, making what used to be the cheapest staple food in Greece the most expensive. There is often talk about a fishing moratorium of a year or two to give the Mediterranean a break, but the economic consequences are simply too overwhelming for the idea to go past the talking stage. On the plus side, tourist concerns about clean beaches (and Greece now proudly claims the cleanest in Europe) have resulted in proper sewage systems on most islands and a noticeable decline in litter and junk, although there is still work to do here. The Greeks may return their beer bottles but they recycle absolutely nothing, not glass, not paper, not plastic.

Many birds use the islands as stepping stones on their migratory paths—swallows, storks, pelicans, herons and egrets all pass at one time of the year or another, and there is a wide variety of indigenous birds to keep them company. Eagles and vultures float over the mountains and cliffs, including the massive Griffon vulture and the rare lammergeyer, with wingspans of nearly 10 feet. Closer to the ground, Greece's extraordinary variety of wildflowers—some 6000 native species—draws an equally colourful array of butterflies. All suffer in the annual forest conflagrations, which are nearly all set by local arsonists (in spite of loud accusations directed at the CIA, Turks and other bogeys). In the summer of 1997, when the Minister of Agriculture Stefanos Tsoumakas suggested giving in and legalizing buildings erected on burned land since 1975, there was an encouraging outcry from voters— especially when the beautiful forest in the hills above Thessaloníki was immediately torched, as if in response. Vagueness about the law and jurisdictions continued to encourage arsonists in an epidemic of forest fires in 1998.

As for creatures unfortunately *not* on the endangered list, the wily mosquito tops the list for pure incivility. Most shops stock the usual defences: lotions, sprays and insect coils; or best of all, pick up one of those inexpensive electric mosquito repellents that plug into a wall socket. Greek skeeters don't spread malaria, but bites from their sand-fly cousins can occasionally cause a nasty parasite infection. Wasps have a habit of appearing out of nowhere to nibble that honey-oozing baklava you've just ordered. Pests lurk in the sea as well: harmless pale brown jellyfish (*méduses*) may drift in anywhere depending on winds and currents, but the oval transparent model (*tsoúchtres*) are stinging devils that can leave scars on tender parts of your anatomy if you brush against them; pharmacies sell soothing unguents. Pincushiony sea urchins live by rocky beaches, and if you're too cool to wear rubber swimming shoes and you step on one, it hurts like hell. The spines may break and embed themselves even deeper if you try to force them out; the Greeks recommend olive oil, a big pin and a lot of patience. Less common but more dangerous, the *drákena*, dragon (or weever) fish, with a poisonous spine, hides in the sand waiting for its lunch. If you step on one (rare, but it happens), you'll feel a mix of pain and numbness and should go the doctor for an injection.

Greece's shy scorpions hide out in between the rocks in rural areas; unless you're especially sensitive their sting is no more or less painful than a bee's. Avoid the back legs of mules, unless you've been properly introduced. The really lethal creatures are rare: there are several species of small viper that live in the nooks and crannies of stone walls, where they are well camouflaged, and only come out occasionally to sun themselves. Vipers will flee if possible, but if they feel cornered they will make a hissing sound like radio static before attacking. Since the time of Homer mountain sheepdogs have been a more immediate danger in outer rural areas; by stooping as if to pick up a stone to throw, you might keep a dog at bay.

The Real Beast

It's a little known fact outside Biblical scholarship, but in the early years of Christianity there was more than one 'Apocalypse' floating around, most of which have since been classified as pseudographia (books attributed to earlier, venerated figures to give them an aura of authority). There is, for instance, an Apocalypse of Peter, and another supposedly by Paul, and a once popular one ascribed to the Virgin Mary. The one that actually made it into the New Testament only squeaked past the early Fathers of the Church because they sincerely believed that it was written by Jesus' beloved disciple John. Modern New Testament scholarship, however, disagrees and posits yet another John, known as John 'of Patmos'.

The pseudographic Apocalypses offer the usual previews of the end of the world and tours of hell (specifying in great detail who went there, and what punishment awaited—not surprisingly, persecutors of Christians were given a good deal of attention). Whoever he was, Patmos John had other fish to fry as well. His Revelation, at least in its time, was intended and read as a prophecy of the fall of the whole persecuting complex: Rome. *'Fallen, fallen, is Babylon the great, she who made all nations drink the wine of her impure passion'* (14:8). John spoke up for all the people who had their doubts whether Rome had done the world a favour by conquering it: the persecuted Christians, the captive nations of the Empire, the victims of the insatiable Roman tax collector, the millions of slaves, the serious men who hated the abomination of Emperor-worship.

> ...and on her forehead was written a name of mystery: 'Babylon
> the great, mother of harlots and of the earth's abominations.'
> And I saw the woman drunk with the blood of the saints and the
> blood of the martyrs of Jesus.

(17:4–6)

The Harlot rides a seven-headed beast, which an angel explains to John represents seven hills (of Rome), and the waters that surround her are 'the peoples and multitudes and nations and tongues' over which she has dominion. And what of the Beast, whom John rather murkily identified with the Antichrist, the son of Satan, whose coming precedes the end of time?

> Here is wisdom. He who has understanding, let him calculate the
> number of the beast, for it is the number of a man; and its
> number is six hundred and sixty-six.

(13:18)

Occultists and Biblical scholars alike have been racking their brains about this number since the Middle Ages. The answer has often been sought in the Hebrew Cabbala, where letters have numerical equivalents useful in conjuring and finding hidden connections. Using the Cabbala, 666 is supposed to be the sum of the letters in the name *Nero Caesar*.

The truth, however, lies in something a bit different: a magic square. Magic squares have fascinated mystics and mathematicians for a long time; Pythagoras himself (from Sámos, just north of Pátmos) is said to have invented them. You'll recall that a magic square is an arrangement of numbers where each column adds up to the same sum, vertically, horizontally, and even diagonally. They come in all sizes, and the mystics long ago got the habit of associating each with one of the seven planetary spheres. The sphere of the sun was given the 6 by 6 square, a very big and complex magic square. Each of the columns adds up to 37 (666=37x18), and the sum of all the numbers in the square (the integers 1 to 36) is 666.

What does the sun have to do with it? Ever since the beginnings of monotheism in Egypt, there was a tendency to associate the One God with the sun, and the Romans cleverly appropriated the symbolism to the emperor-worship that was the foundation of their state. The cult of the Emperor was the cult of Sol Invictus, the Unconquerable Sun. In the Roman Empire, you could believe in any god you liked as long as you also rendered unto Caesar by sacrificing to the Emperor; not to do so was treason. To the hard-headed Christians, this was abomination. They refused, and got fried for it.

To any educated Christian of John's time, there would be no doubt who the Antichrist really was, or where he resided. The seat of evil on earth was Rome, and the Beast was an oppressive tyrant and a false sun-god rolled into one. The number has nevertheless added a certain spice to a certain kind of Christian discourse even today. Fundamentalist preachers have used 666 to prove through numerology that the Antichrist is the Coming Russian Dictator, or the Likely Democratic Presidential Candidate. A dissenting minority once made much of the six letters in the names Ronald Wilson Reagan. In America, one often hears late-night radio reverends pointing the finger at the European Union, which has seemingly usurped the Antichrist position long held by the popes in Rome, in Protestant eyes at any rate. You may even notice some 666 graffiti while travelling in Greece: when the European Union issued its decree no.666 proposing a pan-European ID card, the Greek Orthodox hierarchy went ballistic and sponsored demonstrations in the streets. It was all the proof they needed that Brussels was in league with the devil, or, in Patmos John's own words:

> Also it [the Beast] causes all, both small and great, both rich and
> poor, both free and slave, to be marked on the right hand or the
> forehead, so that no one can buy or sell unless he has the mark,
> this is the name of the Beast or the number of its name.

(13:16)

After all, the European Union was founded with the Treaty of where? Rome!

On *Kéfi*, Music and Dancing

In the homogenized European Union of the late 1990s, the Spaniards, Irish and Greeks are among the very few peoples who still dance to their own music with any kind of spontaneity, and it's no coincidence that both have untranslatable words to describe the 'spirit' or 'mood' that separates going through the motions and true dancing. In Spain, the word is *duende*, which, with the hard-driving rhythms of flamenco, has an ecstatic quality; in Irish it's good *craic*, in Greek, the word is *kéfi*, which comes closer to 'soul'. For a Greek to give his all, he must have *kéfi*; to dance without it could be considered dishonest. The smart young men in black trousers and red sashes who dance for you at a 'Greek Night' taverna excursion don't have it; two craggy old fishermen in a smoky *kafeneíon* in Crete, who crank up an old gramophone and dance for their own pleasure, do. It has no age limit: teenagers at discos pounding out all the international hits of the moment are really only waiting for 1 or 2am, when the clubs switch over to Greek music and the real dancing and *kéfi* can start. You can feel the *kéfi* at Easter when an entire village joins hands to dance an elegant *kalamatianó*, an act as simple and natural as it is moving, an enhanced celebration of community that the rest of us are lucky ever to experience.

Greek music has been influenced by Italy (most notably on the Ionian islands), Turkey, the Middle East and the Balkans, all of whom were once influenced by the Byzantines, who heard it from ancient Greeks, who heard it from the Phrygians—and so on. Traditional island songs, *nisiótika*, are played on bagpipes (*tsamboúna*), clarinet (*klaríno*) and various stringed instruments—the *laoúto* (a large mandolin, used for backing, traditionally picked with an eagle's quill), the *lýra* (a three-string fiddle, held upright on the knee, played on Crete and the southern Dodecanese), the violin (*violí*), the guitar (*kítara*) and the double-stringed hammer dulcimer (*sandoúri*), once limited to Greek Anatolia and now heard most often on the eastern islands. The best time to hear *nisiótika* is during a summer saint's day feast (*panegýri*) or at a wedding; cassettes are increasingly available, but few are good.

Contemporary composers like Mikis Theodorákis often put modern poetry to music, providing splendid renderings of the lyrics of George Seferis, Odysseas Elytis and Yánnis Rítsos; sung by the deep-voiced Maria Farandouri, they are spine-tingling, even if you don't understand a word. Even current Greek pop has surprisingly poetic moments. It owes much of its origins to *rembétika*, the Greek equivalent of the blues, brought over and developed by the more 'sophisticated' Asia Minor Greeks in the 1920s' population exchange, who in their longing and homesickness haunted the hashish dens of Athens and Piraeus. *Rembétika* introduced the *bouzoúki*, the long-necked metallic string instrument that dominates Greek music today, to the extent that nightclubs are called *bouzoúkia*—rougher ones are known as *skilákia*—'dog' shops, where popular singers croon throbbing, lovelorn, often wildly melodramatic music with a Middle Eastern syncopation that offers Greeks some of the catharsis that ancient tragedies gave their ancestors. Although expensive, a night out at one of these nightclubs is an experience not to be missed. Turn up after midnight, buy a bottle of white wine and some fruit, and emote. As the evening wears on, members of the audience may take over the microphone, or the singer may be covered with flowers, or may even make the enthusiasts forget the law against *spásimo*, or plate-breaking. If enough *kéfi* is flowing, you may see middle-aged bank managers dance with wine glasses or bottles on their heads. When the matrons begin to belly-dance on the table, it's time to leave.

Summer festivals and village weddings are the places to see traditional dancing. Every island has its own dances or slight variations, some preserved, some rapidly being forgotten. Cretan dances are among the most vigorous and ancient and enthusiastically danced, fuelled by massive intakes of *rakí*; the *pedektó* demands furious, machine-gun fire steps and hops, which resound under tall Cretan boots. Beginning Greek dancers would do better starting with a *syrtó*, with slow and somewhat shuffling pace throughout, or perhaps the *kalamatianó*, a 12-step *syrtó*, *the* national dance for many people; everyone joins in, holding hands at shoulder-level, while men and women take turns leading and improvising steps. Nearly as common is the dignified *tsamikó*, where the leader and the next dancer in line hold the ends of a handkerchief; if the leader is especially acrobatic, the handkerchief seems to be the only thing that keeps him from flying away altogether. Women are the centre of attention in the *tsíphte téli*, a free-spirited, sensuous belly dance from Asia Minor for the loose-limbed, swivel-hipped and well-oiled, but just as often men (usually old and fat) steal the show.

Other dances are normally but not exclusively performed by men. The *zeybékiko* is a serious, deliberate, highly charged solo (or sometimes duo) dance with outstretched arms, evoking the swooping flight of the eagle; a companion will go down on one knee to encourage the dancer, hiss like a snake and clap out the rhythm. An introspective dance from the soul, the performer will always keep his eyes lowered, almost in a hypnotic state; because it's private, you must never applaud. Another intense dance, the *hasápiko*, or butchers' dance, is perhaps better known as the Zorba dance in the West. The *syrtáki* is more exuberant, traditionally performed by two men or three men, often to the *rembétika* tune; the leader signals the steps and it requires some practice but is well worth learning—as Alan Bates discovered, when he finally began to fathom *kéfi* from Anthony Quinn at the end of the film *Zorba the Greek*.

The Knights of St John

The Knights who ruled Rhodes and the other Dodecanese with such swagger for two centuries came from a venerable tradition of service to pilgrims in the Middle East. They weren't the first: according to the chronicles, the first hostels, *hospitia* or *xenodochia,* were established in Jerusalem by the 9th century, and belonged to different nations; among the first on the scene were the Franks, Hungarians and the Amalfitani. Some time in the very early 12th century a new, autonomous hospice was founded by the church of the Holy Sepulchre by a certain Gerard (according to a Bull of Paschal II dated 1113, addressed to *Geraudo institutori ac praeposito Hirosolimitani Xenodochii*). The hospice was known as the Hospitallers of Jerusalem.

Gerard was a canny organizer, and he profited by the presence of the Crusaders and their enthusiastic generosity to acquire lands and money-making properties in the new Latin Kingdom of Jerusalem as well as in Europe. At first they only lodged the poor and weary, but under Gerard's successor, Grand Master Raymond of Provence (1120–60), the Hospitallers of Jerusalem added an infirmary, creating a hospital in the modern sense of the word.

Raymond of Provence gave the Hospitallers their Rule (similar to that of the Augustinians), regulating their conduct as religious brothers and infirmarians. As donations poured in and the armies of Islam regrouped against the Crusaders, Raymond added another novelty to the order: an armed escort, recruited exclusively from the nobility, to accompany pilgrims. The escort soon grew into an army of heavy cavalry comprised of ex-Crusaders under a marshal, and Turcopoles (light cavalry armed with Turkish gear) recruited from natives of mixed blood, commanded by a Turcopolier. Later Grand Masters themselves went into battle, and by 1200 AD the military branch of the Order of St John was given its own Rule. Its members fell into two categories: secular knights, who served only for a time, and noble knights, who took vows of obedience, poverty and chastity and wore black mantles with white crosses.

Together with that other aristocratic military-religious order, the Knights Templars, the Knights of St John held the front lines in the Holy Land. Both orders held the same rank in the Church and shared the most dangerous tasks on the battlefield. A grateful papacy rewarded them with extensive privileges, autonomy and exemptions from tithes, as well as the right to have their own chapels and clergy. But unlike the mixed Order of St John the Templars were founded uniquely as a military order and claimed precedence in the Holy Land, resulting in a rivalry that in part led to the fall of the Latin Kingdom of Jerusalem.

At the peak of their influence the Hospitallers possessed seven castles and 140 estates in the Holy Land, but also some 19,000 revenue-making *manses* scattered across Europe. Thanks to these, the order was able to survive the capture of Jerusalem by Saladin (1187) and took refuge on Cyprus, where they were given a residence by King Amaury. On Cyprus, the Hospitallers acquired their first ships to harass the Muslims by sea and protect pilgrims who continued to flock to Jerusalem.

With the conquest of Rhodes in 1309 the Order evolved again, when Grand Master Foulques de Villaret became temporal ruler of the ecclesiastical principality of Rhodes. Although one of his first acts was to build a hospital, it always took second place to the military and religious side of the Order, especially as the Ottomans inexorably continued their expansion close to home, in Turkey.

The Order received a tremendous boost in wealth after 1312, when their old rivals the Knights Templars were suppressed by the Pope and King of France on charges of heresy. The Knights of St John were among the biggest heirs of the Templars' properties, and with their windfall they built the tremendous walls that defend Rhodes to this day, as well as lavish inns for themselves. Each was dedicated to a certain 'tongue' or nation and was subdivided into 24 priories, each of which was subdivided again into 656 *commanderies* in charge of collecting income. Each of the eight tongues had a bailiff and dignitary, and each was given a position of authority at the top of the hierarchy: Aragon provided the standard-bearer; Castile the grand chancellor; Provence the grand commander; Germany the grand bailiff; England the turcopolier; France the grand hospitaller; Auvergne the marshal; and Italy, the great sea power of the age, provided the admiral. The grand master could be elected from any of the above, although the French, who had the biggest 'tongue', usually won.

Another change on Rhodes was the transformation of the Knights into corsairs, to chase down Muslim pirates and exact tributes from Muslim shipping. They grew ever more fearless, even pillaging the rich ports of Smyrna (1341) and Alexandria (1365). Their audacity brought down the fury of the Ottoman Turks, who at last put an end to the knightly menace in 1522 under Sultan Suleiman the Magnificent, who in honour of their courage allowed them to leave Rhodes with all their goods (*see* p.110). The Knights retreated to their various *commanderies*, regrouped, then asked Emperor Charles V to grant them the island of Malta. In 1530 Charles V agreed, as long as they paid the king of Spain the famous nominal rent of a falcon a year. There the now Knights of Malta built themselves a fabulous new set of walls and a whole new city, Valletta, and resumed their career as the bane of Muslim shipping. In 1565 Suleiman II, regretting his earlier magnanimity, gathered all his forces to dislodge the Knights. In the four-month siege of Malta, the Turks slew half the knights and 8000 soldiers before Malta was delivered by an army from Spain. The Ottomans regrouped again, only to have their fleet dealt a fatal blow by the combined European powers in the battle of Lepanto (1571).

With the elimination of the Ottoman threat, the Knights of Malta turned their attention to the Barbary pirates, freeing hundreds of Christian galley slaves and selling their captives in turn to Christian galleys. The Order's morals, however, took a rapid decline: revolts were frequent, especially against any Grand Master who attempted to enforce the vows of chastity and poverty. The Reformation further weakened the Order, when its *commanderies* in Protestant lands were either given to the Protestant nobility, or simply suppressed; even in Catholic countries, sovereigns increasingly claimed control over the once autonomous *commanderies* of St John. When Napoleon made his expedition to Egypt in 1798, the then Grand Master, Count von Hompesch, ignominiously surrendered Malta without a fight.

After that, even in Catholic countries, the Order's properties were secularized. In 1831 the Knights returned to their original goals and re-formed as a hospital-funding organization in Rome, making their headquarters the Convent of Santa Maria del Priorato on the Aventine, where members continue to enjoy a small degree of autonomy, including special car number-plates; they wear the eight-pointed Maltese cross on their lapels and are answerable to the Pope, who chooses the Grand Master. Any Catholic man of full legal age who can claim nobility of sixteen quarterings, integrity of character and corresponding social position is invited to join. The English branch of the Order, revived in the 19th century, established the St John Ambulance and the St John Ophthalmic Hospital back where it all started, in Jerusalem. Another descendant of the Order, the Knights of St John International, with its Ladies Auxiliary, is run as a benevolent social club; the

Knights raise funds for local causes and St Vincent de Paul charities in the United States, Nigeria, Ghana, Sierra Leone, Liberia, Trinidad and Panama, and in America, at least, have a lot of bowling tournaments, too.

An Orthodox Life

With the exception of a few thousand Catholics in the Cyclades and Protestants in Athens, all Greeks belong to the Orthodox, or Eastern church; indeed, being Orthodox and speaking Greek are the criteria in defining a Greek, whether born in Athens, Alexandria or Australia. Orthodoxy is so fundamental that even the greatest sceptics can hardly conceive of marrying outside the church, or neglecting to have their children baptized, even though Papandréou's government legalized civil marriages in the early 1980s.

One reason for this deep national feeling is that, unlike everything else in Greece, Orthodoxy has scarcely changed since the founding of the church by Emperor Constantine in the 4th century. As Constantinople took the place of Rome as the political and religious capital, the Greeks believe their church to be the only true successor to the original church of Rome: a true Greek is called a *Romiós* or Roman, and the Greek language is sometimes called *Roméika*. The Orthodox church is considered perfect and eternal and beyond all worldly change; if it weren't, its adherents could not expect to be saved. One advantage is that the Greeks have been spared the changes that have rocked the West, from Vatican II and discussions over women in the clergy and married priests to political questions of abortion, birth control and so on. Much emphasis is put on ceremony and ritual, the spiritual and aesthetic, and yet at the same time the service can be powerfully moving, especially at Easter.

This determination never to change explains the violence of Iconoclasm, the one time someone tried to tinker with the rules. Back in the early 8th century, Byzantine Emperor Leo III, shamed by what his Muslim neighbours labelled idolatry, deemed the images of divine beings to be sacrilegious. The Iconoclasm opened up a first major rift with Rome, and it worsened in 800 when the patriarch of Rome, aka the Pope, crowned Charlemagne as emperor, usurping the position of the Emperor of Constantinople. Further divisions arose over the celibacy of the clergy (Orthodox priests may marry before they are ordained) and the use of the phrase *filioque*, 'and the son', in the Holy Creed. This phrase was the straw that broke the camel's back, causing the final, fatal schism in 1054 when the Papal legate Cardinal Humbert excommunicated the Patriarch of Constantinople and the Patriarch excommunicated the Pope. Ever since then the Orthodox hierarchy has kept a patriarchal throne vacant, ready for the day when the Pope returns to his senses.

After the fall of the Byzantine Empire (that 'thousand-year-long mass for the dead' as one Greek writer recently put it), the Turks not only tolerated the Orthodox church but had the political astuteness to impart considerable powers to the Patriarch. The church helped to preserve Greek tradition, education and identity through the dark age of Ottoman rule; on the other hand it left Greece a deeply conservative country and often abused its power, especially on a local scale. According to an old saying, priests, headmen and Turks were the three curses of Greece and the poor priests (who are usually quite amiable fellows) have not yet exonerated themselves from the list they now share with the king and the cuckold.

The fantastic quantity of churches and chapels on most islands has little to do with the priests, however. Nearly all were built by families or individuals, especially by sailors, seeking the protection of a patron saint or to keep a vow or to thank a saint for service rendered. All but the tiniest have an *iconóstasis*, or altar screen, made of wood or stone to separate the *heirón* or sanctuary, where only the ordained are allowed, from the rest of the church. Most of the chapels are locked up thanks to light-fingered tourists; if you track down the caretaker, leave a few hundred drachmae for upkeep.

The vast majority of all these chapels have only one service a year, if that, on the name day of the patron saint (name days are celebrated in Greece rather than birthdays: 'Many years!' (*Chrónia pollá!*) is the proper way to greet someone on their name day). This annual celebration is called a *yiortí* or more frequently *panegýri*, and if it happens in the summer it's cause for feasts and dancing the night before or after the church service. If feasible, *panegýria* take place directly in the churchyard; if not, in neighbouring wooded areas, tavernas, town squares or even specially built halls. The food will be basic but plentiful; for a set price you receive more than your share of stewed goat. *Panegýria* (festivals) are also places for traditional music and dancing. Apart from Easter, the Assumption of the Virgin (15 August) is the largest *panegýri* in Greece. The faithful sail to Tínos, the Lourdes of Greece, and to a dozen centres connected with Mary, making mid-August a very uncomfortable time to island-hop—ships are packed to the brim, the *meltémi* huffs and puffs, and Greek matrons, the most ardent pilgrims of all, are also the worst sailors.

Orthodox weddings are a lovely if long-winded ritual. The bride and groom stand solemnly before the chanting priest, while family and friends in attendance seem to do everything but follow the proceedings. White crowns, bound together by a white ribbon, are placed on the heads of bride and groom, and the *koumbáros*, or best man, exchanges them back and forth. The newlyweds are then led around the altar three times, while the guests bombard the happy couple with fertility-bringing rice and flower petals. After congratulating the bride and groom, guests are given a small *boboniéra* of candied almonds. This is followed by the marriage feast and dancing, which in the past could last up to five days.

Baptisms are cause for similar celebration. The priest completely immerses the baby in the holy water three times (unlike Achilles, there are no vulnerable spots on modern Greeks) and almost always gives the little one the name of a grandparent. For extra protection from the forces of evil, babies often wear a *filaktó*, or amulet, the omnipresent blue glass eye bead. If you visit a baby at home you may be sprinkled first with holy water, and chances are there's a bit of beneficial garlic squeezed somewhere under the cradle. Compliments should be kept to a minimum: the gods do get jealous. In fact many babies are given other pet names until they're christened, to fool supernatural ill-wishers.

Funerals in Greece, for reasons of climate, are usually carried out within 24 hours, and are announced by the tolling of church bells. The dead are buried for three to seven years (longer if the family can pay) after which time the bones are exhumed and placed in the family box to make room for the next resident. *Aforismós*, or Orthodox excommunication, is believed to prevent the body decaying after death—the main source of Greek vampire stories. Memorials for the dead take place three, nine and forty days after death, and on the first anniversary. They are sometimes repeated annually. Sweet buns and sugared wheat and raisin *koúliva* are given out after the ceremony. But for all the trappings of Christianity, the spirit of Charos, the ferryman of death and personification of inexorable nature, is never far away, as beautifully expressed in perhaps the most famous of myrologies, or dirges, still sung in some places:

> *Why are the mountains dark and why so woebegone?*
> *Is the wind at war there, or does the rain storm scourge them?*
> *It is not the wind at war there, it is not the rain that scourges,*
> *It is only Charos passing across them with the dead;*
> *He drives the youths before him, the old folk drags behind,*
> *And he bears the tender little ones in a line at his saddle-bow.*
> *The old men beg a grace, the young kneel to implore him,*
> *'Good Charos, halt in the village, or halt by some cool fountain,*
> *That the old men may drink water, the young men play at the stone-throwing,*
> *And that the little children may go and gather flowers.'*
> *'In never a village will I halt, nor yet by a cool fountain,*
> *The mothers would come for water, and recognize their children,*
> *The married folk would know each other, and I should never part them.'*

The *Períptero* and the Plane Tree

In Greece you'll see it everywhere, the greatest of modern Greek inventions, the indispensable *períptero*. It is the best-equipped kiosk in the world, where people gather to chat, make phone calls, or grab a few minutes' shade under the little projecting roof. The *períptero* is a substitute bar, selling everything from water to ice-cream to cold beer; an emergency pharmacy stocked with aspirin, mosquito killers, condoms and Band Aids; a convenient newsagent for publications, from *Ta*

Néa to *Die Zeit*; a tourist shop offering maps, guides, postcards and stamps; a toy shop for balloons and plastic swords; a general store for shoelaces, cigarettes, batteries and rolls of film or an instant breakfast (just add hot water). In Athens they're at most traffic lights. On the islands they are a more common sight than a donkey. You'll wonder how you ever survived before *perípteros* and the treasures they contain.

The other great meeting centre of Greek life is the mighty plane tree, or *plátanos*, for centuries the focal point of village life, where politics and philosophy have been argued since time immemorial. Since the time of Hippocrates, the Greeks have believed that plane shade is wholesome and beneficial (unlike the enervating shadow cast by the fig), and there's no better proof than the remarkable 'Hippocrates' plane tree' in Kos town, a national monument so old that it has to be propped up on scaffolding. In Greek the expression *cheréte mou ton plátano* loosely translates as 'go tell it to the marines', presumably because the tree has heard all that nonsense before. The *plátanos* represents the village's identity; the tree is a source of life, for it only grows near abundant fresh water, its deep roots a symbol of stability, continuity and protection—a huge majestic umbrella, as even the rain cannot penetrate its sturdy leaves. Sit under its spreading branches and sip a coffee as the morning unfolds before you; the temptation to linger there for the day is irresistible.

Some rather amusing recent statistics confirm what any previous visitor to Greece had already suspected: no people in Europe spend more time each day doing exactly that, just sitting around the plane tree or 'relaxing'. The European average is 62.5 minutes a day; the Greek spends twice that, 118.6 minutes. The Greeks are also at the top of the Euro-charts in two other categories: the average Hellene spends 61.2 minutes 'socializing', triple the European average of 20.5 minutes, and they spend a greater portion of their income (36.8 per cent) on food, drink and tobacco. No one should be too surprised to learn that their exact antitheses are the Swedes, who only relax 21.7 minutes a day, socialize a meagre 2.6 minutes, and only spend 19.2 per cent on self-indulgence (although per gallon they drink the most coffee).

Lamp Chops and Sweat Coffee

For a country cursed with a mindlessly pedantic system of public education, where rote memorization is the only key to academic success, the Greeks speak astonishingly good English. The Greek dislike of, not to mention their thorough incompetence at, dubbing the likes of *Miami Vice* and *Santa Monica* may have something to do with it, as well as the dogged efforts of thousands of *frontistérion* (private school) teachers, whose task is to get their pupils through their proficiency exams in spite of Greek public education.

All of the above is enough to make the devoted observer of Greek ways suspect that the English mistakes on taverna menus are no accident, but rather part of some crafty plot worthy of Odysseus to keep tourists out of the locals' own secret haunts by making taverna menus such compelling reading that by the time you've spotted the Lamp Chops, Eye Eggs (i.e. sunnyside up), or Sandwitches you're laughing too hard to go anywhere else. Will you have the Rabeet Soupee, Brawn Beans, Stuffed Vine Lives, String Deans, Sours Various, You Court with Gurig and Gogumbers, Eggfish, Chief's Salad or Beet Poots to start? For main course, the Harmbougger sounds distinctly threatening; perhaps it's best to stick with dishes you know the Greeks do well: Scabby Shrimps, Staffed Tomatoes, Reformed Schnitzel, Sguids in Spies, See Food Various, Chicken Pain (i.e. breaded), Souvlaki Privates, Grumps Salad, T-Buogne Rum Stake, Veal Gogglets and Shrimp Shave, or vegetable dishes such as Zucchini Bulls, Cheek Pees, Jacked Potatoes, or perhaps Grass Hill (it turned out to be a small mound of boiled greens). On Skópelos, you can smack your lips over a Rude Sausage or Rude Meat Pie; on Páros, you can ponder where your parents went wrong over a Freud Juice or Freud Salad; in Mytilíni, either sex can enjoy a delicious (and perfectly correct) Fish in Lesbian Sauce; cannibals can find solace at a place on Kos where 'We Serve Hot Tasty Friendly Family!' Then it's off to the Snake Bar for a Sweat Coffee, Kaputsino, or perhaps a Ouisgi before driving off in your Fully Incurable Rent-a-Care from the Vague Travel Agency of Piraeus.

A Traditional Greek Island Calendar

If the Greek islands were the cutting edge of European culture from 2000 to 500 BC, the past thousand years or so have shoved them into such an out-of-the-way corner that in recent times they have proved to be goldmines of old beliefs and traditions, some going back to deepest antiquity. On the Dodecanese, Kárpathos and rural Rhodes have proved especially rich sources for ethnologists—though they may not be for much longer, in the face of rural depopulation, mass tourism and television. Nevertheless, if you were to spend a year in an island village, you would find that St Basil, the Greek Santa Claus, still comes with gifts from Caesarea on **New Year's Eve** (rather than on Christmas Day) and gold coins are still baked in pies called *vassilopíta* that bring good luck to the finder; in the morning children sing *kalenda*, or carols in honour of Basil. Since ancient times **January** has also been closely associated with the Fates; everyone gambles, and readers of palms, coffee grounds, and tarot cards are in demand. Pomegranates, symbols of abundance and fertility, are smashed on thresholds, a stone is cast to give the household health and 'hard heads' against headaches. On 6 January, **Epiphany** (Theofánia, or Ta Fóta, the feast of lights, Christ's baptism), houses are sprinkled with holy water, and ashes from the hearth kept ablaze since Christmas to ward off werewolves and goblins (the *kallikántzaroi*) are scattered for good luck; in many places the priest will toss a crucifix in the sea and men dive after it, hoping to be the lucky finder.

February has a reputation for lameness and wetness; one of its names, Flevarius, suggests opening of veins (*fleva*) of water; a dry February means Greece is in for a drought. The first finches are a harbinger of spring. Olive groves are ploughed in **March**, a very variable month with strange nicknames—the Five-Minded, the Grumbler, the Flayer and *Paloukokáftis*, 'the Burning Pale'. A little bracelet of red and white thread called a *Mertoátano* is tied on children's wrists to protect them from the sun; on Kárpathos they say they tie up 'fatness, beauty, whims and the March sun.' The first swallows come back on Annunciation Day; in Chálki they are greeted with 2000-year-old Swallow Songs.

On Rhodes, **April** used to be called the Goggler; food supplies put up in the autumn would run out, leaving everyone 'goggle-eyed'—hungry. Conveniently, most people are fasting anyway for Lent. Wildflowers are gathered to decorate each church's **Good Friday** *Epitáphios*, or bier of Christ; the flowers or candles used in the service are in great demand for their special power against the evil eye. Easter eggs are dyed red, doors are painted with blood from the Easter lamb, and just after midnight when the priests announces the Resurrection (*Christós Anésti! Christ has risen!*), general pandemonium breaks out as bells ring, fireworks explode, and candles are lit and passed from person to person, and greetings and kisses are exchanged—on Kálymnos and Sými men go even further and throw dynamite, sometimes blowing themselves to smithereens. Families return home with lighted candles, mark the sign of the cross on the doorpost, and tuck into a special meal of *magirítsa,* a soup made of minced lamb's tripe that soothes the stomach after the long Lenten fast. On Easter Day everyone dresses up for the service of Divine Love, then spends the day feasting on spit-roast lamb with all the trimmings, drinking, singing and dancing into the night; in many places effigies of Judas are burned.

May is the month of flowers, when dead souls live, according to popular belief, granted a brief return to earth between Easter and Whitsun. In ancient times temples and statues would be purified then, and to this day it's a month for mischief and sorcery. On 1 May it's important to get up early and eat garlic before the first donkey brays or first cuckoo sings to avoid being 'stuffed'—losing the appetite, or being made somehow asinine. Everyone, even the urbane Athenians, goes to the countryside to 'fetch the May' and make wreaths to bring spring's blessing to the house. However, it's bad luck to lend anything or be married—unless you're a king or a donkey. Ascension Day is traditionally time for the first swim of the year, to 'go to the 40 waves', and if you find a stone with 'sea fluff' on it to take home and put under your bed, all the better.

In **June** wheat and barley are harvested (often a corner of the field is left 'because the hare must eat, too'), cherries, apricots and peaches are picked and the first tomatoes, aubergines, beans and pulses are ripe. Bonfires are lit for St John's Eve and the young people take turns leaping over the flames. As the year changes with the summer solstice, so does luck. A widespread custom is the *kledónas*, 'prophecy': water is silently drawn by young girls named Maria to fill an urn, where everyone deposits a personal item and makes a wish, usually in verse. The water is left open to the stars and on St John's Day, as the wishes are recited or sung, a Maria pulls the items out of the urn; the owner of each item as it is drawn forth gets the wish being sung at the moment. This usually results in a good deal of hilarity.

Hot **July** is the month for threshing and gathering herbs; the first melons, watermelons, figs and grapes are ripe. On 17 July, songs summon Ag. Marína to cure the bites and stings of snakes, scorpions and insects; on 20 July it's the turn of Prophet Elijah, the saint of mountaintop chapels who inherited Zeus' meteorological tasks, controlling the rain, winds and sun. Cretans say anyone who sees a headless shadow at noon will not survive the year. **August** is known as the Vintner, as the grape harvests begin then, or the Fig-gatherer or the Table-bearer for the abundant fruits that are ripe. 'August, my beautiful month, come twice a year,' is an old saying. It is especially sacred to the Virgin, who has feast days on the 15, 23 and 31 August (her birthday) and it's the best month to eat mackerel as well as fruit and vegetables. However, the first six days, the *Drymes*, are unlucky, associated with nymphs, who make hair fall out if it's washed or combed. The pious fast two weeks before the Assumption of the Virgin on 15 August, celebrated everywhere in Greece: among the Dodecanese, Astypálaia, Kárpathos and Kremastí (Rhodes) have the biggest celebrations. **September** is the month of wine-making. In Byzantine times 1 September was New Year's Day (and still is in the Orthodox ecclesiastical calendar), the day when Archangel Michael gets out his book and notes all the souls he will take during the coming year. On Kos children make New Year's garlands of garlic, grapes, pomegranates and a leaf from Hippocrates' plane tree. Sowing begins after 14 September, but take care not to cross a woman en route to the fields.

October usually has the first rains but generally fine weather; Greek Indian summer is the 'little summer of Ag. Dimítros'. Cranes fly south to Africa, chrysanthemums adorn the tables, priests bless and open the first wine barrel. **November**, 'the showery', signals the beginning of the olive harvests. Flocks are brought down from the mountain pastures, and in some places icons are placed around the newly sown fields. Pancakes are made on 30 November for St Andrew, who is mysteriously known as *Trypanoteganitís*, the 'frying pan piercer'; a good housewife will use all her frying pans that day to keep them from getting holes. **December** is called 'good morning, good evening' for its short days. Eating sweet things on 4 December, St Barbara's Day, was believed to ward off smallpox, and women hide their brooms and refrain from cooking beans. Her holiday generally elides with that of St Nikólaos, the protector of sailors, on the 6th, when boats are decorated and icons paraded around the shore. Christmas Eve marks the beginning of the twelve-day holiday period when the demonic *kallikántzaroi* and werewolves are afoot but can be kept at bay by not letting the hearth fire go out, so everyone chooses the fattest 'Christ log' they can. Pigs are slaughtered, and in the villages pork is the tra-ditional Christmas meal. Among the many cakes are sweets made with flaky filo pastry to represent Christ's swaddling clothes.

A Quick Who's Who in Greek Mythology

Like all good polytheists, the ancient Greeks filled their pantheon with a colourful assortment of divinities, divinities perhaps more anthropomorphic than most, full of fathomless contradictions, subtleties and regional nuances. Nearly every island has stories about their doings; some have become part of the familiar baggage of western civilization, others read like strange collective dreams or nightmares. But as classical Greek society grew more advanced and rational-minded, these gods were rounded up and made to live on the sanitized heights of Mount Olympos as idols of state religion, defined (and already ridiculed) in Homer. The meatier matters of birth, sex, death and hopes for an afterlife—i.e. the real religion—went underground in the mysteries and chthonic cults, surviving in such places as Eleusis (Elefsína) near Athens and at the Sanctuary of the Great Gods on Samothráki. On Kálymnos, the Képhalas cave sanctuary of Zeus may have been similarly used.

The big cheese on Olympos was **Zeus** (Jupiter, to the Romans), the great Indo-European sky god, lord of the thunderbolt with a libido to match, whose unenviable task was to keep the other gods in line. He was married to his sister **Hera** (Juno), the goddess of marriage, whose special role in myth is that of the wronged, jealous wife, and who periodically returned to her special island of Sámos to renew her virginity. Zeus' two younger brothers were given their own realms: **Poseidon** (Neptune) ruled the sea with his wife Amphytron, while **Hades** (Pluto) ruled the underworld and dead and rarely left his dismal realm. Their sister was **Demeter** (Ceres), goddess of corn and growing things, who was worshipped in the mysteries of Eleusis. **Aphrodite** (Venus), the goddess of love, is nearly as old as these gods, born when Zeus overthrew their father Cronus (Saturn) by castrating him and tossed the bloody member in the sea foam. She first landed at Kýthera but later preferred Cyprus.

The second generation of Olympians were the offspring of Zeus: **Athena**, the urbane virgin goddess of wisdom, born full-grown straight out of Zeus' brain and always associated with Athens, her special city, although she was also worshipped from earliest times at Líndos, on Rhodes; **Ares** (Mars), the whining bully god of war, disliked by the Greeks and associated with barbarian Thrace; **Hermes** (Mercury), the messenger, occasional trickster and god of commerce; **Hephaistos** (Vulcan), the god of fire and the forge and metalworking, married to Aphrodite; **Apollo**, the god of light, music, reason, poetry and prophecy, often identified with the sun, and his twin sister **Artemis** (Diana) the tomboy virgin moon goddess of the hunt, both born and worshipped on the little island of Délos; Léros too was sacred to Artemis. Their cross-dressing half-brother **Dionysos** (Bacchus) was the god of wine, orgies and theatre. In addition to the twelve Olympians, the Greeks had an assorted array of other gods, nymphs, satyrs and heroes, the greatest of which was **Herakles** (Hercules), the mighty hero who earned himself a place on Olympos, and gods such as **Helios** (Sol), the unassuming sun god, whose special island has always been Rhodes. **Asklepios**, the god of healing (made immortal even after Zeus blasted with him a thunderbolt for daring to bring a dead patient back to life) was diligently worshipped on Kos.

.

Athens and Piraeus

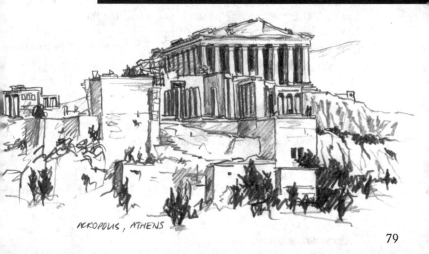

ACROPOLIS, ATHENS

Love for Athens, a city once famous, wrote these words, a love that plays with shadows, that gives a little comfort to burning desire... Though I live in Athens I see Athens nowhere: only sad, empty, and blessed dust.

Michael Akominátos, 12th century

Travellers to the Dodecanese often find themselves in Athens, and although it has perked up considerably since the days of Michael Akominátos it's rarely love at first sight. Look closely, however, behind the ugly architecture and congestion, and you may be won over by this urban crazy quilt—small oases of green parks hidden amidst the hustle and bustle; tiny family-run tavernas tucked away in the most unexpected places; the feverish pace of its nightlife and summer festivals of wine and song; and best of all, the Athenians themselves, whose friendliness belies the reputation of most city dwellers. Another plus: Athens is the least expensive capital in the European Union.

Getting Around

by bus

The free map of Athens distributed by EOT (*see* p.102) marks the main city bus (the blue ones) and trolley routes. Purchase tickets (75dr) before boarding, and punch in the machine; if you're caught without a ticket the fine is 2000dr. Note that all trolleys except 1, 10 and 12 pass in front of the National Archaeology Museum; for the Acropolis and Thesion, catch bus no.230 from Sýntagma Square's post office. For info, call ✆ 185 between 7am and 9pm.

by metro

The metro is an important means of getting across Athens, especially from Piraeus. It runs as far as Kifissiá, stopping at Thissío (Theseum), Monastiráki (flea market, near Pláka), Omónia (Athens' Times Square), and Plateía Viktorías (near Areos Park). The network is being extended 20km with major excavations throughout the city; work is supposed to be finished in 2000, and might be, if the quibbling stops.

by taxi

Compared to other Western cities, Athenian taxis are cheap, but a pain in the butt. Because fares are so low, the only way cabbies can make a decent living is by sharing, which makes hailing a cab a sport not for the fainthearted; the usual procedure is to stand by the street, flag down any passing cab and, if they slow down and cock an ear, shout out your general destination. If the taxi is going that way, the driver will stop; if not, not. If there are more than two of you, flagging a cab is hopeless, and you might as well walk to the nearest taxi stand or call a radio taxi. Check the meter when you board (although some taxis now have two meters) and pay from there, with a small surcharge, but more often than not the cabbie will try to nail you to the full fare on the meter. The only thing to do is start writing down the taxi's licence number and threatening to go to the police, which usually settles the issue on the spot.

The meter starts at 200dr, and the 60dr per kilometre doubles if you leave central Athens. There's a 300dr airport surcharge, a 150dr bus station/port surcharge, 50dr per bag luggage surcharge, and all prices double from midnight to 5am and on major holidays such as Easter. A taxi between Athens and the airport should cost about 1500dr. Piraeus is particularly prone to cowboys preying on unsuspecting tourists heading from and to the ferries; take proper yellow taxis with meters and official licence numbers or be prepared to be ripped off. **Radio taxis** charge a 300dr callout fee. Some numbers to try: ✆ 513 0640; ✆ 922 1755; ✆ 411 5200; ✆ 582 1292.

driving

Just don't. If evil chance finds you behind a wheel, note that parking in the central Athens Green Zone is forbidden outside designated areas. Green Zone borders are the following streets: Sékeri, Botássi, Stoúrnara, Marni, Menándrou, Pireás, Likourgoú, Athinás, Mitropóleos, Filellínon, Amalías and Vassilís Sofías.

Orientation: Athens in a Nutshell

Sýntagma (ΣΨNTAΓMA) (**Constitution**) **Square** is the centre of the city, site of the **Parliament Building** which backs on to the **National Gardens** and **Záppeion Park**, a cool haven of green and shade to escape the summer heat, with ducks to feed and benches to snatch forty winks. Traffic is slowly being siphoned away, so you can hear yourself think at the outdoor tables of the overpriced cafés and the great big McDonald's. The McPresence may be a golden arch-blasphemy for old Athens hands, but it's packed just the same, mostly with Greeks who don't give a hang about culture pollution. At the time of writing Sýntagma Square is further convulsed with the construction of the new $2.8 billion metro; a 3rd-century AD Roman bath and villa with lovely murals, an 11th-century BC grave and the tomb of a little dog were found under all the traffic; archaeological finds from the digs will be displayed in a smart underground concourse.

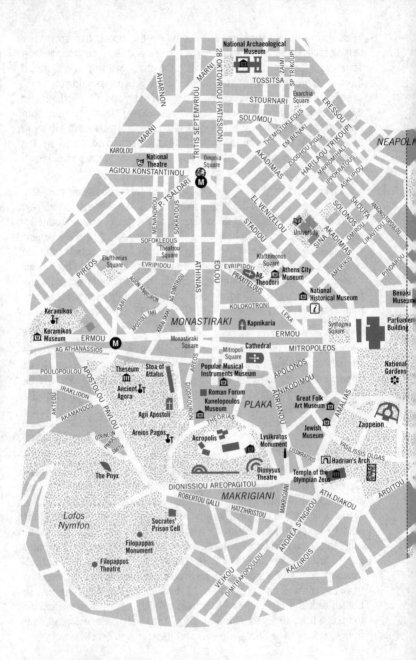

Lycavitos Theatre

Lycavitos Hill

KOKALI

EAPOLI

Ag.Georgios

Funicular Railway

VASILISSIS SOFIAS

ARISTIPOU

PAPADIAMANDOPOULOU

PINDAROU

Dexameni

CHARITOS

PATRIARHI IOAKIM

PLOUTARHOU

National Gallery

KOLONAKI

Goulandris Museum of Cycladic Art

SOFIAS

MIHALAKOPOULOU

Benaki Museum

VASSILIS

War Museum

Byzantine Museum

IRODOU ATIKOU

National Gardens

VASSILEOS KONSTANDINOU

PANGRATI

Zappeion

Athens Stadium

N

500 metres
500 yards

From Sýntagma Square it's a short walk down to the **Pláka** (ΠΛΑΚΑ), the medieval centre under the Acropolis, where many of the older houses have been converted into intimate tavernas or bars, each tinkling away with its own bouzouki. This is also a good place to look for mid-priced accommodation now that cars have been banished. On the very top of Pláka, at the foot of the Acropolis, **Anafiótika** (ΑΝΑΦΙΟΤΙΚΑ) is a charming uncommercialized enclave left by the builders of Otho's palaces, who came from the island of Anáfi and, homesick, tried to re-create their village here.

During the day meander through Athens' nearby flea market district, to the west of **Monastiráki** (ΜΟΝΑΣΤΙΡΑΚΙ) **Square** (and the metro station), where bulging shops sell everything from good quality woollen goods and fake Caterpillar boots to furniture and second-hand fridges. Several streets en route all claim to be the flea market, but are nothing more than tourist trap alley; aim for Avysinias Square. Just north of Monastiráki, across Ermoú, **Psirri** is an inner-city workers' neighbourhood of winding little streets that in the past couple of years has become one of the trendiest spots to eat and play in Athens, where retro is definitely in. A ten-minute walk east from Sýntagma will take you to **Kolonáki Square**, Athens' Knightsbridge in miniature, complete with fancypants shops, upmarket restaurants and plenty of well-heeled 'Kolonáki Greeks'—Athenian Sloane Rangers—to patronize them. Above the square rises **Lykavitós** (ΛΥΚΑΒΕΤΟΣ) hill, illuminated like a fairytale tower at night (a long walk, but there's a funicular every 10 minutes from the corner of Aristippoú and Ploutarchoúis). The summit offers the best panoramic views of Athens and Piraeus, *néfos* permitting, and the chapel of **St George**, a restaurant/bar, a lovely outdoor theatre and a cannon fired on national holidays.

For something different, a 15-minute walk north of Sýntagma past the University (Panepistímou) will bring you to funky **Omónia** (ΟΜΟΝΙΑ) **Square**, the Athenian Times Square, open 24 hours a day and embracing a useful metro stop, as well as fast food, huge news-stands, porn-mongers and screwballs. The **National Archaeology Museum** is further north, and behind it lies **Exárchia**, Athens' Latin Quarter, home of trendies, students and literati. Terra incognita for tourists, Plateía Exárchia is one of the city's liveliest centres after dark, with traditional *ouzeries* and *boîtes* where you're likely to find rave alongside bluesy, smoke-filled *rembétika* clubs. For establishment Athens, Exárchia is synonymous with Anarchia, and home to druggies, disaffected youth and graffiti-sprayers. But it's tame by London or New York standards. Two other areas off the tourist trail and pleasant places to stay are residential **Veikoú** and **Koukáki**, reached from the southern slopes of the Acropolis or Filopáppou Hill, both on the nos.1, 5 and 9 trolley-bus routes. Proper Greek neighbourhoods, the local shops, tavernas and *ouzeries* have few concessions to tourism and excellent, authentic food. Good places to go for a leisurely lunch or to round off an evening.

A 20-minute walk from Sýntagma, along Vass. Sofías, brings you to the Hilton Hotel, a useful landmark. Behind it are the essential Athenian neighbourhoods of **Ilíssia** and **Pangráti**, the best place to get a feel for everyday life in the city. Lose yourself in their back streets and you may find your own little taverna (of which there are plenty), rather than restrict yourself to the tourist haunts in the centre. Across Konstantínos Avenue from Záppeion Park, the landmark is the big white horseshoe of the **Olympic Stadium**, site of the 3rd-century BC original used during the Panathenaea festival, and rebuilt for the first modern Olympics, in 1896. Behind this you'll find **Mets**, an old-fashioned neighbourhood popular with artists and media folk with some fine old houses and small pensions: it's a good place to stay with authentic tavernas and *kafenéions*.

From Záppeion Park buses run frequently down to the coast and suburbs of **Glyfáda**, **Voúla** and **Vouliagménis**. Glyfáda, close to the airport, is a green and pleasant suburb that has grown into a busy resort and rival of fashionable Kolonáki. Smart city dwellers shop at the ritzy boutiques and berth their gin palaces in the swish marina, ready for weekend jaunts over to Kéa and other nearby islands. At the other end of the scale it's the hub of British package holidays to the so-called Apollo Coast. Here and further down the coast at Voúla are pay beaches run by EOT, usually jammed with well-heeled Athenians. There are all kinds of facilities and the sea is cleaner at some than others—watch out for that sewage outfall—but nothing like the crystal waters of the more remote islands. There's also good swimming beyond Voúla in the rocky coves at Vouliagménis, a smart place for a fish lunch and haven for Greek yachties. En route, **Kavoúri** has excellent fish restaurants, ideal for a romantic dinner overlooking the sea. Beyond Vouliagménis, the road continues along the coast to **Várkiza**, another beach playground, and winds to stunning **Cape Soúnion** and its **Temple of Poseidon** (440 BC), famous for its magnificent position and sunsets and where there's always at least one tourist searching for the column where Byron carved his name.

Major Museums and Sites in Athens

The Acropolis

© 321 0219; open summer Mon–Fri 8–6.30, Sat and Sun 8–2.30; winter Mon–Fri 8–4.30, Sat and Sun 8.30–2.30; adm exp.

Acropolis in Greek means 'top of the town', and many Greek cities have similar naturally fortified citadels crowned with temples, but Athens has *the* Acropolis, the ultimate, standing proud above the city from a hundred different viewpoints. First inhabited at the end of the Neolithic Age, it had a Cyclopean wall and the palace of Athens' Mycenaean king, although this was later replaced by a temple of Poseidon and Athena, after the two divinities took part in a contest to decide who would be the patron of the city. With his trident Poseidon struck the spring Klepsydra out of the rock of the Acropolis, while Athena invented the olive tree, which the Athenians judged the better trick. In later years the tyrant Pisistratos ordered a great gate to be constructed in the Mycenaean wall, but Delphi cursed it and the Athenians dismantled it. In 480 BC the temple's cult statue of Athena was hurriedly bundled off to Salamis, just before the Persians burnt and smashed the Acropolis. Themistocles built a new rampart out of stones of the old Parthenon, and under Pericles the Acropolis as we see it today took shape.

The path to the Acropolis follows the Panathenaic Way, laid out at the consecration of the Panathenaic Festival in 566 BC. The Acropolis entrance is defended by the **Beulé Gate** (named after Ernest Beulé, the archaeologist who found it); the monumental stairways were built by the Romans and the two lions are from Venice. Themistocles' reconstructed Panathenaic ramp leads to the equally reconstructed **Propylaia**, the massive gateway built by Pericles' architect Mnesikles to replace Pisistratos' cursed gate. The ancient Greeks considered the Propylaia the architectural equal of the Parthenon itself, although it was never actually completed because of the Peloponnesian War. On either side of the Propylaia's entrance are two wings; the north held a picture gallery (Pinakothéke) while the smaller one to the south consisted of only one room of an unusual shape, because the priests of the neighbouring Nike temple didn't want the wing in their precinct. The original entrance had five doors, the central one pierced by the Panathenaic Way.

Temple of Athena Nike

The Ionic Temple of Athena Nike, or *Wingless Victory*, was built by the architect Kallikrates in 478 BC of Pentelic marble. It housed the cult statue of Athena, a copy of a much older wooden statue; its lack of wings, unlike later victory statues, gave the temple its second name. In 1687 the Turks destroyed the temple to build a tower. It was rebuilt in 1835 and again in 1936, when the bastion beneath it threatened to crumble away. Cement casts replace the north and western friezes which were taken to England by Lord Elgin. From the temple of Athena Nike the whole Saronic Gulf could be seen in pre-*néfos* days, and it was here that King Aegeus watched for the return of his son Theseus from his Cretan adventure with the Minotaur. Theseus was to have signalled his victory with a white sail but forgot; at the sight of the black sail of death, Aegeus threw himself off the precipice in despair and, although he was miles from the water at the time, gave his name to the Aegean Sea.

The Parthenon

The Parthenon, the glory of the Acropolis and probably the most famous building in the world, is a Doric temple constructed between 447 and 432 BC under the direction of Phidias, the greatest artist and sculptor of the Periclean age. Originally called the Great Temple, brightly painted and shimmering with gold, it took the name Parthenon (Chamber of Virgins) a hundred years after its completion. Constructed entirely of Pentelic marble, it held Phidias' famous chryselephantine (ivory and gold) statue of Athena, who stood over 36ft high. The builders of the Parthenon wrote the book on mathematical perfection, subtlety, grace and *entasis*, the art of curving a form to create the visual illusion of perfection. Look closely, and you'll see that there's not a straight line to be seen: the foundation is curved slightly to prevent an illusion of drooping caused by straight horizontals. The columns bend a few centimetres inward, and those on the corners are wider to complete the illusion of perfect form. The outer colonnade consists of 46 columns and above them are the remnants of the Doric frieze left behind by the beaverish Lord Elgin: the east side portrayed the battle of giants and gods, the south the Lapiths and Centaurs (mostly in the British Museum today), on the west are the Greeks and the Amazons, and on the north the battle of Troy. Little remains of the pediment sculptures of the gods. Above the interior colonnade, the masterful Ionic frieze designed by Phidias himself shows the quadrennial Panathenaic Procession in which the cult statue of Athena in the Erechtheion was brought a golden crown and a new sacred garment, or *peplos*.

The Parthenon, used as a church and then a mosque, was intact until 1687, when a Venetian bomb hit the Turks' powder stores and blew the roof off; an earthquake in 1894 was another serious blow. Entrance within the Parthenon has been forbidden, to save on wear and tear. Preserving the building, as well as undoing the damage of previous restorations, has been the subject of intense study over the past 15 years, when the alarming effects of the *néfos* on the marble could no longer be ignored: while discovering how to use hot, pressurized carbon dioxide to re-harden stone surfaces, Greek scientists have learned about ancient building techniques, and after all these years are picking up the pieces to reconstruct as much of the temple as possible, stringing column drums on new non-rusting titanium rods.

The Erechtheion

The last great monument on the Acropolis is the Erechtheion, a peculiar Ionic temple that owes its idiosyncrasies to the various cult items and the much older sanctuary it was built to encompass. Beneath the temple stood the Mycenaean House of Erechtheus, mentioned by Homer, and the primitive cult sanctuary of Athena; on one side of this grew the Sacred Olive Tree created on the spot by Athena, while under the north porch was the mark left by Poseidon's trident when he brought forth his spring. The tomb of the snake man Kekrops, the legendary founder of Athens, is in the Porch of the Caryatids, where Erechtheus died at the hand of either Zeus or Poseidon. Within the temple stood the ancient primitive cult statue of Athena Polias, endowed with the biggest juju of them all, solemnly dressed in the sacred *peplos* and crown. After the Persian fires, the sanctuary was quickly restored, but the marble temple planned by Pericles was not begun until 421 BC. Converted into a church in the 7th century, the Turks made it a harem and used the sacred place of the trident marks as a toilet.

Basically the Erechtheion is a rectangular temple with three porches. Inside were two cellas, or chambers: the East Cella dedicated to Athena Polias, the smaller to Poseidon-Erechtheus. Six tall Ionic columns mark the north porch where the floor and roof were cut away to reveal Poseidon's trident marks, as it was sacrilegious to hide such divine work from the view of the gods. The famous maidens or caryatids gracefully supporting the roof on their heads are another Ionian motif. Lord Elgin nicked parts of this temple as well, including one of the six caryatids (now in the British Museum); the other girls, said to weep every night for their missing sister, have also come in from the *néfos* and have been replaced by casts.

The Acropolis Museum

This was built to house sculptures and reliefs from the temples, in particular the Erechtheion's caryatids, the statues of Kores, or Maidens offered to Athena, and the 6th-century BC Calf Bearer (*Moschoforos*). Anti-*néfos* filters have been installed to show the British parliament that Greece is ready to care for the Elgin marbles properly, if they should ever vote to give them back. Below the Acropolis to the west is the bald **Areópagos**, or hill of the war god Ares, with a marble portal to mark the seat of the High Council, who figured so predominantly in Aeschylus' play *The Eumenides* where mercy defeated vengeance for the first time in history during the trial of the matricide Orestes. Although Pericles removed much of the original power of the High Council, under the control of the ex-archons it continued to advise on the Athenian constitution for hundreds of years.

Beyond it, tucked in the side of Philopápou hill, is the **Pnyx**, where the General Assembly of Athens met and heard the speeches of Pericles and Demosthenes. On assembly days citizens were literally rounded up to fill the minimum attendance quota of 5000, but they were paid for their services to the state. Later the assembly was transferred to the theatre of Dionysos. On the summit of the big hill is the **Philopáppos Monument** (AD 114) built in honour of Caius Julius Antiochos Philopáppos, a Syrian prince and friend of Athens. Come up here for the romantic sunsets and views of the Acropolis; just below is the Dora Stratou Theatre, where Athens' folk dance troupe performs nightly.

The Theatres

Two theatres are tucked into the south flank of the Acropolis. The older, in fact the oldest in the world if you don't count the 'theatre' at Knóssos, is the **Theatre of**

Dionysos (*open daily 8.30–2.30, adm*). Built in the 6th century BC when Thespis created the first true drama, it was continually modified up to the time of Nero. Here 17,000 could watch the annual Greater Dionysia, held in honour of Dionysos, the god of wine and patron divinity of the theatre; the dramatic competitions were awarded prizes, many of which went to the works of Aeschylus, Sophocles, Aristophanes and Euripides. The stage that remains is from the 4th century BC, while the area before the stage, or *proskenion*, is decorated with 1st-century AD scenes based on the life of Dionysos. A couple of streets east in Pláka, the **Monument of Lysikrates** was built by an 'angel' who funded the play that won top prize in 334 BC. It later passed into the hands of Capuchin friars, who hosted Lord Byron; another Lord, Elgin, wanted to take the monument to London but was thwarted this time by the friars.

The second theatre, the **Odeon of Herodes Atticus** (AD 161) was originally covered with a roof when it was built by the Rockefeller of his day, Herodes Atticus (whose life reads like something out of the *Arabian Nights*: he inherited his extraordinary wealth from his father, who found a vast golden treasure outside Rome). The Odeon hosts the annual mid-May and September **Festival of Athens**, where modern European and ancient Greek cultures meet in theatre, ballet, and classical music concerts performed by companies from all over the world.

The Heart of Ancient Athens: the Agora, Theseum & Stoa of Attalus

© 321 0185; open 8.30–2.45, closed Mon; adm.

The Agora was not only the market but the centre of Athenian civic and social life. Here citizens spent as much time as possible, where they discussed the issues of the day and were buttonholed by Socrates. After the Persians destroyed all the buildings of the Agora in 480 BC, it was rebuilt on a much grander style; since then many landmarks have suffered, mostly from angry Romans, firebug barbarians or Athenians in need of cheap building stone. Only the foundations remain of the council house or **Bouleuterion** and the neighbouring Temple of the Mother of the Gods, the **Metroön**, built by the Athenians as reparation for the slaying of a priest from her cult. The round **Tholos** or administration centre is where the *prytanes* worked, and, as some had to be on call day and night like modern police, kitchens and sleeping quarters were included. To the right of the Tholos is the **horos**, or boundary stone; a path from here leads to the foundations of the prison where Socrates spent his last days and drank the fatal hemlock. Opposite the Metroön, only a wall remains of the **Sanctuary of the Eponymous Heroes of Athens**, the ten who gave their names to Kleisthenes' ten tribes. The **altar of Zeus Agoraios** received the oaths of the new archons, a practice initiated by Solon.

The 4th-century **Temple of Apollo** was dedicated to the mythical grandfather of the Ionians, who believed themselves descended from Apollo's son Ion; the huge cult statue of Apollo it once held is now in the Agora museum. Almost nothing remains of the **Stoa Basileios** (or of Zeus Eleutherios), the court of the annual archon, where trials concerning the security of the state were held. By the Stoa of Zeus stood the **Altar of the Twelve Gods**, from which all distances in Attica were measured. Alongside it ran the sacred **Panathenaic Way**, the ceremonial path that ascended to the Acropolis, where devotees celebrated the union of Attica; some signs of its Roman rebuilding may be seen by the Church of the Holy Apostles. South of the Altar of Twelve Gods stood a Doric **Temple to Ares** (5th century BC). The **Three Giants** nearby were originally part of the **Odeon of Agrippa** (15 BC); parts of the orchestra remain intact after the roof collapsed in AD 190. Both the site and giants were reused in the façade of a 5th-century AD gymnasium, that a century later became the University of Athens, at least until Justinian closed it down. Near the **Middle Stoa** (2nd century BC) are ruins of a **Roman temple** and the ancient shops and booths. On the other side of the Middle Stoa was the people's court, or **Heliaia**, organized by Solon in the 6th century BC to hear political questions; it remained active well into Roman times.

Between the **South and East Stoas** (2nd century BC) is the 11th-century **Church of the Holy Apostles** (Ag. Apóstoli), built on the site where St Paul addressed the Athenians; it was restored, along with its fine paintings, in 1952. Across the Panathenaic Way run the remains of **Valerian's Wall** thrown up in AD 257 against the barbarians, its stone cannibalized from Agora buildings wrecked by the Romans. Between Valerian's Wall and the Stoa of Attalos are higgledy-piggledy ruins of the **Library of Pantainos**, built by Flavius Pantainos in AD 100 and destroyed 167 years later. Artefacts found in the Agora are housed in the **museum** in the **Stoa of Attalos**, the 2nd-century BC portico built by one of Athen's benefactors, King Attalos II of Pergamon, and reconstructed by a later benefactor, John D. Rockefeller of Cleveland, Ohio. Adjacent to the agora, the mid 5th-century BC **Theseum** is nothing less than the best-preserved Greek temple in existence. Doric in order and dedicated to Hephaistos, the god of metals and smiths, it may well have been designed by the architect of the temple at Sounion. It is constructed almost entirely of Pentelic marble and decorated with *metopes* depicting the lives of Herakles and Theseus (for whom the temple was misnamed in later centuries). Converted into a church in the 5th century, it was the burial place for English Protestants until 1834, when the government declared it a national monument.

National Archaeology Museum

Patission and Tossítsa Streets, ℂ 821 7717, open Mon 12.30–6.45; Tues–Fri 8–6.45, Sat and Sun 8.30–2.45; adm exp.

This is the big one, and deserves much more space than permitted here. It contains some of the most spectacular and beautiful works of the ancient Greek world—the Minoan frescoes from Santoríni, gold from Mycenae (including the famous 'mask of Agamemnon'), statues, reliefs, tomb stelae, and ceramics and vases from every period. The Cycladic collection includes one of the first known musicians, the 2500 BC sculpture of a harpist that has become the virtual symbol of the Cyclades. The star of the sculpture rooms is a virile bronze of Poseidon (5th century BC) about to launch his trident, found off the coast of Evia in 1928; around him are some outstanding archaic Kouros statues and the Stele of Hegeso, an Athenian beauty, enveloped by the delicate folds of her robe, seated on a throne. Don't miss the so-called Antikýthera Mechanism, the world's first computer, made on Rhodes *c.* 70 BC (*see* p.119). The museum has a shop on the lower level, with reproductions of exhibits by expert craftsmen, so accurate that each piece is issued with a certificate declaring it an authentic fake so you can take it out of the country.

Other Museums and Sites in Athens

Benáki Museum: On the corner of Vassilís Sofías and Koumbári Street, ✆ 361 1617, c*losed indefinitely for renovation; shop open.* Byzantine and Islamic treasures from 6th–17th centuries, two icons painted by El Greco, folk art, and a superb collection of costumes and artefacts from the Ionian islands to Cyprus.

Goulandris Museum of Cycladic and Ancient Greek Art: 4 Neofýotou Doúka (just off Vass. Sofías), ✆ 722 8321, *open 10–4, Sat 10–3, closed Tues and Sun.* The Goulandris' collection of Cycladic figurines and other art going back to 3000 BC, as well as ancient art from other parts of Greece, may be second to the collection in the National Museum, but it's better documented and intelligently displayed.

Greek Folk Art Museum: 17 Kydathinaíon St, Pláka, ✆ 322 9031, *open 10–2, closed Mon; adm.* Exquisite Greek folk art, embroideries, wood carvings, jewellery, and nearby, in a renovated mosque, a superb collection of ceramics.

Jewish Museum: 36 Amálias, ✆ 323 1577, *open Mon–Fri 9–2.30 and Sun 10–2.30, closed Sat.* Most of Greece's Jewish population arrived in the 16th century, escaping the Spanish Inquisition, and most of their descendants were killed in the Second World War; documents and artefacts chronicle the time in between.

National Gallery: 50 Vass. Konstantínou, across from the Athens Hilton, ✆ 723 5937, *open 9–3, Sun and holidays 10–2, closed Tues; adm.* The National Gallery concentrates on painting and sculpture by modern Greek artists.

National Historical Museum: 13 Stadiou Street, ✆ 323 7617, *open 9–1.30, closed Mon; adm.* In the imposing neoclassical Old Parliament of Greece, guarded by a bronze equestrian Theodóros Kolokotrónis, hero of the War of Independence, are exhibits on Greek history, concentrating on the War of Independence.

Roman Forum: Located between the Agora and the Acropolis, at Pelopia and Eolou Sts, ✆ 324 5220, *open 8.30–3, closed Mon; adm.* At the end of the Hellenistic age the Romans built their own marketplace, or Forum, feeling uncomfortable in the Greek Agora, especially after they wasted it. The Forum contains the celebrated 1st-century BC **Tower of the Winds**, or Clock of Andronikos, which was operated by a hydraulic mechanism, so the Athenians could know the time, day or night. Note the frieze of the eight winds that decorates its eight sides, although it has lost its ancient bronze Triton weathervane. The Forum also contains the **Gate of Athena Archegetis**, built by money sent over by Julius and Augustus Caesar; there is also a court and ruined stoa, and the Fehiye Camii, the Victory or Corn Market Mosque.

Temple of Olympian Zeus: Vass. Ólgas and Amalías, © 922 6330, *open 8.30–3, closed Mon; adm.* Fifteen columns recall what Livy called 'the only temple on earth of a size adequate to the greatness of the god'. The foundations were laid by the tyrant Pisistratos, but work ground to a halt with the fall of his dynasty, only to be continued in 175 BC by a Roman architect, Cossutius. It was half finished when Cossutius' patron, Antiochos IV of Syria, kicked the bucket, leaving the Emperor Hadrian to complete it in AD 131. Nearby are the ruins of ancient houses and a bath and at the far end stands **Hadrian's Arch**, in Pentelic marble, erected by the Athenians to thank the emperor for his help; the complimentary inscription reads on the Acropolis side: 'This is Athens, the ancient city of Theseus', while the other side reads: 'This is the city of Hadrian, not of Theseus'. The Athenians traditionally come here to celebrate the Easter Resurrection.

Byzantine Churches and Monasteries

Agii Theódori: This 11th-century church in Klafthmónos Square at the end of Dragatsaníou St is notable for its beautiful door; the bell tower is more recent.

Kapnikaréa: A few blocks from Agii Theódori, on Ermoú Street, is the tiny Kapnikaréa (the chapel of the University of Athens), built in the late 11th century in the shape of a Greek cross, its central cupola supported by four columns.

Panagía Gorgoepikoos: 'Our Lady who Grants Requests Quickly', the loveliest church in Athens is in Mitropóleos Square. Known as the little cathedral, it was built in the 12th century almost entirely of ancient marbles: note the ancient calendar of state festivals and the signs of the zodiac. The adjacent 'big' **Cathedral** or Metropolitan was built in 1840–55 with the same collage technique, using bits and pieces from 72 destroyed churches. The Glucksberg Kings of Greece were crowned here between 1863 and 1964, and it contains the tomb of the unofficial saint of the Greek revolution, Gregory V, the Patriarch of Constantinople, hanged in 1821.

Athens © (01–)   **Where to Stay in Athens**

Athens is a big noisy city, especially so at night when you want to sleep—unless you do as the Greeks do and take a long afternoon siesta. If you can't find a room, try the Hotel Association's booking desk in Sýntagma Square, in the National Bank building (*open Mon–Thurs 8.30–2, Fri 8.30–1, Sat 9–1, ✆ 323 7193*).

luxury

The beautiful **Grande Bretagne**, Sýntagma Square, ✆ 333 0000, ✆ 322 8034 (*lux*) was built in 1862 for members of the Greek royal family who couldn't squeeze into the palace (the current Parliament building) up the square. It is the only 'grand' hotel in Greece worthy of the description, with a vast marble lobby and elegant rooms (now air-conditioned and appointed with modern conveniences). Down from the Grande Bretagne on Sýntagma Square the **Meridian Athens**, 2 Vass Geórgiou, ✆ 325 5301, ✆ 323 5856 (*lux*) is a modern favourite with a very respectable restaurant.

On a less exalted level, but with a far more fetching view, is the **Royal Olympic Hotel** at 28 Diákou, ✆ 922 6411, ✆ 923 3317 (*lux*), facing the Temple of Olympian Zeus and Mount Lykavitós. There are a number of family-sized suites, and if you have the misfortune to get a room without a view, there's a wonderful panorama from the rooftop bar. In Kolonáki, **St George Lycabettus**, 2 Kleoménous (Plateía Dexaménis) ✆ 729 0711, ✆ 729 0439 (*lux*) has an intimate, family-run atmosphere, pool, and views of the Parthenon or out to sea.

expensive

Close to Pláka, the **Electra Palace** at 18 Nikodímou, ✆ 324 1401, ✆ 324 1875 (*A*) has views of the Acropolis and a wonderful rooftop swimming pool in a garden setting. More reasonable, just off Sýntagma Square, the **Astor**, 16 Karagiórgi Servías, ✆ 325 5555, ✆ 325 5115 (*A*) has a rooftop garden restaurant. The **Parthenon**, 6 Makrí St, ✆ 923 4594, ✆ 923 5797 (*A*) is not far from the Acropolis, and has a pretty outdoor breakfast area. **Titania**, 52 Panepistímou, ✆ 330 0111, ✆ 330 0700 (*B*) has a rooftop terrace planted with old olive trees, and gorgeous views over the Acropolis and Lykavittós. The **Athenian Inn**, 22 Cháritos in swanky Kolonáki, ✆ 723 8097, ✆ 724 2268 (*C*) was the favourite of Lawrence Durrell.

moderate

Adam's, 6 Herefóntos, ✆ 322 5381 (*C*) is in a quiet but central location on the edge of the Pláka; rooms are traditional, comfortable, and good value. Also in Pláka, the 19th-century **Akropolis House**, 6–8 Kodroú, ✆ 322 3244, ✆ 324 4143, has modernized rooms but in a traditional style, with antique furnishings, frescoes and a family welcome. **Pension Adonis**, 3 Kódrou, ✆ 324 9737, is a gem, clean and well-run by the Greek who managed the Annapolis Hilton. All rooms have balconies, and there are lovely breakfasts, a roof garden, and bar with views (rates include breakfast).

Museum, 16 Bouboulínas, ✆ 360 5611, ✆ 380 0507 (*C*), right at the back of the Archaeology Museum, has similar rooms, but the prices are a bit higher. **Tembi**, 29 Eólou, ✆ 321 3175, ✆ 325 4179 (*D*) , near Monastiráki, is nothing special, but is cheaper, with kind owners, and washing facilities. **Hermes**, 19 Apollónos, ✆ 323 5514, ✆ 323 2073 (*C*) near Sýntagma is comfortable and friendly, with a small bar and roof garden with Acropolis views. **Hera**, 9 Falírou at Veikoú, ✆ 923 6683, ✆ 924 7334 (*C*) is modern but tasteful with a garden on the ground and roof.

Out in posh Kifissiá, **Katerina**, 3 Mykónou, ✆ 801 9826 (*C*) is one of the least expensive and friendliest places. In Chalándri, a bit closer to Athens, the **Akropol**, 71 Pentélis Ave, ✆ 682 6650, ✆ 684 5057 (*C*) is very nice with a garden, popular with business people, American tourists and anyone who wants to stay above the *néfos* line. **Art Gallery** at Eréchthiou 5, Veíkoú, ✆ 923 8376, ✆ 923 3025 (*E*) is a pleasant place at the lower end of this category, though Pláka is a 20-minute walk.

inexpensive

The first six on this list are in Pláka: **Phaedra**, 16 Cherefóndos St, ✆ 323 8461 *(D)* just off Filellínon St, has free hot showers, an unreconstructed pre-war interior, and pleasant staff. **John's Place**, 5 Patróou St, ✆ 322 9719 (near Metropóleos St) (*E*) is simple and cheap, with bathrooms down the hall. **Kouros**, 11 Kódrou St (just off Kidathinéou St), ✆ 322 7431 (*E*) is an old house in a quietish backwater near the Greek Folk Art Museum, opposite the small park area on Kidathinaíon. The **Student Inn**, 16 Kidathinéon, ✆ 324 4808, is ideal for the rowdy younger crowd (1.30am curfew). Very near Monastiráki, the **Pella Inn**, Ermou 104, ✆ 321 2229, is simple but welcoming. **Aphrodite**, Apollonos 21, ✆ 322 3357, ✆ 322 6047, has little character, but good rooms on a quiet street. In Exárchia, book early for **Dryades**, E. Benáki 105 and Anaxartísias, ✆ 382 7191, ✆ 380 5193 (*D*); the top three rooms have lovely views (the same owner also runs the even cheaper **Orion** (*D*) adjacent). **Marble House**, 35 A. Zínni, in Koukáki, ✆ 923 4058 (*E*) is a comfortable Greek-French-run pension. The **Student's Hostel** at 75 Damaréos St, Pangráti, ✆ 751 9530, ✆ 751 0616, is central and not a member of the YHA. Athens' nearest **campsites** are at Dafní Monastery and down on the coast at Voúla.

hotels near the airport

If you have an early or delayed flight, or just a day in Athens, there are a few hotels by the airport. They do tend to be desperately noisy—some are practically on the runway. **Emmantina**, 33 Vass. Georgíou, Glyfáda, ✆ 898 0683, ✆ 894 8110 (*A; exp*) is one of the better ones, with a pool on the roof and an airport shuttle bus. Convenient, moderate choices in

Glyfáda include: the **Blue Sky**, 26 Eleftherías, ✆ 894 7722, 📠 894 3445; **Avra**, 5 Gr. Lambraki, ✆ 894 7185 📠 898 1161; and **Beau Rivage**, 87 Vass. Geórgiou, ✆ 894 9292. **Kreoli**, 17 Vass. Georgíou, ✆ 894 4301, 📠 894 8986 (*B*) is basic, but friendly and family-run, with a pool and breakfast room. Front room and ear plugs essential, air-conditioning extra.

Eating Out in Athens

Athenians rarely dine out before 10 or 11pm, and they want to be entertained afterwards. If it's warm they'll drive to the suburbs or the sea. Glyfáda, near the airport, and outer Piraeus (Kalípoli) are popular on a summer evening: the cool sea breeze is a life-saver after the oppressive heat of Athens. The following places are all Greek, but ethnic food, especially Asian, is just as easy to find.

Pláka

Pláka is the place to head for pleasant restaurants and al fresco dining in the evening—the tinkling glasses, music, chatter and laughter ricochet off the medieval walls. **Platanos**, 4 Diogénis, ✆ 322 0666, the oldest taverna in Pláka, is near the Tower of the Four Winds and serves good wholesome food in the shade of an enormous plane tree (*around 3000dr*). *Closed Sun.* In the heart of Pláka, in Filomousón Square, where you will land up sooner or later, you can eat well at **Byzantino**, 18 Kidathinéon, ✆ 322 7368, which serves big portions (the fish soup and lamb fricassée are excellent) at its tables under the trees (*3000dr*). It's also one of the few decent places open for Sunday lunch. **Bacchus**, 10–12 Thrasyllou, ✆ 322 0385 has a lovely cloistered outdoor dining area under the Parthenon; try one of the savoury pies (*around 4000dr*). For a cut above taverna fare, dine at **Daphne's**, 4 Lysikrátous (by the Lysikratos monument) ✆ 322 7971, a neoclassical mansion with an elegant dining room with Pompeiian frescoes and beautiful courtyard—a rarity in Athens—serving refined, traditional Greek and international dishes (*around 9000dr a head*). Athens' oldest vegetarian restaurant, **Eden**, is at 12 Lissíou and Mnissikléous, ✆ 324 8858, with vegetarian quiches and soya moussakas (*around 2500dr*). *Closed Tues.*

Under Pláka: Psirri/Monastiráki/Thísio

Among the many new restaurants and *ouzéries* in Psirri, the first remains outstanding for fun: **Taki 13**, at 13 Táki, ✆ 325 4707, has a superb atmosphere with simple food but a great party bar, often featuring live music (jazz/blues Tuesday and Wednesday, Greek on weekends) and sing-songs till 1.30 am. Weekend afternoons bring similar outbursts of drinking and singing at the more bohemian **Café Abysinnia**, in Place Abysinnias, in the centre of Monastiráki, ✆ 321 7047; so-so food but excellent atmosphere. *Closed Mon.* If you have a hankering for an excellent *souvláki* and *gýros*, get yourself to **Thanassis**, 69 Mitropoléos, in Monastiráki, ✆ 324 4705, open till 2am. **Vrachakia**, Ortynon 7, nearer the Thesion, overlooks the Acropolis and offers a bizarre 1950s ambience to go with its taverna classics (*5000dr*). In the same area, **Phanari**, Irakleidon 19A, has some of the best and most economical fish dinners in Athens (*from 4000dr*) and tables in the middle of a street that comes alive after dark.

Kolonáki and Around

The legendary **Gerofinikas**, 10 Pindárou, ✆ 362 2719, still has the ancient palm tree that gave it its name, growing right out of the middle of the restaurant; the food is famous, expensive (*around 7000dr a head*) and the whole meal an experience. *Closed holidays.* Behind the Hilton, the Cypriot restaurant **Othello's,** 45 Mikalakopoúlou, ✆ 729 1481, serves delicious, authentic cuisine (*around 4500dr for a meal*). Out towards the US embassy, **Vlassis**, 8 Pasteur St, ✆ 642 5337 is a superb family-run taverna, *the* place to find true Greek cuisine and one of the rare ones with excellent wines and desserts, too (*around 5000dr*). *Book. Closed Sun.* **Salamandra**, Matzarou 3, ✆ 361 7927, has some of the least expensive but tastiest food in Kolonáki, served in a pretty old house (*under 3000dr*). *Closed Sun.*

Around Omónia Square

Sleazy Omónia Square is a great place to try Greek street food. If you're anywhere near the Central Market, don't miss one of the best *mageiria* in Athens: **Diporto**, Theatrou and Sofokléous, an Athens institution, serving simple but delicious dishes and salads with barrelled retsina (*lunch only, around 3000dr*). **Athinaiko**, 2 Themistokléous, east of Omónia, ✆ 383 8485 is a great place to fill up on tasty *mezédes* and swordfish kebabs while watching the passing crowds. On the same street, at No.18, **Andreas**, ✆ 362 1522, offers tasty seafood at reasonable prices, and tables outside. The traditional Greek hangover cure, tripe soup (*patsas*), and meaty Hellenic soul food is dished up in the early hours to trendy drunkards at **Monastiri**, the butchers' restaurant in the central meat market.

Exárchia

In Exárchia, **Kostayiannis**, 37 Zaími, ✆ 821 2496, behind the National Archaeology Museum, has a succulent display of food in the glass cabinets near the entrance preparing you for a memorable culinary evening. Apart from the superb seafood, the 'ready food' is unbeatable—roast pork in wine and herb sauce or the rabbit *stifádo*, accompanied by barrelled retsina. Prices here are very reasonable (*3500dr for a full evening meal*). To enjoy the after-theatre ambience, don't get there too early. *Closed lunchtimes, Sun, and Aug.* **Galatia**, 50 Valtetsiou, ✆ 380 1930, offers authentic Cypriot fare in relaxed surroundings. For a night out, book a table at **Strephis**, Athineas 5 and Poulcherias 8, ✆ 882 0780, in a historic house at the foot of Stefi hill, where Xanthis, owner and disciple of Theodorakis leads the public in old Greek songs; good, plentiful food (*evenings only; around 4500dr*). Among several tavernas along Methonis street, try **Ama Lachi**, at No.66, ✆ 384 5978, cheap, good and pleasant; there's another clutch of inexpensive places around Plateía Exárchia.

Entertainment and Nightlife

The summer is filled with festivals attracting international stars from around the world; at other times, classical music fans should try to take in a performance at the **Mégaron**, on Vass. Sofías and Kokkáli, ✆ 728 2333, Athens' brand new acoustically wonderful concert hall. Maria Callas got her start at the **Greek National Opera House**, 59-61 Academías St, ✆ 361 2461, which is shared with the national ballet. From May to September there are nightly folk dance performances at the **Dora Stratou Theatre** on Philapapou Hill (✆ 921 4650. *Rembétika*, the Greek blues, is in full revival in Athens; the real thing may be heard live at **Stoa Athanaton**, Sophokleous 19, ✆ 321 4362 (*closed Sun*) or **Rota**, Ermou 118, ✆ 325 2517 (*closed Mon and Tues*), and often at **Diogenis Palace**, 259 Syngroú (also a useful street for big bouzouki clubs, or if you're looking for a transvestite), ✆ 942 4267. Irakleidon street in Thissio has popular rock bars, such as **Stavlos** and **Berlin**. For jazz, try **French Quarter**, 78 Mavromicháli in Exárchia, ✆ 645 0758 or **Half Note**, Trivonianou 17 in Mets, ✆ 923 3460, which alternates between Greek and foreign artists. In summer, young fashion slaves and beautiful Athenians head out to the bars and clubs in Glyfáda or by the airport: here you'll find **Vareladiko**, 4 Alkondidon St, ✆ 895 2403, the first 'hyper-club' in Greece, with the latest Greek hits; **Romeo**, 1 Ellinikikou, ✆ 894 5345, a *skyladiko* club for a wild Greek night out, and **Amfitheatro**, Vass. Georgiou , ✆ 894 4538, Athens' biggest rave venue. Gay Athens gathers in Makrigiánni, the neighbourhood just south of the Acropolis: **Splash**, **Lamda** and **Granazi** are popular dancing bars with cover charges, all along Lembessi St, off Syngroú. In the summer, outdoor cinemas are a treat and all the films are in their original language: two of the nicest are in Kolonáki: **Dexameni**, in Dexameni Square halfway up Lykavittós, ✆ 360 2363 and **Athinaia**, 50 Charitos St, ✆ 721 5717.

The port of Athens, Piraeus (ΠΕΙΡΑΙΑΣ)—pronounced pi-ray-A or the old way, Pirevs—was the greatest port of the ancient world and remains today one of the busiest in the Mediterranean. In Greece, a country that derives most of its livelihood from the sea in one way or another, Piraeus is the true capital, while Athens is merely a sprawling suburb where the bureaucrats live. Still, it takes a special visitor to find much charm in the tall grey buildings and dusty hurly-burly in the streets, although Marína Zéa and Mikrolimáni with their yachts, brightly-lit tavernas and bars are a handsome sight, as are the neon signs flashing kinetically as you sail from Piraeus in the evening.

Historical Outline

Themistocles founded the port of Piraeus in the 5th century BC when Pháliron, Athens' ancient port, could no longer meet the growing needs of the city. From the beginning Piraeus was cosmopolitan and up-to-date: the Miletian geometrician Hippodamos laid it out in a straight grid of streets that have changed little today. The centre of action was always the huge agora in the middle of the city. In the shelter of its *stoae* the world's first commercial fairs and trade exhibitions were held, including some on an international scale. All religions were tolerated, and women were allowed for the first time to work outside the home.

As Piraeus was so crucial to Athens' power, the conquering Spartan Lysander destroyed the famous Long Walls that linked city and port in 404 BC, at the end of the Peloponnesian War. Piraeus made a brief come-back under Konon and Lykurgos, who rebuilt its arsenals. After the 100-year Macedonian occupation and a period of peace, Sulla decimated the city to prevent any anti-Roman resistance, and for 1900 years Piraeus dwindled away into an insignificant village with a population as low as 20, even losing its name to become Porto Leone (after an ancient lion statue, carved in 1040 with runes by future king of Norway Harald Hadraada and his Vikings, then later carted off by Morosini to embellish Venice's Arsenal). With Athens the capital of independent Greece, Piraeus has regained its former glory as the reigning port of a seagoing nation, although nearly everything dates from after 1944, when the departing Germans blew the port sky-high.

Getting Around

In Piraeus this usually means getting out of town as quickly as possible. **Ships** are grouped according to their destination (*see* map) and almost anyone you ask will be able to tell you the precise location of any vessel. The cluster of ticket agents around the port is very competitive, but prices to the islands are fixed, so the only reason to shop around is to

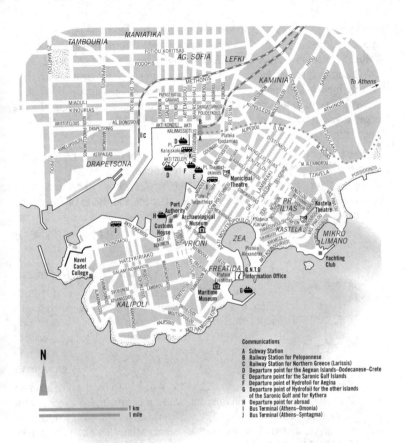

Communications

A   Subway Station
B   Railway Station for Peloponnese
C   Railway Station for Northern Greece (Larissis)
D   Departure point for the Aegean Islands–Dodecanese–Crete
E   Departure point for the Saronic Gulf Islands
F   Departure point of Hydrofoil for Aegina
G   Departure point of Hydrofoil for the other islands
       of the Saronic Gulf and for Kythera
H   Departure point for abroad
I   Bus Terminal (Athens–Omonia)
J   Bus Terminal (Athens–Syntagma)

N

1 km
1 mile

see if there is an earlier or faster ship to the island of your choice. For complete non-biased ferry schedules call the **Piraeus Port Authority** ✆ 422 6000.

The **metro** is the quickest way into central Athens, while **buses** on the main 'Green' line (no.040) will take you directly to Sýntagma Square/Filellínon St. The express line no.19 bus service to East and West Airport leaves from Karaiskáki Square.

The Sights

Piraeus has its own fine **Archaeology Museum** at 31 Char. Trikoúpi Street, ✆ 452 1598 (*open 8.30–3, closed Mon*) with an above-average collection of antiquities, many discovered off the Attica coast; pride of place goes to the five bronzes found in the port in 1959: an archaic Kouros, two Artemises, the Piraeus Athena and a tragic mask, as well as the fine 7th-century BC Protoattico amphora. The **Maritime Museum** on Akti Themistoklés by Freatídos Street, ℰ 451 6822 (*open 8.30–2, Sun 9–1, closed Mon*), has intriguing plans of Greece's greatest naval battles, ship models and mementoes from the War of Independence. If you find yourself in Piraeus with time to kill on a Sunday morning, prowl through the flea market in and around Hippodamias Square, where you may well happen across some oddity brought back by a Greek Sinbad.

Beaches are not far away, although the sea isn't exactly sparkling. Kastélla is the closest, followed by Néo Fáliron. Buses go to Ag. Kósmos by the airport, where you can play tennis or volleyball; at Glyfáda and Vouliagméni, further east, there's more wholesome swimming and a golf course. Zéa, Glyfáda and Vouliagméni are the three **marinas** organized by the National Tourist Organization. Piraeus is also the place to charter yachts or sail boats, from 12ft dinghies to deluxe twin-screw yachts, if you've missed your island connection (*see* p20).

Where to Stay in Piraeus

Hotel accommodation in Piraeus is geared towards businessmen, and less so towards people who have arrived on a late-night ship or plan to depart on an early-morning one. There are plenty of sleazy hotels within a 10-minute walk of the metro station.

expensive

Kastella, 75 Vass. Pávlou, ℰ 411 4735, ℰ 417 5716 (*B*) is a nice place on the waterfront beyond Mikrolimáni, with a roof garden. Even more swish is the **Cavo d'Oro**, 19 Vass. Pávlou, ℰ 411 3744 (*B*), with a restaurant and disco, and the most expensive of all, **Mistral**, Vass. Pávlou 105, ℰ 412 1425, ℰ 412 2096 (*B*) comes equipped with a pool, restaurant and air-conditioning.

moderate

If you want to be within walking distance of the docks, the **Triton**, 8 Tsamadou, ℰ 417 3457, ℰ 417 7888 (*B*) is one of the best of the many in the area. **Lilia**, 131 Zéas, Passalimáni, ℰ 417 9108, ℰ 411 4311 (*C*) is pleasant and offers free transport to the port. The **Ideal**, 142 Notará, ℰ 429 4050, ℰ 429 3890 (*C*), 50m from the customs house, offers air-conditioning, but should be renamed the So-So.

inexpensive

Known to seasoned travellers as the One Onion, the **Ionian**, 10 Kapodistríou, ℰ 417 0992 (*C*) is getting smellier by the year but is very convenient for an early ferry or if you've just fallen off one. Others are

Achillion, 63 Notará Street, ℗ 412 4029 (*D*), **Aenos**, near the main harbour, ℗ 417 4879 (*C*), **Santorini**, ℗ 452 2147 (*C*), and **Acropole**, ℗ 417 3313 (*C*), all used to backpackers.

Eating Out in Piraeus

Around the port the fare is generally fast food or tavernas so greasy it's a wonder they don't slide off the street. The bijou little harbour of Mikrolimáni, once the traditional place to go, is now an overpriced tourist trap. On the other hand, Piraeus has one of Greece's top seafood restaurants in the elegant **Varoulko**, 14 Deligiorgi, near Zéa Marina, ℗ 411 2043 (*book*), where the denizens of the deep are exquisitely prepared and brought to you without a menu; huge wine cellar and prices over 10,000dr to match. *Closed Sun.* Its chief rival, **Thalassinos**, is just behind the Onassis hospital in Kallithéa, at Liskratous 32, ℗ 930 4518, serving more utterly fresh seafood, beautifully prepared, in the same price range. *Closed Sun eve and Mon.* On Piraeus' highest hill (it's worth taking a taxi), **Rigas** is an excellent family taverna. It's a favourite destination for Sunday lunch, with a huge choice of starters, and some unusual main courses to go along with the old favourites (*around 3500dr*). Nip across the road and top it off with a coffee on the terrace of the **Bowling Club** opposite to enjoy the superb view over Piraeus. But if it's fish you must have, head over to Fratídas, around from the Zéa Marína yacht harbour, where several moderately priced places offer fresh fish and sea views or, better still, continue along the coast to Kalípoli (bus 904 or 905 from the Metro) where *ouzeries* and fish tavernas line the road, and you can watch the ferries pass and the sun set over Salamína. **Diasimos**, 306 Aktí Themiksoleous, ℗ 451 4887, is one of the best in this area; Athenians drive down on Sundays to enjoy the sea views and seafood. For something less pricey but equally memorable, try to locate the Naval School near here: the favourite for excellent fish, salad and wine is **Margaro**, at the gate on Hatzikyriakoú St, ℗ 451 4226. Although there's absolutely no view at all, the variety, freshness and reasonable price of the seafood is its own reward.

An alternative if it's packed: walk up the road away from the Naval School, pass the traffic lights and look out for the *psarotaverna* **Anna**.

Towards the airport at Kalamáki, the **Apaggio**, 8 Megístis Street, ℗ 983 9093, specializes in Greek regional dishes. The menu changes daily, but often includes rarely seen delicacies such as lamb with prunes and almonds and onion pie. It's one of the in-places for Greek foodies and will set you back around 6000dr. *Bookings essential; closed Mon.*

tourist information

The National Tourist Organization (EOT) has thankfully opened a proper tourist information office in the heart of Athens, after 20 years of waiting. It's right near Sýntagma Square at 2 Amerikis Street, ℭ (01) 331 0561 (*open Mon–Fri 9–6.30, Sat 9–2, closed Sun*). EOT also have a branch at the **East Airport:** ℭ (01) 969 9500. On Internet try Welcome to Athens with maps, hotels, and practical info at *http://agn.hol.gr/hellas/attica/athens.htm.*

emergencies

Ambulance: ℭ 178. Doctors on duty: ℭ 105. Fire: ℭ 199. Police: ℭ 100. Pharmacies: ℭ 107.

The Athens tourist police are out at Dimitrakopoúlou 77, Koukáki, ℭ 925 3396, ℰ 924 3406, but they have a magic telephone number—**171**; Agent 171 not only speaks good English, but can tell you everything from ship departures to where to spend the night, 24 hours a day. Piraeus tourist police are in the cruise ship New Passengers Terminal on Aktí Miaoúli, ℭ 429 0665.

left luggage

Pacific LTD, 26 Níkis (just down from Sýntagma Square), ℭ 324 1007, offers a left luggage service; open regular business hours. In Piraeus, the left luggage store next to the HML ticket agency is open 7am–midnight.

lost property

If you leave something on a bus, taxi or metro, try ℭ 642 1616.

shopping

To find bargains, visit the Monastiráki flea market in the morning (don't miss the arcade off Andrianou, selling traditional crafts); to spend lots of money, the latest in Greek designer fashion (Carouzos, Prince Oliver, Parthenis, etc.) is on display in the boutiques along Kolonáki's Tsakalof and Milioni streets. For food, Athens' **Central Market** is on Athinás Street, between Evripidou and Sophokleous; food shops continue all the way to Omónia Square. On a number of islands you can visit workshops where women make carpets, but there's only one place to buy them: **EOMMEX**, 9 Mitropoleos St, ℭ 323 0408. Other fine handicrafts are on sale at the shops run by the **National Welfare Organization**, at 6 Ipatiás and Apóllonos Sts, ℭ 325 0524 and at 135 Vass. Sofiás, ℭ 646 0603.

If you need a good book in English try **Eleftheroudakis**, 4 Níkis, ℭ 322 9388 or **Compendium**, 28 Níkis ℭ 322 1248, both near Sýntagma; also **Pantelides**, 11 Amerikí, ℭ 362 3673, with a wide selection of more academic titles. For used books, try **Koultoura**, 4 Mantazarou, ℭ 380 1348 or **Bibliopolion**, 22 Ifestou St, in Monastiráki. **Metropolis**, 64 Panepistímiou, ℭ 383 0404, has the biggest selection of old, rare and new Greek recordings.

Rhodes/Ródos (ΡΟΔΟΣ)

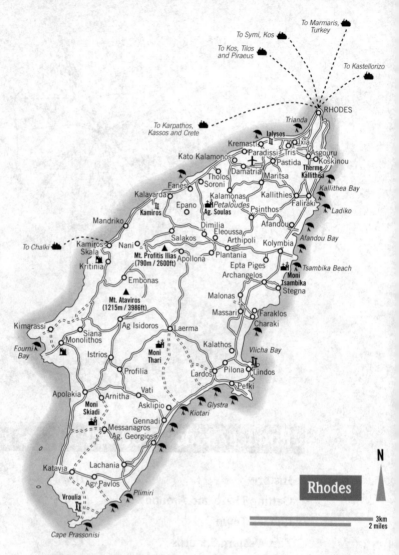

To Marmaris, Turkey

To Symi, Kos

To Kos, Tilos and Piraeus

To Kastellorizo

RHODES

To Karpathos, Kassos and Crete

Trianda

Ialysos

Kremasti

Ixia

Paradissi

Tris

Asgourou

Kato Kalamonos

Pastida

Koskinou

Damatria

Maritsa

Therme Kallithea

Tholos

Fanes

Soroni

Kalamonas

Kallithies

Kallithea Bay

Kalavarda

Epano

Kamiros

Ag. Soulas

Petaloudes

Psinthos

Faliraki

Ladiko

Mandriko

Dimilia

Afandou

Eleoussa

Salakos

Arthipoli

Afandou Bay

To Chalki

Kamiros Skala

Nani

Apollona

Plantania

Kolymbia

Kritinia

Mt. Profitis Ilias (790m / 2600ft)

Epta Piges

Archangelos

Tsambika Beach

Embonas

Moni Tsambika

Stegna

Mt. Ataviros (1215m / 3986ft)

Malonas

Kimarassi

Ag Isidoros

Laerma

Massari

Faraklos

Charaki

Fourni Bay

Siana

Monolithos

Moni Thari

Kalathos

Vlicha Bay

Istrios

Profilia

Lardos

Pilona

Lindos

Apolakia

Arnitha

Vati

Pefki

Moni Skiadi

Asklipio

Glystra

Gennadi

Kiotari

Messanagros

Ag. Georgios

Katavia

Lachania

Ag. Pavlos

Vroulia

Plimiri

Cape Prassonisi

N

Rhodes

3km
2 miles

Rhodes, 'more beautiful than the sun' according to the ancient Greeks, is the largest and most fertile of the Dodecanese, ringed by sandy beaches, bedecked with flowers, blessed with some 300 days of sun a year, dotted with handsome towns and villages full of monuments evoking a long, colourful history—in a nutshell, all that it takes to sit securely throned as the reigning queen of tourism in Greece. As a year-round resort for cold northerners and top international package destination (in increasingly swanky, fancy-pants packages) it's not quite fair to compare it with Greece's other islands. Rhodes is a holiday Babylon, Europe's answer to Florida, a glittering, sun-drenched chill pill in the sea, where people shed their inhibitions with their woollens, if not always their black socks with their sandals. Germans, Brits and Scandinavians outnumber everyone (there's even a special post box for Sweden at the central post office) but Israelis, Czechs and even Turks are now adding some different accents to the Babelling brew.

When and if you get fed up with the hordes, head inland, or for the southern half of Rhodes, beyond Líndos and Péfkos, and watch the sun set to see if you can find any lingering hints of the island evoked from Lawrence Durrell's imagination in his *Reflections on a Marine Venus*, written just after the war: 'Ahead of us the night gathers, a different night, and Rhodes begins to fall into the unresponding sea from which only memory can rescue it. The clouds hang high over Anatolia. Other islands? Other futures? Not, I think, after one has lived with the Marine Venus. The wound she gives one must carry to the world's end.'

Mythology

In myth, Rhodes is the subject of a messy number of very ancient and very often contradictory traditions. According to one, the first inhabitants of Rhodes were the Children of the Sea, the nine dog-headed enchantresses called Telchines, who had flippers for hands. In spite of this apparent handicap, they made the sickle that Cronos used to castrate Uranus; they carved the first statues of the gods, and founded Kámiros, Ialysós and Líndos before moving to Crete. There Rhea, the great mother goddess of the earth, made them the nurses of her son Poseidon, and they forged the sea god's trident.

Poseidon fell in love with the Telchines' sister, Alia, and had six sons and a daughter by her. The daughter, the nymph Rhodos, became the sole heiress of the island when Zeus decided to destroy the Telchines for meddling with the weather (they were fond of weaving magical mists), although their real crimes was belonging to a pre-Olympian matriarchal religion. He flooded Rhodes, but the Telchines managed to escape in various forms, most notoriously as the hounds of Artemis who tore Actaeon to bits.

The same cast of characters are on stage in another version, although this time the Telchines change sex and shed their dog heads and flippers. The sons of Pontos and Thalassa (the sea), they were artisans, magicians and ministers of Zeus. They had the same sister, the nymph Alia, who was loved by Poseidon and gave birth to Rhodos and a number of sons. When these sons refused to let Aphrodite dock as she sailed between her favourite islands of Kýthera and Cyprus, the goddess of love put a curse of incestuous passion on them and they raped their mother. In despair Alia flung herself into the sea and became 'Lefkothea' (the White Goddess). The wicked sons hid in the bowels of the earth and became demons as Poseidon in his wrath flooded Rhodes (the Telchines, tipped off by Artemis, escaped before the deluge).

The sun god Helios later fell in love with Rhodos, evaporated the stagnant waters with his hot rays and married the nymph. They had a daughter and seven sons, known as the Heliades. Athena gave them wisdom and taught them nautical and astrophysical lore. But the wisest of the Heliades, Tenagis, was killed in a jealous fit by four of his brothers, who fled to Lésbos, Kos, Ikaría and Egypt. The two innocent brothers, Ohimos and Kerkafos, remained and founded the city of Achaia. Ohimos' daughter Kydippi, a priestess of Hera, married her uncle Kerkafos and had three sons, Lindos, Kamiros and Ialysos, who founded the three city-states that bear their names.

A later, tidier, Olympian version of the story as related by Pindar tells that while the gods were dividing up the world's real estate Zeus realized that he had forgotten to set aside a portion for Helios. Dismayed, Zeus asked Helios what he could do to make up for his omission. The sun god replied that he knew of an island just emerging from the sea off the coast of Asia Minor which would suit him admirably. Helios married Rhodos and their seven sons, famous astronomers, ruled the island. One of the sons, or perhaps Tlepolemos (who led the ships of Rhodes to Troy), refounded the ancient Telchine towns.

Kámiros even has another possible founder: Althaemenes, son of the Cretan King Katreus and grandson of Minos. When an oracle predicted that Katreus would be slain by one of his offspring, Althaemenes tried to avoid destiny by going off to Rhodes, where he founded Kámiros and built an altar of Zeus, surrounding it with magical metal bulls that would bellow if the island were invaded. In later life Katreus sailed to Rhodes to visit his son, whom he missed dearly. He arrived at night, and what with the darkness and the bellowing of the metal bulls Althaemenes failed to recognize his father and fellow Cretans and slew them. When he realized his error in the morning he piteously begged Mother Earth to swallow him up whole, which she did.

History

Inhabited since Palaeolithic times, Rhodes was colonized by the Minoans, who built shrines to the moon at Filérimos, Líndos and Kámiros. When the Achaeans took over in the 15th century BC they founded the town of Achaia. Before settling on Rhodes for its name, the island was often known as Telchinia (*see* above), or Ophioussa, for its numerous vipers; even today villagers wear snake-repelling goatskin boots when working out in the fields. The Achaeans were supplanted in the 12th century BC by the Dorians, whose three cities—Líndos, Ialysós and Kámiros—dominated the island's affairs. According to Homer, they sent nine ships to Troy, led by Tlepolemos, son of Herakles, who met an unhappy end before the Trojan walls. Positioned along the main Mediterranean trade routes, Rhodes was important early on in both trade and naval power, especially after the three cities became the most influential members of the Dorian Hexapolis (*c.* 1000 BC).

The Founding of Rhodes City, and its Colossus

Rhodes sided with the Persians in both of their major campaigns against Greece, but upon their defeat quickly switched sides and joined the Delian confederacy. In 408 BC, in order to prevent rivalries and increase their wealth and strength, Líndos, Ialysós and Kámiros united to found one central capital, Rhodes, or Ródos, 'the rose'. Hippodamos of Miletus, the geometrician, designed the new town on a grid plan similar to the one he provided for Piraeus, and the result was considered one of the most beautiful cities of ancient times. It was huge, its walls encompassing a much greater area than that enclosed by the existing medieval walls. Celebrated schools of philosophy, philology and oratory were founded, and the port had facilities far in advance of its time. Although Líndos, Kámiros and Ialysós continued to exist, they lost all their importance and most of their populations to the new capital.

One reason for Rhodes' prosperity was its unabashedly expedient foreign policy. During the Peloponnesian War, it adroitly sided with whichever power was on top, and was far enough from the action to avoid intra-Greek entanglements. But not those from Asia Minor; in 355 BC Rhodes was grabbed by Mausolus, satrap of Caria, ally of Persia and Phoenician Tyre. The Carians compelled Rhodes to go to Tyre's aid against Alexander the Great in 336 BC, which led to another forced submission to a Macedonian garrison. Nevertheless, Alexander favoured Rhodes at the expense of hostile Athens and enabled the island to dominate Mediterranean trade; like Athens in Classical times, Rhodes ruled the waves and policed the seas of the Hellenistic era and set up trade counters all over the known world.

In the struggles between the Macedonian generals to divide up the conquests after Alexander's death, Rhodes' neutrality was compromised when another of Alexander's generals, the powerful Antigonas, ordered Rhodes to join him against Ptolemy (the general who had taken Egypt). Egypt was one of Rhodes' most lucrative trading partners and the Rhodians refused. To change their minds, Antigonas sent his son Dimitrios Poliorketes (the Besieger) at the head of the 40,000-man Syrian army and the Phoenician fleet to besiege the uppity islanders.

The ensuing year-long siege (305–304 BC) by one of the greatest generals of all time against the greatest city of the day has gone down in history, not only as a contest of strength and endurance, but as a battle of wits. Over and over again Dimitrios would invent some new ingenious machine, such as the ten-storey Helepolis siege tower, only to have it ingeniously foiled by the Rhodian defenders (who tripped up the Helepolis with a hidden shallow ditch). After a year both sides grew weary of fighting and made a truce, Rhodes agreeing to assist Dimitrios' father Antigonas in wars except in battles against Ptolemy.

So Dimitrios departed, leaving his vast siege machinery behind. This the Rhodians either sold or melted down, earning the enormous sum of 300 talents which they used to construct a great bronze statue of Helios, their patron god of the sun. The famous sculptor from Líndos, Chares, was put in charge of the project, and in 290 BC, after twelve years of work and at a cost of 20,000 pounds of silver, Chares completed the Colossus, or didn't quite: he found he had made a miscalculation and committed suicide just before it was cast. Standing somewhere between 100 and 140ft tall (at her crown the Statue of Liberty is 111ft), the Colossus did not straddle the entrance of Rhodes harbour, as is popularly believed, but probably stood near the present Castle of the Knights, gleaming bright in the sun, one of the Seven Wonders of the Ancient World. But of all the Wonders the Colossus had the shortest lifespan; in 225 BC an earthquake cracked its knees and brought it crashing to the ground. The Oracle at Delphi told Rhodes to leave it there (there are suspicions that Rhodian officials paid off the Oracle, wanting to use the money on improving their fleet instead) and it lay forlorn until AD 653 when the Saracens, who had captured Rhodes, sold it as scrap to a merchant from Edessa. According to legend, it took 900 camels to transport the bronze to the ships.

After the great earthquake, rulers from all over the Hellenistic world sent funds to repair the town and it was rebuilt grander than ever, with an estimated population of 80,000. New troubles arose when Philip V of Macedon, eager to expand in the area at the expense of the Ptolemies, paid pirates to attack Rhodian shipping. Rhodes declared war on Philip, in alliance with Byzantium and Pergamon. In 201 Philip's continuing mischief in the area sent the Rhodians to complain to Rome, beginning a cooperative relationship that brought the island to the summit of its influence. Assistance in Rome's war against Antiochus meant the island acquired, briefly, large possessions in Caria and Lycia in 188 BC. Alexandria was their only rival in wealth, and they had no rivals in Mediterranean trade until the Romans granted tiny Delos duty-free trade concessions in 166 BC; that same year the island's tax revenues fell from a million drachmae to a mere 150,000 drachmae.

In 164 BC Rhodes signed a peace treaty with Rome obliging it to contribute troops to Roman wars, which brought down upon it sieges by Rome's enemies, especially Mithridates of Pontus. At the same time, the famous School of Rhetoric on Rhodes attracted all the top Romans of the day—Pompey, Cicero, Cassius, Julius Caesar, Brutus, Cato the Younger and Mark Antony. When Caesar was assassinated, Rhodes as always backed the right horse, in this case Augustus; only this time the wrong horse, Cassius, was in the neighbourhood. Having studied on the island, he knew it well, and he sacked the city, captured its fleet, and sent its treasures to Rome (43–42 BC). It was a blow from which Rhodes never recovered. She lost control of her colonies and islands, and other Roman allies muscled in on her booming trade. In AD 57 St Paul preached on the island and converted many of the inhabitants; by the end of the Roman empire, Rhodes was a sleepy backwater.

Two Hundred Years of Knights

Byzantium brought many invaders and adventurers to Rhodes: Arabs and Saracens (including in 804 a siege by the great Harun al-Rachid, of *Arabian Nights* fame). The Genoese, the Venetians and the Crusaders all passed through; in 1191 Richard the Lionheart and Philip Augustus of France stopped by to recruit mercenaries to fight Saladin. After the second (and last) fall of Jerusalem in 1291, the Knights Hospitallers of St John (*see* p.67), dedicated to protecting pilgrims and running hospitals in the Holy Land, took refuge on Cyprus, but by 1306 they had become interested in the wealthier and better positioned Rhodes. They asked the Emperor Andronicus Palaeologus to cede them the island in return for their loyalty, but after 1204 the Byzantines had learned better than to trust the Franks. The Knights, under Grand Master Foulques de Villaret, then took the matter into their own hands and purchased the Dodecanese from their current occupants: Genoese pirates. The Rhodians weren't impressed, and the Knights had to spend their first three years subduing the natives.

By 1309, with a little help from the Pope, the Knights were secure in their possession and began to build their hospital and inns in Rhodes town. They built eight inns or *auberges* in all, one for each of the 'tongues', or nationalities (England, France, Germany, Italy, Castile, Aragon, Auvergne and Provence). There were never more than 650 Knights on Rhodes and, although nominally dedicated to caring for pilgrims (their hospital still exists), their focus shifted to their role as free-booting, front-line defenders of Christendom. With their new funds derived from the suppression of the Knights Templars in 1312, the Knights of St John replaced the fortifications—and continued to replace them up until the 16th century, hiring the best Italian fortification engineers until they could claim one of the most splendid defences of the day.

Meanwhile, the Knights had made themselves such a thorn in the side of Muslim shipping that Rhodes was besieged by the Sultan of Egypt in 1444 and by

Mohammed II, the Conqueror, in 1480, with 70,000 men. Both times their tremendous walls won the day. But enough was enough: in 1522 Suleiman the Magnificent attacked Rhodes with an unprecedented 400 ships and 200,000 men; the defenders of Rhodes (there were 6000 of them, plus 1000 Italian mercenaries and 650 Knights) bitterly joked that the Colossus was now coming back at them in the form of cannon balls. After a frustrating six-month siege Suleiman was on the point of abandoning Rhodes when a German traitor informed him that of the original Knights only 180 survived, and they were on their last legs. The Sultan redoubled his efforts and the Knights were at last forced to surrender. In honour of their courage, Suleiman permitted them to leave in safety, with all their Christian retainers and possessions.

Ottomans and Italians

The remaining Greeks were forced to move outside the inner walls, leaving the heart of the city to become the exclusive domain of the Turkish and Jewish populations of the island. Suleiman built a mosque to celebrate his victory and over the years the Ottoman rulers added a few others, but in general the Turks left things as they were, content to enjoy Rhodes, which they regarded as a kind of paradise on earth. When the Rhodians attempted to revolt during the War of Independence the Turks reacted with atrocities; their popularity dropped even more in the Great Gunpowder Explosion of 1856, when lightning struck a minaret and exploded a powder magazine, blowing a large chunk of the Old Town to bits and killing 800 people.

The Italians took Rhodes from the Turks after a siege in 1912. They cheekily claimed that the island was their inheritance from the Knights of St John, and Mussolini, fancying himself as a new Grand Master, had their palace reconstructed to swan around in. He never saw it. War intervened; after 1943 the Germans took over until May 1945, long enough to send most of the island's Jewish community, 2000 strong, to the concentration camps. Rhodes, with the rest of the Dodecanese, officially joined Greece in 1948, whereupon the government declared it a free port, boosting its already great tourist potential.

Rhodes (0241–) **Getting There and Around**

By air: Rhodes airport, the third busiest in Greece, © 92 839, has just been enlarged. There are numerous UK, German and Scandinavian direct charters from April to mid October and nearly a million charter arrivals during the season. Domestic flights from **Olympic** (Iérou Lóchou 9, © 24 555) include at least four daily flights to Athens, and frequent connections with Thessaloníki, Crete (Herákleon), Kárpathos, Kos, Kastellórizo, Kássos, Mýkonos and Santoríni. **Air Greece** also has a flight to Athens, a bit cheaper than Olympic, © 21 690. **Airport Flight Information Desk:**

✆ 83 214 or 83 200 or 83 202. The bus to Parádissi passes near the airport every 30 minutes or so until midnight; taxi fares to town are around 2500dr. If your return flight is delayed—charters always seem to be—it's only a three-minute walk to the nearest bar and taverna (Anixis) in Parádissi, and the latter stays open until 2am.

By sea: international **ferries** from the **Commercial Harbour** once a week to Limassol, Cyprus, and Haifa, Israel, on Salamis Lines; daily ferry to Piraeus, Pátmos, Léros, Kálymnos, Kos and Sými; frequently to Níssyros and Tílos; twice a week to Kastellórizo, Páros, Íos, Kárpathos, Kássos, Crete (Heráklion) and Santoríni; once a week to Astypálaia, Lipsí, Ikaría, Foúrni, Náxos, Sýros, and Marmaris, Turkey (*see* p.139). Daily **excursion boats** and *Sými I* and *Sými II* ferries from **Mandráki Harbour** to Líndos and beaches at Lárdos, Tsambíka, Faliráki, Kallithéa, Ladiko, Kolymbia and Sými. **Hydrofoil**: daily to Kos, Pátmos and Sými, also connections to Léros, Tílos, Níssyros, Kálymnos, Samos (Pythagório), Chálki and Marmaris (currently 5000dr round trip). **Port authority**: ✆ 28 666 and 28 888.

By road: there is a frequent **bus service**: east coast buses are yellow and depart from the Sound and Light square; west coast buses are white and blue, departing from around the corner by the Market. Taxis are plentiful and reasonably priced. The central **taxi rank** is in Mandráki Harbour, ✆ 27 666. **Radio taxis** run 24hrs and come a bit more expensive, ✆ 64 712, ✆ 66 790, ✆ 64 734. It's worth hiring wheels to get off the beaten track, especially in the interior; nearly anything from four-wheel-drive beach buggies to motorbikes is available; out of high season prices are negotiable. Note that petrol stations are closed Sunday, holidays and after 7pm.

The **Dodecanese Association of People with Special Needs**, ✆ 73 109, will, with 48-hour notice, provide free transport in special vans to any destination on Rhodes, between 7am and 3pm.

Rhodes (0241–)   ***Tourist Information***

The **Greek National Tourist Organisation** (EOT) office on the corner of Papágon and Makaríou Street, ✆ 23 255 or 21 921, ✎ 26 955, has very helpful multilingual staff and a wide range of maps, leaflets and information (*open Mon–Fri, 8–3*); **tourist police** have a 24-hour multilingual number, ✆ 27 423, for any information or complaints. **City of Rhodes Tourist Information Centre**, Rimini Square, ✆ 35 945 (*open Mon–Fri, 9–6, Sat 9–12 noon, closed Sun*) is mostly a money exchange. Hotels and both tourist offices have copies of the free and helpful English-language newspaper, *Ródos News*. For **recorded info**, ✆ 78 489.

Consulates

US: the Voice of America station at Afándou may help, ✆ 52 555.
British: Mr and Mrs Dimitriádis, 111 Amerikís, ✆ 27 306/27 247.
Irish: Mr Skevos Mougros, 111 Amerikís, ✆ 22 461.

Festivals

Lenten carnival **just before Easter**; **14 June**, Profítis Amós at Faliráki; **20 June,** Scandinavian midsummer festivities in Rhodes town, organized by tour operators (yes, really); **28 June** at Líndos; **first 10 days in July:** musical meetings in Rhodes; **29–30 July**, Ag. Soúla at Soroní, with donkey races; **26 July**, Ag. Panteleímonos at Siána; in **August**, dance festivals at Kallithiés, Maritsa and Embónas; **14–22 August**, Tis Panagías at Kremastí; **26 August**, Ag. Fanoúrious in the Old Town; **5 September**, Ag. Trías near Rhodes town; **7 September**, at Moní Tsambíkas (for fertility); **13 September**, Ag. Stávros at Apóllona and Kallithiés; **26 September**, Ag. Ioánnis Theológos at Artamíti; **18 October**, Ag. Lukás at Afándou; **7 November** at Archángelos.

Rhodes Town

Spread across the northern tip of the island, Rhodes (POΔOΣ) (pop. 50–60,000, of the 98,000 on the island) is the largest town and capital of the Dodecanese, and celebrated its 2400th anniversary in 1993. It divides neatly into Old and New Towns. Tourism reigns in both, although these days the New Town is increasingly filling up with designer boutiques aimed at the prosperous Rhodians and visiting upmarket Greeks who come to shop duty-free. The medieval city is so remarkably preserved that it looks like a film set in places, and has often been used as such (most recently in *Pascali's Island*).

Rhodes presents an opulent face to the sea, and sailing in is much the prettiest way to arrive and get your bearings. The massive walls of the Old Town, crowned by the Palace of the Grand Masters, rise out of a lush subtropical garden; graceful minarets and the arcaded waterfront market, bright with strings of lightbulbs at night, add an exotic touch. Monumental pseudo-Venetian public buildings trying to look serious decorate the shore to the left, while opposite three 14th-century **windmills** (down from the original 15) turn lazily behind a forest of masts. Yachts, smaller ferries and excursion boats dock at the smallest of three harbours, **Mandráki** (MANΔPAKI). The entrance is guarded by the lighthouse and fort of **Ag. Nikólaos**, built in the 1460s to take the brunt of the Turkish attacks (plans are afoot to make it a naval museum), and a **bronze stag and doe**, marking where the

Colossus may have stood. Under the Knights a chain crossed the port here and every ship that entered had to pay a two per cent tax of its cargo value towards the war effort. Larger ferries, any craft to Turkey, and cruise ships enter the **commercial harbour** (ΕΜΠΟΡΙΚΟΣ ΛΙΜΕΝΑΣ) nearer the Old Town walls.

These **walls** (currently being restored) are a masterpiece of late medieval fortifications, and, although you'll often be tempted to climb up for a walk or view, access is by guided tour only (*Tues and Sat, meet in front of the Palace of the Grand Master at 2.30; adm*). Constructed over the old Byzantine walls under four of the most ambitious Grand Masters, d'Aubusson, d'Amboise, del Carretto and Villiers de l'Isle Adam, they stretch 4km and average 38ft thick. Curved the better to deflect missiles, the landward sides were safeguarded by a 100ft-wide dry moat. Each national group of Knights was assigned its own bastion and towers to defend, except the Italians, who were the best sailors and were put in charge of the Knights' fleet.

Of the many gates that linked the walled Old Town with the village outside, the most magnificent is the Gate of Emery d'Amboise (**Píli Ambouaz**, in Greek) near the Palace of the Grand Masters, built in 1512 (entrance off Papagou Street). Under the Turks, all Greeks had to be outside the walls by sundown or forfeit their heads.

The Old Town (ΠΑΛΑΙΑ ΠΟΛΗ)

The medieval town within these walls was fairly dilapidated when the Italians took charge. They restored much, but fortunately lost the war before they could get on with their plan to widen all the streets for cars and build a ring road. To keep any such future heretical notions at bay, UNESCO has declared the Old Town a World Heritage Site, and is providing funds for historical restorations and infrastructure and burying electric and phone lines.

Entering the aforementioned Gate d'Amboise, passing the tablecloth sellers and quick-draw portrait artists, you'll find yourself in the inner sanctum or **Collachium**, where the Knights could retreat if the outer curtain wall were taken. By the gate, at the highest point, a castle within a castle, stands the **Palace of the Grand Masters,** built over a temple of Helios; some archaeologists believe that the Colossus actually stood here, overlooking the harbour (*open Tues–Fri, 8–7, Sat and Sun 8–3, Mon 12.30–7; adm exp*). Construction of this citadel was completed in 1346, modelled after the Popes' palace in Avignon—not by accident: 14 of the 19 Grand Masters on Rhodes were French and French was the official spoken language of the Order. Underground rooms were used as storage and as a refuge for the civilian population in case of attack. The Turks used the whole as a prison, even after the Great Gunpowder Explosion of 1856, when the first floor caved in, and the Italians did the same until Mussolini ordered that it be reconstructed as his summer villa. The Italians covered the floors with lovely Roman mosaics from Kos, brought in a hotch-potch of Renaissance furniture, and installed a lift and modern plumbing, but the war broke out and ended before the Duce could enjoy its 158 rooms (don't panic; only a tenth are open to the public).

Note the huge marble coat of arms on one of the fireplaces: 'Restored by Vitt. Eman., III, King and Emperor 1939.' On the ground floor, two excellent permanent exhibitions have been set up: *The City of Rhodes from its Foundation to the Roman Period* and *Rhodes from the 4th century to its Capture by the Turks*, with English translations, full of curious sidelights on lightweight Rhodian bricks (used for the dome of Hagia Sophia in Constantinople) and the Knights' production of sugar, an item worth its weight in gold in the Middle Ages. There's a collection of detached frescoes, coins, icons, and the tombstone of the Grand Master Villiers de l'Isle Adam, who defied Suleiman the Magnificent for six months even though outmanned nearly 40 to one.

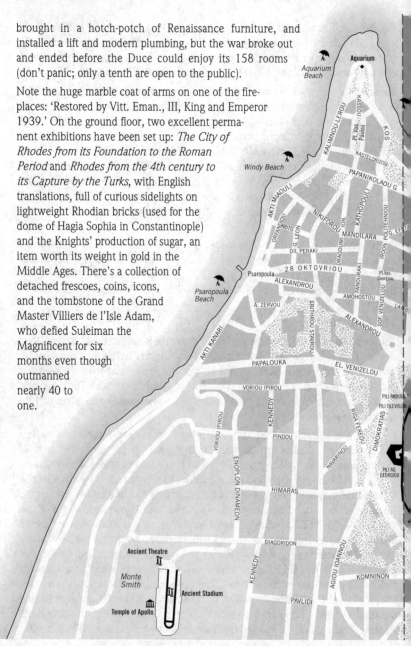

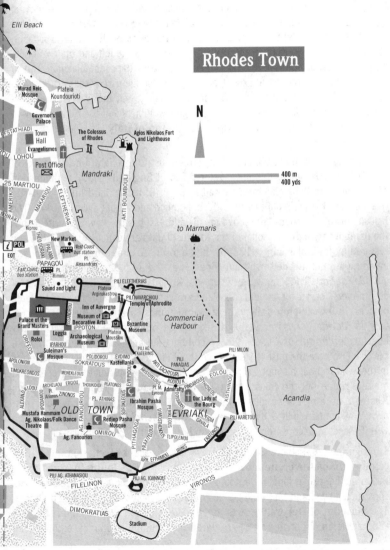

Rhodes Town

Elli Beach

Murad Reis Mosque

Plateia Koundourioti

Governor's Palace

EFSTATHIADI

Town Hall

The Colossus of Rhodes

Agios Nikolaos Fort and Lighthouse

Evangelismos

ROU

LOHOU

Post Office

N

Mandraki

PL. ELEFTHERIAS

25 MARTIOU

AMERIKIS

MAKARIOU

400 m

400 yds

AMVRAKI

PL. Kiprou

THEO DORAKI

New Market

West Coast bus station

AKTI BOUMBOULI

to Marmaris

EOT

PAPAGOU

PALAMA

PL. Alexandrias

East Coast bus station

PL. Rimini

PILI ELEFTHERIAS

ISIDOROU

Sound and Light

Plateia Argirokastrou

PILI NAVARCHIOU

Temple of Aphrodite

Commercial Harbour

Inn of Auvergne

Museum of Decorative Arts

IPPOTON

Byzantine Museum

Palace of the Grand Masters

Plateia Moussiou

Roloi

Loggia

Archaeological Museum

PILI AG. EKATERINIS

PILI MILON

ORFEOS

APOLONION

IPARHOU

Suleiman's Mosque

POLIDOROU

EVDIMO

Kastellania

PILI PANAGIAS

ANTI SACHTOURI

TIMOKREONDOS

SOKRATOUS

MENEKLEOUS

ARISTOTELOUS

RODIOU K.

PINDAROU

FEOLOU

KISTHINIOU

PILI KARETOU

ALEXANDRIDOU

ARCHELAOU

ERGIOU

THOUKIDIDI

PLATONOS

PL. M. Evreon

DIMOSTHENOUS

PERIKLEOUS

Acandia

Arionos

ZINONOS

PL. ATHINAS

Admiralty House

Our Lady of the Bourg

HIPPODAMOU

SOFOKLEOUS

Ibrahim Pasha Mosque

DOSIADOU

PERAKLEOUS

FIDIA

GAVALA

Mustafa Hammam

OLD TOWN

AG. FANOURIOU

EVRIAKI

Ag. Nikolaos/Folk Dance Theatre

Redjep Pasha Mosque

SYNAGOGA

OMIROU

Ag. Fanourios

PITHAGORA

PRAXITELOUS

TUPOLEMOU

IRINIS

EXATHNOS

PILI AG. ATHANASIOU

PILI AG. IOANNOU

ARH. EFTHIMIOU

FILELINON

VIRONOS

DIMOKRATIAS

Stadium

115

The main street descending from the palace into the heart of the Collachium is a favourite of film makers: quiet, evocative, cobblestoned **Odós Ippotón** (Knights' Street), beautifully restored by the Italians. It passes under the arcaded **Loggia** that originally linked the Palace to the Knights' 14th-century cathedral of St John where the Grand Masters were buried; after this was shattered in the Gunpowder Explosion a Turkish school was built in the midst of the ruins. Ippotón has most of the Knights' inns, where they had meetings and meals. There were eight, divided into 'tongues', and each is emblazoned with the arms of the Grand Master in charge when they were built: the **Inn of Provence** on the left and the two buildings of the **Inn of Spain** on the right, then the French chapel and elaborate **Inn of France** (1509), adorned with escutcheons and crocodile gargoyles; as there were always more French knights than any other 'tongue', their inn was the most spacious. Next door stands a townhouse, belonging to Villiers de l'Isle Adam; opposite was the Knights' entrance to the Hospital. The **Inn of Italy** (1519) stands at the foot of the street.

Two squares open up at the end of the street; just to the right, on the corner of Plateía Moussion, stands the much restored **Inn of England** (1483), abandoned in 1534 when the Pope excommunicated Henry VIII. It was hard hit by an earthquake in 1851, then rebuilt by the British, bombed and rebuilt again in 1947. The British consul of Rhodes (*see* above for the address) has the key. Opposite stands the flamboyant Gothic Hospital of the Knights, built between 1440 and 1481 and restored by the Italians in 1918, now home to the **Archaeology Museum**, still awaiting a much needed overhaul (*open Tues–Fri 8–7, Sat and Sun 8–3, Mon 12.30–7; adm*). The long ward, where the Knights' surgeons (from the ranks of commoners) cared for patients in elaborate canopy beds, still has its heraldic devices. In the sculpture gallery the star attraction is Lawrence Durrell's 3rd-century BC *Marine Venus* (marine because she was found in the sea) and the pretty kneeling *Aphrodite of Rhodes* (90 BC), combing out her hair after emerging from the sea; also note the bust of Helios from the 2nd century BC, complete with holes in the head to hold his metal sunrays. Ceramics, stelae, Mycenaean jewellery and mosaics round out the collection. In the adjacent square, 11th-century **Panagía Kastrou**, used by the Knights as their cathedral of St Mary until they built their own, now contains a little **Byzantine Museum** (*open 8.30–3, closed Mon; adm*), with frescoes and icons from disused churches across the island and Chálki.

Through the arch, charming Plateía Argyrokástro has the loveliest inn, the 15th-century **Inn of Auvergne** (now a cultural centre) with a **fountain** made from a Byzantine baptismal font. Here, too, is the 14th-century **Palace of the Armeria**, constructed by Grand Master Roger de Pins as the Knights' first hospital on Rhodes. The **Museum of Decorative Arts** (*open 8.30–3, closed Mon; adm*) has folk arts and handicrafts from all over the Dodecanese, including costumes, embroideries and a reconstruction of a traditional room. In Plateía Sýmis, the next square north, are the ruins of a 3rd-century BC **Temple of Aphrodite**, discovered by the Italians in 1922. Fragments of another temple of the same epoch, dedicated to **Dionysos**, are in a corner behind the Ionian and Popular Bank. The Italians reopened the two harbour gates that the Turks had blocked up, **Píli Eleftherías** to Mandráki ('Freedom Gate', named by the Italians who regarded themselves as Rhodes' liberators) and **Píli Navarchio** (Arsenal Gate) to the marina and Commercial Harbour.

The Medieval Town

South of the Collachium of the Knights is the former Turkish bazaar and shopping district, centred around bustling **Sokrátous Street**, to this day thick with tourist and duty-free luxury shops. Midway along, at no.17, the Turkish-owned *kafeneíon* has remained steadfastly unchanged for the past century: some say, ditto its coffee-drinking, backgammon-playing clientele. At the top of Sokrátous Street stands the slender minaret of the lovely, faded red **Mosque of Suleiman** (*now closed*), built in 1523 by Suleiman the Magnificent to celebrate his conquest of Rhodes. The **Muselman Library** (1793) opposite contains rare Persian and Arabian manuscripts and illuminated copies of the Koran. Two precious 700-year-old Korans stolen in 1990 and worth 100 million drachmae have now been recovered and are back on show. Behind Suleiman's mosque, the Byzantine clock tower, **To Roloi**, has splendid views over the town, if you're lucky enough to find it open.

South of Sokrátous Street the Turkish Quarter dissolves into a zigzag of narrow streets, where charming Turkish balconies of latticed wood project beside crumbling stone arches and houses built directly over the street. On tatterdemalion Plateía Arionos, off Archeláos Street, the **Mustafa Mosque** keeps company with the atmospheric **Mustafa Hammam**, or Turkish baths, built in 1558 and remodeled in 1765 when the relaxation rooms were added. Still heated by a ton of olive logs a day, it has mosaic floors and marble fountains and a lovely ceiling, divided into men's and women's labyrinthine sections (*open Tues–Fri 11–7, Sat 8–6, Sun, Mon closed, bring own soap and towels; adm*). Another old mosque, **Ibrahim Pasha** (1531), is off Sofokléous Street; executions took place in front of it.

On Hippocrátes Square, where Sokrátous turns into Aristotélous Street, stands the picturesque Gothic-Renaissance **Kastellania**, built by d'Amboise in 1507, perhaps as a tribunal or commercial exchange for the Knights. It stands at the head of Pithágora Street, the main street of **Evriakí**, the Jewish quarter; according to Josephus the community dates from the 1st century AD and later chronicles cite them among the Rhodes' defenders against the Turks.

Continuing east along Aristotélous Street, the **Plateía Evrión Martyrón** (the Square of Hebrew Martyrs) honours the memory of the Rhodians sent off to die in the concentration camps. The so-called **Admirality** is on the square, with a bronze seahorse fountain; it was more likely the seat of Rhodes' bishop. From here, Pindárou Street continues to the impressive ruins of **Our Lady of the Bourg**, once the largest Catholic church on Rhodes, built by the Knights in thanksgiving for their defeat of the Turks in 1480 but never the same after it took a British bomb in the war. The Turkish and Jewish Quarters offer many other little cobbled lanes to explore, dotted with old frescoed churches converted into mosques and converted back again: it's worth trying to find little 13th-century **Ag. Fanourios** with its fine frescoes off Omirou, hidden behind a modern building, near the abandoned **Redjep Pasha Mosque** (1588), once completely coated with colourful Persian tiles. The gate at the end of Pithagora Street, **Píli Ag. Ioánnou,** or Red Door, is another demonstration of the walls' strength.

The New Town

Outside the walls, the row of seafront cafés look enticingly over Mandráki harbour, but they're overpriced and mainly aim at dragging in unsuspecting greenhorns. Just behind them, in the Italian-built octagonal **New Market**, tomatoes and water-melons have been replaced by gýros and *souvláki* stands. Further along Mandráki is an austere ensemble of Mussolini-style public buildings built in the 1920s—post office, theatre, town hall. The Italians also left Rhodes some rather more light-hearted architectures: the **Governor's Palace**, a pseudo-Doge's Palace decorated with a garish red diaper pattern, and the cathedral **Evangelísmos**, a copy of St John's, the cathedral blown up in the Gunpowder accident. The fountain is a copy of Viterbo's Gothic Fontana Grande.

The Turks regarded Rhodes as an island paradise, and many Muslim notables in exile (including a Shah of Persia) chose to spend the rest of their lives here. Many lie buried in the cemetery north of the municipal theatre, next to the **Mosque of Murad Reis**, named after the admiral of the Egyptian Sultan who was killed during the siege of Rhodes in 1522 and buried in a turban-shaped tomb or *turbeh*. The mosque has a lovely minaret reconstructed by the Greek government. Stretching along the shore from here is Rhodes' busiest strand, shingly **Élli Beach**, sheltered from the prevailing southwest winds and packed chock-a-block with parasols and sunbeds; signs everywhere warn about illegal beach touts poisoning people with out-of-date food. There's a diving platform for high divers and a lifeguard, but people floating on airbeds should beware being swept out to sea.

At the northernmost tip of the island is the **Aquarium** (*open daily 9–12; adm*), built by the Italians in 1938 and the only one in Greece, with tanks of Mediter-ranean fish and sea turtles, a pair of which are over 100 years old, and a startling collection of stuffed denizens of the deep, their twisted grimaces the result not of any prolonged agony but of amateur taxidermy. Local farmers have contributed an eight-legged calf and four-legged chicken for more horror-show fun. On the head-land, **Aquarium Beach** has deep water but its breezes make it more popular for windsurfing and paragliding rather than sunsoaking; ditto **Windy Beach**, which stretches down to Aktí Miaoúli. A bit further south, **Psaropoúla** is a safe, sandy beach running from the Hotel Blue Sky to the Belvedere. Although often breezy, the biggest danger is crossing the busy road to get to it. South of Psaropoúla are numerous small coves with safe swimming unless the wind is strong. Women should beware another drawback: the area is nicknamed Flasher's Paradise.

Just Outside Rhodes Town

City bus no.5 heads south of the New Town to the ancient acropolis of Rhodes, **Monte Smith**, named after Admiral Sydney Smith who in 1802 kept track of Napoleon's Egyptian escapades from here; today most people come up for the romantic sunset. On the way (North Epírou Street) are the ruins of an **Asklepeion**, dedicated to the god of healing, and a **Cave of the Nymphs**. On the top of Monte Smith, the Italians have partly reconstructed a 2nd-century BC Doric **Temple of Pythian Apollo** who was later associated with Rhodian Helios, and the 3rd-century BC **Stadium,** which sometimes hosts Classical dramas in the summer. A few columns of the temples of Zeus and Athena were ham-handedly re-erected. The **Ancient Theatre** is the only square one found on any Greek island.

City bus no.3 will take you the two kilometres out to **Rodíni Park**, with its cypresses, pines, oleanders, maples, peacocks and new **Deer Park** (the Delphic oracle told the ancient Rhodians to import deer to solve their snake problem, and they have been here ever since). Rodini Park marks the spot where Demosthenes' rival Aeschines established his celebrated School of Rhetoric in 330 BC, where the likes of Apollonius taught and the likes of Julius Caesar and Cicero learned how to speak so persuasively—there's a rock-cut tomb from the 4th century BC, the so-called 'Tomb of Ptolemy', and the ruins of a Roman aqueduct. The Knights grew their medicinal herbs here, and now merry drinkers can join Rodíni's peacocks for the **Rhodes Wine Festival**, recently resurrected by the council during three weeks in late July–early August with music, dance and food. Special buses transport revellers from the hotels to and from Mandráki harbour. During the evenings you can try Rhodes' own wines: *Chevaliers de Rhodes*, *Ilios*, the prize-winning premium red from CAIR, *Archontiko*, the excellent Emery white *Villaré*, and other Greek vintages.

The World's First Computer

During his days at the School of Rhetoric, Cicero was greatly impressed with something that he described as a 'future telling astronomical device', and it might have been on his orders that a Roman galley sailed to Rhodes to fetch it to the Urbs, along with the usual swag of statues and art that Rome was in the habit of relocating to itself. The ship, however, sank on its return in the treacherous seas south of the Peloponnese, off the tiny island of Antikýthera. It was the 22nd day of the ancient Greek month of Mounichon, in the first year of the 180th Olympiad (5 May, 59 BC). How is it possible to know the day that a ship was wrecked over 2000 years ago? Because Cicero's 'future telling astronomical device' was in fact the world's first computer.

The wreck was discovered by chance in 1900 by sponge divers from Sými, who had sheltered in a storm off an inaccessible coast of Antikýthera. After the storm passed, a few divers donned their gear and went to see if there might be any sponges in the neighbourhood. Instead they were startled to see a man beckoning to them—the famous 4th-century bronze *Ephebe of Antikýthera*, now one of the stars in the National Museum in Athens and one of the few sure testimonials in Greece of Rhodes' once renowned school of bronze sculpture. The Greek archaeological service was notified and sent down a warship to haul up what was the world's first underwater archaeological dig. Among the statues, vases and glass they brought up a peculiar lumpish thing. As the months passed and the sea mud dried, a wooden cabinet about a foot high was revealed. This quickly deteriorated on contact with the air, leaving a calcified hunk of metal that broke into four bits. Archaeologists were astonished to see that they belonged to a mechanical device inscribed with ancient Greek script.

At first dismissed as a primitive astrolabe, the Antikýthera mechanism sat forgotten in the National Museum in Athens until 1958, when a young British historian of science, Derek de Solla Price, was allowed to examine it and became the first to recognize it as an astronomical computer, which by its setting was shown to have been made on Rhodes in 82 BC. The days of the month and signs of the zodiac were inscribed on bronze dials, with pointers to indicate the phases of the moon and position of the planets at any given time, the whole operated within by a complex mass of clockwork: bronze cog wheels with triangular teeth, connected to a large four-spoke wheel, driven by a crown gear shaft, which probably had a key of some sort for winding. A moveable slip ring allowed for Leap Year adjustments and alignments. As far as anyone can judge it was last set by the Roman sea captain the day his ship went down. As Derek Price wrote: 'It is a bit frightening to know that just before the fall of their great civilization, the Ancient Greeks had come so close to our age, not only in their thought, but also in their scientific knowledge'. The next similar device to be noted anywhere was in 11th-century India, by the Iranian traveller al-Biruni.

Shopping

Rhodes' duty-free status has made for some odd sights; it may be the island of the sun, but nowhere on earth will you find more fur shops, or more umbrella shops: a popular model opens up to reveal Michael Jackson's mug in alarming proportions. In the Old Town Sokrátous is the main bazaar street and Sakhellaridis, in Plateía Moussíou, is the place to look for Greek music. The New Town near Mandráki is full of designer shops and a Marks and Spencer for the homesick. For shoes, try Plateía Kýprou; for a reasonably priced tailor-made suit made from the finest British fabrics, the Kakakios Brothers, 47 G. Labráki, who made them for the likes of Gregory Peck and Anthony Quinn. The biggest market in the Dodecanese takes place on Zefiros Street (by the cemetery) every Saturday morning; get there early if you want to find a bargain. Another one takes place on Wednesdays, at Vironas by the Stadium.

Rhodes Town ✉ *85100,* ✆ *(0241–)*   **Where to Stay**

Rhodes has a plethora of accommodation in every class and price from one of the most expensive hotels ever to be built in Greece to humble village rooms. Most places are booked solid by package companies, some for winter breaks too, so if you're island-hopping in high season it's worth phoning ahead. On the Internet *www.helios/forthnet.gr/dis/ rhodes/index.html* has more info on hotels and sights, while *www. helios.gr/hotels/* offers on-line descriptions and bookings for a selection of luxury to C class hotels across the island.

luxury

Most of the luxury hotels are in Ixiá and Triánda although the mega-luxury, seven-star suites at the **Rodos Park**, next to the historic centre at 12 Riga Fereou, ✆ 24 612, ✐ 24 613, in town overlooking the park, are just as opulent, with private jacuzzis, pool, health club, ballroom and every other amenity. The **Grand Hotel Summer Astir Palace** on Aktí Miaoúli, ✆ 26 284, ✐ 35 589, has the island's casino, a nightclub, tennis courts and what's reputed to be the largest swimming pool in the country.

expensive

The **Plaza** on Ieroú Lóchou, ✆ 22 501, ✐ 22 544 (*A*) has been done up and is centrally situated with a pool, baby-sitting and English buffet breakfast. **So Nikol**, 61 Ippodámou, ✆ 34 561, ✐ 32 034 (*E*) offers atmospheric accommodation in a lovely old house in the heart of the Old Town with excellent bed and breakfast, large garden and rooftop terrace with great views. The Greek/Danish proprietors also have new apartments to sleep four nearby. Booking essential.

moderate

It was good enough for Michael Palin on his *Pole to Pole* jaunt so the **Cavo d'Oro**, ✆ 36 980, is well worth a try. The delightful 13th-century house at 15 Kisthiníou, near the Commercial Harbour, has been beautifully restored by the owner and his German wife and he'll even meet you from the ferry. **Victoria**, 22 25th Mariou, ✆ 24 626, ✉ 36 675 (*C*) is central, family-run, and the owner's son, a UK-trained doctor, has consulting rooms next door.

If you want to be in Mandráki Harbour, then the **Spartalis**, ✆ 24 371 (*C*) is basic but handy and just over the road from the quay with a nice breakfast terrace and sea views. Recently renovated **Marie**, 7 Kos, ✆ 30 577, ✉ 22 751 (*C*) is near Élli beach, and offers a pool, sea sports and satellite TV. Near the Old Town **Popi**, Stratigou Zisi and Maliaraki 21, ✆ 23 479, ✉ 33 453, has studios in the old fashioned Greek style, each sleeping four. **Hermes**, 1 N. Plastira, ✆ 27 677 (*C*), near the quay at Mandráki, is also useful if you're just passing through and allows you to store luggage. **Paris**, Ag. Fanouríou 88, ✆ 26 354 (*D*) has nice rooms and a quiet courtyard with shady orange and banana trees, and prices at the bottom of this range.

inexpensive

One of the best value is the **Ambassadeur**, 53 Othonos and Amalías, ✆ 24 679 (*C*). In the heart of the Old Town, **Attiki**, Theofiliskou, ✆ 27 767 (*E*) is quietly tucked away in the corner in a medieval building, a bit dishevelled but children welcome. *Open all year*. **La Luna**, ✆ 25 856 (*E*) and its bar are in a perfectly quiet courtyard next to a tiny church on Ierokleous just off Orfeos. *Open all year*.

Some of the cheap backpackers' haunts have become a bit unsavoury, but **Spot**, Perikléous 21, ✆ 34 737 (*E*) is very good value with light, airy rooms plus en suite bathrooms; nearby the **Iliana**, 1 Gavála, ✆ 30 251 (*E*) is in an old Jewish family house and has a small bar and terrace; no charge for childen under 10. **Maria's Rooms**, on Menekléous, ✆ 22 169, are a comfortable choice around a quiet courtyard.

Other budget options include **Athinea** at 45 Pythagóra, ✆ 23 221, with decent rooms and shared facilities. There are also **Minos Pension**, 5 Omírou, ✆ 31 813 and recently restored **Andreas**, 28D Omírou, ✆ 34 156, ✉ 74 285, under friendly French/Greek management, although only a few rooms have a bath.

Rhodes has a cosmopolitan range of eating places from luxury hotel restaurants to dives selling tripe (*patsás*). The Rhodians are to the Greek islands what the Parisians are to France. They are fashionable, often fickle, and love new food trends. Rhodes has several good places serving a Greek version of *nouvelle cuisine,* some just out of town (*see* p.127). In the New Town with its strong Italian influence you can eat great authentic pizza, pasta and other Italian dishes as well as fast food, burgers (the local rivalry is Greece's Goody's vs. Ohio's Wendy's), or Danish, Swedish, Indian, Chinese, French, Mexican, even Yorkshire cuisine on the menu. And then there's Greek...

New Town

Probably the best place for *mezédes* is **Palia Istoria** ('Old Story'), ✆ 32 421 (*exp*), on the corner of Mitropóleos and Dendrínou south of the new stadium. This award-winning restaurant isn't cheap but you get what you pay for—an imaginative array of dishes from celery hearts in *avgolémono* sauce to scallops with mushrooms and artichokes, and a good choice of vegetarian dishes. Food is served out under the pergola in a private house atmosphere; the fruit salad has twenty kinds of fruit. Excellent Greek wine list; booking advisable, splurge for a taxi. **Alatopipero** ('Salt and Pepper'), ✆ 65 494 at 76 M. Petrídi (*exp*; again, you'll probably need a taxi) is another trendy *mezedopoíon* with trays of different, inventive dishes making up your meal. Cyclamen leaves stuffed with rice are among the specialities, but there are giant Butcher's Plates for carnivores, seafood delicacies and an adventurous wine list of rare Greek boutique wines, considered the best in town. Try award-winning *Hatzimichaélis Cabernet* or *Ayiorítiko* made by the monks on Mount Áthos.

Ellinikon, 29 Alexandrou Diákou, ✆ 28 111, is another popular choice with the locals, serving a choice of Greek and international dishes (5000dr). For a real taste of Denmark try **Dania** at Iroon Polytechniou 3, ✆ 20 540 (*mod*), near Royal Scotland Bank, with traditional herring dishes and a running smorgasbord on Sunday evenings. The wacky **7.5 ΘΑΥΜΑ** ('Wonder') at Dilperáki 15, ✆ 39 805 (*exp–mod*), advertises 'food, drink and party hats since 292 BC' and turns out to be Swedish chefs, ancient Greek décor, Eastern-inspired dishes and seriously good food served in a secret garden. One of the best and most authentic tavernas for lunch is **Christos** out in the suburb of Zéfiros beyond the commercial harbour. A favourite with local families and taxi drivers—no problem finding it—food is excellent, ethnic and inexpensive. The New Market is full of holes in the wall offering good 'n' greasy *gýros* with outdoor tables.

Old Town

After an aperitif, plunge into the maze of back-streets—in some industrious shops you'll see tailors and cobblers still hard at work, and you'll find a wide range of eating places, some still untouristy and authentic (**Hippokates**, tucked in narrow Euripidou, is one) others all the rage with trendy locals. **Alexis**, with tables around a Turkish fountain on Sokrátous Street, is one of the top fish restaurants, expensive but good. For cheap and cheerful Greek staples try **Ioannis**, under the Sydney Hotel in Apéllou Street. **Nireas**, 22 Plateía Sofokléous, is ace for Greek home cooking (booking advisable, ℗ 21 703). The adjacent **Sea Star**, ℗ 31 884, is good for fish, if a bit pricey; colourful management compensates. The nearby **Aigaion** is a good bet for local seafood like the unusual *foúskes*, which resemble rocks. Home-style **Dodekanissos**, 45 Plateía Evrión Martyrón, ℗ 28 412 has moderate-priced seafood and an exceptionally good shrimp *saganáki*; another old favourite is **Dinoris**, 14 Plateía Moussíou, ℗ 35 530, tucked down a narrow alley by the museum, with a romantic garden patio and more lovely fish; **Fotis**, 8 Menekleóus St, ℗ 27 359, does excellent grilled fish, simple and delicious.

Cleo's on Ag. Fanouríou is one of the most elegant places to dine in the heart of the medieval city, serving upmarket Italian or French cuisine (to reserve, call ℗ 28 415). Neighbouring **Kamares**, reached through a big archway into a pretty garden, is another good choice for Greek specialities and international dishes. On the other end of the scale, join the working men for a bowl of *patsás* soup at **Meraklis** on Aristotélous 32 or **Patsas Sotiris** in an alley off Sokrátous.

Rhodes (0241–)   ***Entertainment and Nightlife***

Rhodes has something for everyone, with around 600 bars in the town alone. There are discos with all the latest sounds, laser shows and swimming pools, Irish pubs, theme bars, super-cool cocktail bars or live music tavernas in restored old town houses, bars full of gyrating girls and wet T-shirt nights, and even simple *ouzeries* where a game of backgammon is the high spot. The island has all kinds of music from traditional folk sung to the *lýra*, funk, soul, house and rap to vintage Elvis. Traditional Greeks head for the late-night **bouzouki club** at Élli Beach, while for more sophisticated Greek sounds, the **Grand Hotel** on Aktí Miaoúli has the **Moons Rock**, featuring top bouzouki singers and musicians, and a **casino**, ℗ 24 458 (no jeans or shorts), although it now has to compete with a new casino operated by Playboy International in the handsome Hotel des Roses, a 1930s landmark. For a romantic intimate garden evening among the jasmine, there's nearby **Christos**, 59 Dilperaki.

Orfanídou Street just in from Akti Miaouli is known as the street of bars (Irish **Flanagan's**, **Colorado**, **Hard Rock Caffé** (*sic*) and **Live Rock Club** are currently popular) and **Diákou Street** to the south is also heaving with nightlife, British and Scandinavian tourists spilling out of the bars into the road in high season. Rockers should head for the ever-popular **Sticky Fingers**, A. Zervou 6, south of Psaropoula, or to see what Rhodian fashion slaves are up to, there's **To Rodinkon Prytaneion** at Georgious Leontos 25. In the Old Town, **O Mylos**, just off Sokrátous, is a pretty open garden music bar, or join the smart set in the clocktower, **To Roloi**, up the ramp on Orféos, or follow the cognoscenti to the fabulous **Karpouzi**, in a lovely medieval building off Sokrátous in the Old Town with *rembetíka*, wine and *mezédes.*

You can take in a film (subtitled, in the original language) at one of two open-air cinemas: the **Metropol**, corner of Venetoken and Vironos streets near the stadium, or at the **Muncipal Cinema**, by the town hall, with artier fare. The history of Rhodes unfolds at the **Son et Lumière** show in the Palace of the Grand Master (*in English on Mon and Tues at 8.15pm, Wed, Fri and Sat at 9.15pm, Thurs 10.15pm*). Or watch real if coolly professional **traditional Greek folk dances** by the Nelly Dimogloú company in the Old Town Theatre (*June–Oct nightly except Sat and Sun, 9.20pm–11pm; for information ✆ 20 157 or 29 085; dance lessons also available*). Bop till you drop at **Le Palais** disco or **Privato**, 2 Iliadon, ✆ 33 267.

Western Suburbs: To Ancient Ialysós and Mt Filérimos

On the way out of town, look out for the little ethnic houses on the left at **Kritiká**, built by Turkish immigrants from Crete facing their homeland. **Triánda** (ΤΡΙΑΝΤΑ) or Tris, the modern name for Ialysós, has become the island's prime hotel area, and Ialysós Avenue, which runs via **Ixiá** into Rhodes town, is lined with apartments, hotels and luxury complexes out for the conference trade all year round as well as catering for rich summer clientele. The beaches along here are a favourite of windsurfers (nearly every hotel has a pool for calmer swims), the sea is a lovely turquoise colour, and there are views across to Turkey. This coast was settled by Minoans in 1600 BC, and may have been damaged in the explosions and subsequent tidal wave from Santoríni; more recently this golden mile has been devastated by neon-lit bars, fast food places and eateries providing English breakfasts and smorgasbord.

Triánda village occupies the not completely excavated site of **ancient Ialysós**, the least important of the three Dorian cities. When the Phoenicians inhabited Ialysós, an oracle foretold that they would only leave when crows turned white and fish appeared inside the water jars. Iphicles, who besieged the town, heard the prediction and with the help of a servant planted fish in the amphorae and daubed a few ravens with plaster. The Phoenicians duly fled (and whatever the ancient Greek for 'suckers' might have been, we can be sure Iphicles said it). Ialysós was the birthplace of the boxer Diagoras, praised by Pindar in the Seventh Olympian Ode, but with the foundation of the city of Rhodes it went into such a decline that when Strabo visited in the 1st century AD he found a mere village, albeit with a rich, extensive cemetery that yielded the Mycenaean jewellery in the archaeology museum.

The main interest in Ialysós lies in the beautiful garden-like acropolis-citadel above Triánda, on **Mount Filérimos**, thought to be the initial nucleus of the 15th-century BC Achaean settlement of Achaia (*open daily except Mon, 8.30–5; adm; wear modest dress to visit the monastery*). John Cantacuzene defended the Byzantine fortress on the site against the Genoese in 1248 and Suleiman the Magnificent made it his base during the final assault on the Knights in 1522. Built over the foundations of a Phoenician temple are the remains of the great 3rd-century BC **Temple of Athena Polias and Zeus Polieus**, in turn partly covered by Byzantine churches. A 4th-century **Doric fountain** with lionhead spouts has been reconstructed. But the main focal point is the monastery of **Our Lady of Filérimos**, converted by the Knights from a 5th-century basilica church and heavily restored by the Italians. Reached by a cypress-lined flight of steps, the monastery and its domed chapels wear the coat of arms of Grand Master d'Aubusson, under whom the church diplomatically had both Catholic and Orthodox altars. Beneath the ruins of a small Byzantine church with a cruciform font is the tiny underground chapel of **Ag. Geórgios**, with frescoes from the 1300s. The monks will be pleased to sell you a bottle of their own green liqueur called Sette, made from seven herbs.

For more wonderful views, there's an uphill path from the monastery lined with the Stations of the Cross. In 1934 the Italian governor erected an enormous cross on the summit although seven years later the Italians themselves shot it down to prevent the Allies from using it as a target. In 1994 the Lions Club financed the current one, 52ft high, dominating an otherwise very secular coast.

Rhodes ✉ *85100,* ✆ *(0241–)*   **Where to Stay**

The Ixiá and Triánda strip is one long stretch of hotels, with the prime luxury compounds in Ixiá. At the top of the list is the vast **Grecotel Rhodos Imperial**, ✆ 75 000, 📠 76 690 (*lux*), the most luxurious 5-star hotel on the island and the most expensive hotel project in Greece so far, with a range of top restaurants, watersports centre, fitness club, children's mini club, and every delight from *syrtáki* dance lessons to Greek language courses, squash to cabaret. The **Miramare Beach**, ✆ 96 251/4, 📠 90 153 (*lux*) has been revamped for those 'seeking paradise on earth' with swish cottages slap on the beach. Another rival, the **Rodos Palace**,

✆ 25 222, ✉ 25 350 (*lux*) has just undergone a three-year refurbishment to become one of the most up-to-date hotels in the Med, with twin digital state-of-the-art communications systems. The striking domed, heated Olympic-size indoor pool is partly built with Sými's former solar water still; you'll also find three outdoor pools, a sauna, gym, tennis courts and all the trimmings. **Rodos Bay**, ✆ 23 662, ✉ 21 344 (*A; exp*) has a pool and bungalows by its private beach, while the rooftop restaurant has one of Rhodes' finest views. Scores of A and B class hotels and apartments plus cheaper pensions are available all along from here to the airport.

Rhodes ✆ (0241–)   ***Eating Out***

Two of the island's gourmet citadels are here. **Ta Koupia**, ✆ 91 824, in Triánda by Ialysós (take a taxi), is simply the cat's pyjamas among Rhodian trendies and visiting movie stars. Wonderfully decorated with antique Greek furniture, the food matches the décor in quality—excellent *mezé* and upmarket Greek dishes with an Eastern touch. **La Rotisserie**, ✆ 25 222, in the Rodos Palace is the place for French and Greek *nouvelle cuisine*, with an exquisite wine list, followed by dessert trolley and a cigar from the humidor; the Rhodians love the 7000dr set-price lunch that changes daily. **Trata** on Triánda beach is good and much kinder to the pocket. In Ialysós the **Sandy Beach Taverna** right on the beach is a favourite lunchtime haunt with a garden terrace; try its *kopanistí*, cheese puréed with cracked olives. In Ixiá, **Restaurant Tzaki** is known for its *mezédes* and also has bouzouki music.

Down the East Shore to Líndos

Like the windier west shore, the sandy shore southeast of Rhodes town is lined with luxury hotels and holiday resorts, beginning with the safe Blue Flag beaches of **Réni Koskinoú**, popular with families. The inland village of **Koskinoú** is known for its houses with decorative cobblestoned floors and courtyards, the distinctive Rhodian pebble mosaics or *choklákia*, a technique introduced by the 7th-century Byzantines. On the way, industry has taken over **Asgouroú**, a Turkish village; the mosque was originally a church of St John.

Further along the coast the coves of **Kalithéa** are a popular spot for swimming and snorkelling. The waters of Kalithéa were personally recommended by Hippocrates, and now the old, disused thermal spa in a magnificent kitsch Italianate-Moorish building from the 1920s is getting a 600-million-drachma restoration by EOT. There's a small lido and the Rhodes Sub Aqua Centre operating aboard *The Phoenix*. Beyond here, holiday La-La Land begins in earnest with **Faliráki Bay North**, a massive development of upmarket hotel complexes along the sandy beach, complete with a shopping mall. Bad enough, if that's what you've come to a Greek island to escape from, but reserve judgement until you meet the original **Faliráki**, 'the vortex', with its sweeping golden sands, awarded a Blue Flag for excellence and featuring all kinds of watersports and wild nightlife. A playground for the 18–30s, predominantly Brit crowd; fur and jewellery shops rub shoulders with fast food places, bars featuring wet T-shirt contests and local supermarkets that call themselves Safeway, ASDA and Kwik Save, copying the logos from UK carrier bags. If the beach to the south is the nudist hang-out, the rest of Faliráki attracts families with diversions such as sailing catamarans, jumping off Godzilla's Meccano set at the **New World Bungy**, © 76 178, the **Faliráki Snake House** with tropical fish and live reptiles (*open 11am–11pm; adm*) and **Aqua Adventure**, 'the longest waterslide in Greece!' located on the grounds of the Hotel Pelagos. Ironically, as Faliráki tries to become a sunny version of Blackpool, some exclusive hotel complexes in Cycladic village-style are springing up in the area. Faliráki also has the island's only campsite.

Ladiko Bay just south is a small rocky cove also known as Anthony Queen Beach (*sic*) after the actor who bought land from the Greek government (or thought he did—he's never been able to get the title) while filming *The Guns of Navarone* at Líndos; some scenes were shot on the beach. Next door, the hidden village of **Afándou** is less frenetic and has the ultimate rarity in this part of the world—an 18-hole golf course by the sea as well as tennis courts. Once known for its carpet-weaving and apricots, Afándou now relies on tourism (complete with a little tourist choo-choo train and a Chinese takeaway) thanks to its 7km pebble beach, deep crystal waters and excellent fish tavernas; a few people also work at the Voice of America radio station. By this point you may have noticed a plethora of roadside ceramic 'factories' with coach-sized parks, which are exactly what they seem to be.

Next comes **Kolýmbia**, a developing resort with many new large hotels. A scenic avenue of eucalyptus trees leads to **Vágia Point** with some great beaches south of the headland. Local farms are irrigated thanks to the nymph-haunted lake fed by the **Eptá Pigés**, the 'Seven Springs', 5km inland. A wooded beauty spot with scented pines, it's a tranquil place to escape the sun, with strutting peacocks, lush vegetation and a wonderful streamside taverna. You can walk through ankle-deep icy water along the low, narrow tunnel dug by the Italians (claustrophobes have an alternative route, from the road) which opens out into the spring-fed lake. But beware, the Greeks tend to wade back up again, colliding with everyone.

The long sandy bay at **Tsambíka** is very popular, with its tiny white monastery perched high on the cliffs above. Rhodes' answer to fertility drugs, the monastery's icon of the Virgin Mary, attracts childless women who make the barefoot pilgrimage and pledge to name their children after the icon. Their prayers are answered often enough; look out for the names Tsambíkos or Tsambíka, unique to Rhodes. The road leads on to **Stégna**, where charming fisherman's houses are being engulfed by tourist development. There's a shingle beach set in a pretty bay.

Next stop on the main road, **Archángelos** (pop. 3500) is the largest village on Rhodes, with a North African feel, its little white houses spread under a chewed-up castle of the Knights. Its churches, **Archángelos Gabriél** and **Archángelos Michaél**, are two of the prettiest on the island; another nearby, **Ag. Theodóroi**, has 14th-century frescoes. Fiercely patriotic, the villagers have even painted the graveyard blue and white. Archángelos is famous for its ceramics and has several potteries-cum-gift shops, regular stops on island tours. Otherwise the village is still somewhat untouched by tourism and its major industries are agriculture and fruit farming. The villagers speak in their own dialect, and also have a reputation for their musical abilities, carpet-making, and special leather boots that keep snakes at bay in the fields. Local cobblers can make you a pair to order. They fit either foot, but they don't come cheap.

Once one of the strongest citadels on Rhodes, the ruined **Castle of Faraklós** towers on the promontory below **Malónas**, overlooking Charáki and **Vlícha Bay**. They were originally occupied by pirates until the Knights gave them the boot, repaired the walls and used the fort as a prison. Even after the rest of the island fell to Suleiman, Faraklós held out, only surrendering after a long, determined siege. The nearby fishing hamlet of **Charáki** has a lovely shaded esplanade running along a superb crescent-shaped pebble beach. There are good waterside fish tavernas, great swimming and postcard views of Líndos. In **Mássari**, just inland, one of the Knights' sugar refineries was discovered where olives and orange groves now reign.

ⓒ *(0241–)*   ### Where to Stay and Eating Out

Koskinóu ✉ 85100

Most tavernas are like the village itself, small and typically Greek. **O Yiannis**, once cheap and cheerful, has become the place to see and be seen. There'll be queues but it's worth the wait; otherwise head to industrial and unfashionable Asgoúrou 5km out of town on the Líndos road for great *mezédes* at **Ouzadiko To Steki**, ⓒ 62 182, a Rhodian institution with wine and retsina from the barrel. There's no menu, but the food is wonderful with unusual dips and fritters and fresh seafood like clams, crab and stuffed *kalamári. Dinner only.*

Faliráki ✉ 85100

Between Kalithéa and Faliráki, **Esperos Village**, ⓒ 86 046, ⓐ 85 741 (*lux–exp*) set high in its own grounds with Disney-inspired castle gates, is so Cycladic it looks as if it escaped from Tinos. At the other end of the scale there are droves of C-class hotels (any package operator can set you up) and **Faliráki Camping**, ✆ 85 516, now the island's only official campsite, has every comfort. After dark, Faliráki is one big party. **Champers**, ✆ 85 939, is the eighth wonder of the world for young package ravers, with karaoke and dancing on giant barrels among the attractions; young sun-and-fun crowds also head for **Slammer's Pub**.

Afándou ✉ 85103

> **Lippia Golf Resort**, ✆ 52 007, ✉ 52 367 (*A; exp–mod*) is an all-inclusive air-conditioned resort with indoor and outdoor pools as well as proximity to the links; **Reni Sky**, ✆ 51 125, ✉ 52 413 (*B; mod*) has a pool and good-value rooms. For exceptional fish tavernas in Afándou follow the jet-set to **Reni's**, ✆ 51 280 (*exp*), probably the best on the island, or head south to Charáki's excellent **Argo**, ✆ (0244) 51 410, or **Haraki Bay**, ✆ (0244) 51 680, with an enormous selection of *mezédes*.

Líndos

Dramatically situated on a promontory high over the sea, beautiful Líndos (ΛΙΝΔΟΣ) is Rhodes' second town. With its sugar-cube houses wrapped around the fortified acropolis, it looks more Cycladic than Rhodian; it has kept its integrity only because the whole town is classified as an archaeological site, unique in Greece; even painting the shutters a new colour requires permission, and no hotels were allowed to be built within sighting distance of the windows. Líndos was a magnet for artists and beautiful people back in the swinging sixties, when, they say, you could hear the clink of cocktail glasses as far away as Rhodes town. It still has a few showbiz Brits (Pink Floyd's Dave Gilmour), Italians, Germans and Saudi princes and diplomats—who have snapped up many of the lovely old captains' houses. Incredibly beautiful as Líndos is, there's little left of real village life apart from locals selling a few vegetables and other produce in the early morning when most people are sleeping off the night before. In July and August the cobbled streets are heaving with day-trippers and you can literally be carried along by the crowds—around half a million visitors are siphoned through each year. The locals have adjusted to the seasonal invasion and pander to the tourists' every need, from pornographic playing cards to English breakfasts. If you want to avoid the hordes visit in the off season; Greek Easter is wonderful in Líndos. But if you can't take the heat, be warned. Líndos is the frying pan of Rhodes and temperatures can be unbearable in August (several places rent out electric fans). The nightlife also sizzles.

Líndos was the most important of the three ancient cities of Rhodes, first inhabited around 2000 BC; the first temple on its magnificent, precipitous acropolis was erected in 1510 BC. It grew rich from its many colonies, especially Neapolis (modern Naples). Ancient Líndos, four times the size of the present town, owed its precocious importance to its twin natural harbours, the only ones on Rhodes, and to the foresight of its benevolent 6th-century BC tyrant Cleoboulos, one of the Seven Sages of Greece, a man famous for his beauty, his belief in the intellectual equality of women, and his many maxims, one of which, 'measure is in all the best' (moderation in all things), was engraved on the oracle at Delphi. The reservoir and rock tunnels dug by his father, King Evander, supplied water to Líndos until only a few years back. St Paul landed at St Paul's Bay, bringing Christianity to the Lindians; the Knights fortified Líndos, and during the Turkish occupation of Rhodes Lindian merchants handled most of the island's trade. To this day there's a rivalry between the people of Rhodes town and Líndos, and the Lindians are still known for their business acumen.

Getting Around

Besides daily **boats** from Rhodes town, Líndos has its own direct hydrofoil to Sými and to Marmaris, Turkey (*see* p.139); book through Pefkos Rent-a-car, ✆ (0244) 31 387. **Donkey taxis** to the Acropolis cost 1000dr; the possibility of buying a photo of the experience comes with the deal. If you're staying, little three-wheeled vehicles will transport your luggage.

Tourist Information

By the bus stop square: ✆ (0244) 31 900, ✉ 31 282.

A Walk Around Town

The serpentine pebbled lanes and stairs of Líndos are lined with dramatic and unique houses, many of them elegant sea captains' mansions built between the 15th and 17th centuries. Usually built around courtyards with elaborate pebbled mosaics or *choklákia*, secluded behind high walls and imposing doorways, the houses have high ceilings to keep cool and unusual raised living rooms or *sala*, and beds are often on sleeping platforms. According to tradition, the number of cables carved around the doors or windows represented the number of ships owned by the resident captain. Many are now holiday homes or bars, which take full advantage of their flat roofs, great for sunbathing and admiring the views. Some houses still have collections of Lindian ware, delightful plates painted with highly stylized Oriental motifs first manufactured in Asia Minor; legend has it that the Knights of St John once captured a ship full of Persian potters and would not let them go until they taught their craft to the islanders. They used to be displayed in the fancy **Papakonstandís Mansion**, once the museum, now the Museum Bar. As some compensation, stop in at the Byzantine church of the **Assumption**, built on the site of a 10th-century church and restored by Grand Master d'Aubusson in 1489–90. It may take a few moments for your eyes to adjust to the dim light to see its frescoes of the Apostles, painted by the artist Gregory of Sými in 1779 and refurbished in 1927. One has a camel head. The back wall is covered with a scene of the *Last Judgement*, with St Michael weighing souls and a misogynist St Peter welcoming the Elect into heaven's gate.

The Acropolis of Líndos

Floating high over Líndos housing is the **Temple of Lindian Athena** (*open Mon 2.30–6.40, Tues–Fri 8–6.40, Sat and Sun 8.30–2.40; adm exp*), one of the most stunningly sited in Greece, accessible by foot or 'Lindian Taxi'—hired donkey. The steep route up is lined with billowing blouses, embroidered tablecloths and other handicrafts put out for sale by local women, who sit by their wares, mugging passers-by. Líndos' reputation for embroideries dates back to the time of Alexander the Great. Some needlework is authentically hand-made but the vast majority is mass-produced, imported and overpriced.

Just before the Knights' stairway, note the prow of a trireme carved into the living rock. This once served as a podium for a statue of Agissándros, priest of Poseidon, sculpted by Pythokretes of Rhodes, whose dramatic, windblown *Victory of Samothrace* now graces the Louvre. The inscription says that the Lindians gave Agissándros a golden wreath, portrayed on the statue, as a reward for judging their athletics events. At the top of the stair are two vaulted rooms, and to the right a crumbling 13th-century church of **St John**. Continue straight on for the raised Dorian arcade or **Stoa** of Lindian Athena, the patron goddess of the city. She was a chaste goddess; to enter beyond here, any woman who was menstruating or had recently made love had to take a purifying bath, heads had to be covered, and even men were obliged to have clean bare feet, or wear white shoes that were not made of horsehair. From here the 'stairway to Heaven' leads up to the mighty foundations of the **Propylaea** and, on the edge of the precipice, the **Temple of Athena** itself, of which only seven columns are standing. Both were built by Cleoboulos, rebuilt after a fire in 342 BC and reconstructed by the Italians. In ancient times the temple was celebrated for its primitive wooden statue of Athena, capped with gold, and its golden inscription of Pindar's Seventh Olympian Ode, now gone without a trace. When the Persians attacked Líndos in 490 BC, they gave up when they heard the goddess had performed a miracle and provided the citadel with water. On the northern slope of the Acropolis, the **Voukópion** is a small sanctuary in the recess of the rock which was used to sacrifice bullocks in honour of Athena at a distance from her temple, which was presumably to be left uncontaminated by blood.

The views from the Acropolis are stunning, especially over the azure round pool of the small harbour, **St Paul's Bay**, where St Paul landed in AD 58 and where the beach manages to remain fairly detached from the hubbub. Below this, the **Grand Harbour** with the town beach and small but trendy **Pallas Beach** was the home port of ancient Líndos' navy, 500 ships strong. On the far end of this, the cylindrical **Tomb of Cleoboulos** actually pre-dates the king, and in the Middle Ages was converted into the church of Ag. Aililiános.

Villages and Beaches around Líndos

Péfki (ΠΕΥΚΟΙ), just south of Líndos, has a narrow sandy beach fringed by the pine trees which give it its name. Much quieter than Líndos, it's still a fast-developing resort with holiday apartments, mini-markets, cocktail bars, some good tavernas, fish and chips and a Chinese restaurant. Sprawling **Lárdos** (ΛΑΡΔΟΣ), inland west of Líndos, has a pretty valley village as its core, with a charming central square where you can watch the local world go by. Just to the southwest, in the valley of **Keskinto**, farmers in 1893 dug up half of a stone stele from *c.* 100 BC with references to the orbits of Mercury, Mars, Jupiter and Saturn, believed to be the work of Attalus. Keskinto, on the same latitude as the Pillars of Hercules (*aka* Gibraltar), was the site of the observatory believed to have produced the famous Antikýthera Mechanism (*see* p.119).

If you're under your own steam, head 12 km inland to **Laerma**, turn 2km down the Profila road and travel another 2km on a rather dodgy road to **Moní Thari**, founded in the 9th century—the oldest surviving religious foundation on Rhodes, well hidden from pirates and now reoccupied by a charismatic abbot and monks from Pátras. The monastery is said to have been founded by a princess held hostage by pirates, who had a dream from the Archangel Michael promising her that she would soon be free. The princess had a gold ring, and in turn promised St Mike to build as many monasteries as cubits that she flung her ring. She threw it so far she lost it, and ended up building only Thari. The church has some of the finest frescoes on Rhodes, dating back to the 12th century; in places they are four layers thick. Note the more unusual scenes: the *Storm on the Sea of Galilee* and the *Encounter with the Magdalene.*

South of Lárdos the beach on sweeping **Lárdos Bay** has sand dunes bordered by reeds and marshes. This area is being developed with upmarket village-style hotels, but you can still find very peaceful, even deserted beaches further along the coast: **Glystra** is a gem, with a perfect sheltered cove. **Kiotári** now has sophisticated hotel complexes isolated in the surrounding wilderness, while its beach stretches for miles, with a hilly backdrop, stylish international holidaymakers and laid-back seafront tavernas. A detour inland leads to the medieval hill village of **Asklipío** (ΑΣΚΛΗΠΙΕΙΟ) huddled beneath the remains of yet another crusader castle. The church of the recently restored **Monastery of Metamórfossi** dates from 1060, and has frescoes from the 15th century depicting stories from the Old Testament, arranged like comic strips around the walls.

Further south, buses go as far as **Gennádi,** an agricultural town with a beach that looks like a vast pebble mosaic. Nearby **Ag. Georgios** has water sports and refreshments; inland, **Váti,** with its huge plane tree in the centre, is typical of the new Rhodes; only 35 people hold the fort during the week, while everyone else has a flat in the city and returns at weekends. A Bohemian, arty crowd of mostly German expats have livened up the similar one-horse village of **Lachaniá**. Plimíri (ΠΛΗΜΥΡΙ) has a spanking new marina, a fish farm and a popular fish restaurant as well as some wonderful deserted beaches along a California-like coast.

Líndos ✉ *85107,* ✆ *(0244–)*   **Where to Stay**

In Líndos, where it's illegal to build new hotels, nearly every house has been converted into a holiday villa, all but a few with the name of a British holiday company on the door: Direct Greece is one of the bigger agencies (book through London, ✆ (0181) 785 4000). If you do want to take pot luck, try the pensions **Electra**, ✆ 31 226 (*mod*) and **Katholiki**, ✆ 41 445 (*mod*), in a traditional house with garden, built in 1640; **Kyria Teresa**, ✆ 31 765, who has pretty garden rooms in her house or the **Lindos Sun**, ✆ 31 453 (*C; mod*); **Nikolas**, ✆ 48 076 (*exp*) has pricey apartments sleeping from 2–6. **Pallas Travel**, ✆ 31 275, have rooms and villas.

Outside Líndos several excellent hotels are beautifully positioned on Vlícha Bay, 3km from town. The big news here is the **Atrium Palace**, at Kálathos, ✆ 31 601, 📧 31 600 (*lux*), with every amenity. The **Lindos Bay**, ✆ 31 501, 📧 31 500 (*A; exp*) is on the beach with great views of Líndos. The **Steps of Lindos**, ✆ 31 062, 📧 31 067 (*A; exp*) has luxury rooms and facilities, and offers a variety of watersports.

There are plenty of village rooms and pensions beyond Líndos—just look out for the signs. Further down the coast outside Lárdos the **Lydian Village**, ✆ 47 361, 📧 47 364 (*A; lux–exp*) is a stylish club-type complex, exquisitely designed, with white Aegean-style houses clustered around paved courtyards. Furnishings are luxurious but with an ethnic feel, pale blue wooden taverna chairs, and old ceramics. There's every facility, and it's right on the beach, with hills behind.

Eating Out

International cuisine rules; prices are high and a traditional Greek coffee as scarce as gold dust. **Mavriko's** (since 1933) just off the square is good, with an imaginative menu, while nearby **Xenomania** up a rural track also has gourmet dishes if you want to splash out. On a more modest budget, **Dionysos Taverna** in the centre has all the usual Greek favourites in a rooftop setting, while **Maria's** is still very Greek and **Agostino's**, with a romantic roof garden, does tasty grills, village dishes and Embónas wine by the carafe. It's also open for breakfast and brunch. At Péfki, carnivores can head to the **Butcher's Grill**, run by family butchers from Lárdos, with excellent fresh meat and traditional village cooking; while **To Spitaki**, an old house in the village centre, offers Greek dishes with a cordon bleu touch in the peaceful gardens. In the main square at Lárdos, **Anna's Garden Taverna** is as pleasant as it sounds.

Entertainment and Nightlife

Líndos has all kinds of bars that come into their own once the trippers have gone, many in converted sea captains' mansions—the **Captain's House**, with the most elaborate doorway in Líndos, decorated with birds, chains and pomegranate flowers (the symbol of Rhodes); and the 400-year-old **Lindian House**, with painted ceiling and lovely windows; and **Jody's Flat**, encompassing a tree, with English papers and board games. The **Qupi Bar** is an institution, near another, **Lindos By Night**, on three floors with a lovely roof garden just above the donkey station. Three new nightclubs thump away at night: **Namas** and **Akropolis**, half way down to the beach, and **Amphitheatre** on the hillside. Lárdos has a good selection of music bars as well.

The Far South: Windsurfing and Weddings

Kataviá (KATTABIA), the southernmost village on Rhodes, has an end-of-the-line atmosphere, and, more importantly, a petrol station. In July and August it gets invaded by migrating windsurfers who adore the southernmost tip of Rhodes, **Cape Prassonísi**, 'the Green Island', reached by an abominable road from Kataviá. The desolate landscape may as well be the end of the world. A narrow sandy isthmus links Prassoníssi with Rhodes, one side wild and wavy, the other side perfectly calm. There are a couple of tavernas and unofficial camping. Near the isthmus, Danish archaeologists discovered ruins of a 7th–6th-century BC walled settlement at **Vroulia**, set on a panoramic shelf over the sea.

For more grand views over both coasts of Rhodes, take the high corniche road from Kataviá up to **Messanagrós**, an old-fashioned mountain village. Just west, if you get stuck, you can spend the night at **Moní Skiádi**, a hilltop monastery sheltering a miraculous icon of the Panagía and Child which was said to have flowed blood when a 15th-century heretic stabbed the Virgin's cheek. The wound, and stains, are still visible. The unpaved road continues down to the west coast, where there are spectacular views but a wind-battered sea. Sheltered in a valley, **Apolakiá** (ΑΠΟΛΑΚΚΙΑ) is a modern, unexceptional town with a few tavernas and rooms to rent, but which produces the best watermelons and marriage feasts on Rhodes.

Getting Hitched on Rhodes

As marriages or renewing-wedding-vows ceremonies become big business on Rhodes, it's interesting to note that even fifty years ago, real Rhodian weddings were the stuff of folklore and lingering pagan rites. The ceremony began with gifts: the bridegroom presented his fiancée with a braided jacket, a veil embroidered with gold, a skirt and shoes, and the bride reciprocated with a shirt and a tobacco pouch she embroidered herself. To show she was no longer available, the bride's long hair was cut in front in a fringe, while the rest was gathered in numerous small plaits. Her hands were anointed with cinnamon. When she was ready, the wedding musicians were brought in to pass their instruments over her head (a meaningful gesture repeated several times during the wedding day). The bridegroom was given much the same treatment.

After the wedding, the young couple were led to their new home—the bride's dowry (as it often is to this day, although unofficially). The new husband then dipped his finger in a pot of honey and made the sign of the cross on the door, while all the guests cried: 'Be as good and sweet as this honey!' He next stamped on a pomegranate placed on the threshold, its bursting seeds a guarantee of future fertility, while the guests showered the couple with corn, cotton seeds and orange flower water. After the musicians sang the praises of the bride and groom, the bride knelt before the father and mother of the groom and kissed their hands, then was led away by her female friends to eat at a neighbour's house to the wild crashing of cymbals and song. The dancing would begin at night and last for two days.

Up the West Coast: Monólithos, Embónas & Mount Atáviros

Monólithos is the most important village of the region, the monolith in question a fantastical 700ft rocky spur rising sheer above the sea, capped spectacularly by a **castle** built by the Grand Master d'Aubusson. A precarious stairway winds to the top and, within the castle walls, there's the little 15th-century chapel of **Ag. Geórgios** with some interesting frescoes. There are fabulous views, especially at sunset, across to the islands of Alimnia and Chálki; a couple of panoramic tavernas make the viewing easier. There are strong currents off Cape Monólithos, but 5km below the castle, down a tortuous road, the shady bay of **Foúrni** has a sandy beach and a seasonal cantina. There are early Christian cave dwellings round the headland.

The road continues through **Siána**, an attractive old stone village built on a hillside, offering a superb view of the coast and islets. Siána is famous for its wild honey and *suma*, a local firewater reminiscent of schnapps. You can sample both at roadside cafés in the village, where the oldest houses have roofs made of clay. The church of **Ag. Panteléimon** has a beautiful interior and basil growing at the doorway.

Renowned for its wine, olives, tobacco, dancing and festivals, the mountain village of **Embónas** (EMΠΩNAΣ) has tried to preserve its traditional ways. The dances of the women are exceptionally graceful and the *panegýri* in August are among the best on the island, fuelled by the local vintages. Some of the older people still wear local costumes, but only those who don't mind being camera fodder for the Greek Nights and Folk Dance busloads from Rhodes town. Embónas is the centre for the Rhodes winemaking cooperative, **CAIR** (their sparkling white makes a superb Buck's Fizz), and **Emery Winery**, founded by the Triantafýllou family in the 1920s. Visitors are welcome in the handsome tasting room (✆ (0246) 41 208; *open Mon–Fri until 3*). Their mighty red Cava (12.5°) is made from a local grape, *mandilari* (or *amoryianí*), but the wine that has really made them famous, white Villaré, owes its distinctness to the indigenous grape *athiri* that refuses to grow well outside its own microclimate, at 700m altitude on the slopes of the island's highest peak, **Mount Atáviros** (1215m); the summit is a tough 3hr climb from Embónas. Here Althaemenes (*see* 'Mythology') built the temple of Zeus Ataviros, although little remains to be seen. Besides eagle-eye views of the whole island, you can (they say) see Crete on a clear morning; poor Althaemenes used to come up here when he longed, like all Cretans, for his mother island. While up on the roof of Rhodes, head around to **Ag. Isidóros**, like Embónas minus tourists, with vineyards and tavernas. Legend says Althaemenes founded the white hillside village below Embónas, **Kritinía**, which he named in honour of Crete.

Just below Kritinía lies **Kámiros Skála** (ΣKAΛA KAMIPOY), a fishing harbour with two good tavernas that served as the port of ancient Kámiros, 16km north. These days it's where the local ferries depart for Chálki. The ferries link with the buses to and from Monólithos and Rhodes town, taking the children of Chálki to school and the islanders shopping. Towering high above Kámiros Skála, the **Kastéllo** (signposted Kástro Kritinías) is one of the Knights' most impressive ruins, set above lemon groves and pinewoods and affording spectacular views.

Ancient Kámiros

Althaemenes' most celebrated foundation, however, was **Kámiros** (KAMIPOΣ) (*open Tues–Sun 8.30–5; adm*), one of Rhodes' three Dorian cities, built in terraces up the hillside. Destroyed by an earthquake in the 2nd century BC, the city was simply abandoned and forgotten, covered with the dust of centuries until no one remembered it was there. In the 19th century local farmers discovered a few interesting graves, and in 1859 the British Consul, Biliotti, and French archaeologist, Alzman, began excavating. The city they eventually brought to light has been compared to Pompeii: well preserved, untouched by Byzantium, Christianity or the Knights. The cemetery in particular rendered up many beautiful items now in the British Museum, and in archaeological terms the discovery was one of the richest ever in Greece. An excellent water and drainage system, supplied by a large reservoir, served around 400 families in the excavated Hellenistic-era houses.

A second dig carried out in 1914 by the Italians uncovered most of the ancient city: the baths, the Agora with its rostrum for public speeches, the Agora's Great Stoa with its Doric portico, Roman houses, two temples, one 6th-century BC dedicated to Athena of Kámiros and the other Doric from the 3rd century, and an altar dedicated to sunny Helios.

Down on the coast at modern Kámiros there are tavernas for pit-stops. **Fanés**, further north, has a long, narrow stony beach with a few tavernas.

Inland, on a high hill over the village of **Sálakos**, are the ruins of another medieval fort; Sálakos itself is beloved for its shade and fresh water from the Spring of the Nymphs. This region, with its cedar and pine forests and views of the sea, is one of the prettiest for walks. Further up, the road leads to **Mount Profítis Ilías** (790m) and its two derelict Swiss chalet hotels. The trees here belong to the Prophet Elijah, who according to legend strikes down any sinner who dares to cut one down. The chief settlements on its slopes are **Apóllona** with a museum of popular art and **Eleoússa** with a pretty Byzantine church. Nearby **Arthípoli**, with its good tavernas, is a favourite green oasis for lunch.

Back on the Northwest Coast

Theológos (or **Thólos**) announces the proximity of Rhodes town with hotels and a collection of roadside supermarkets and tavernas. Beyond is the straggling village of **Parádissi** (ΠΑΡΑΔΕΙΣΙ) next door to the **airport**. Hardly heaven, it's still a useful place for an overnight stay after a night flight—plenty of 'rooms to let' signs—and there's a small beach, constantly zapped by roaring planes. The strip in neighbouring **Kremastí** (ΚΡΕΜΑΣΤΗ) bustles with foreign tourists and Greek soldiers from the island's main barracks. The village itself is famous for its wonder-working icon, **Panagías Kremastí**, occasioning one of biggest *panegýri* in the Dodecanese, lasting from 15 to 23 August. There's a funfair, *souvláki* stands and all kinds of hawkers selling their wares. At the climax on the 23rd the villagers don traditional costumes and dance a very fast *sousta*.

Inland, a road between Theológos and Parádissi leads to **Káto Kalamónas** and from there to one last enchanting spot, more so if you manage to get there before or after the tour buses: **Petaloúdes**, the **Valley of the Butterflies** (*open daily 9–6*). Sliced by a stream and laughing waterfalls, the long, narrow gorge is crowned by a roof of fairytale storax trees, whose vanilla-scented resin is used to make frankincense. From June to September rare Quadrina butterflies (actually moths, *Callimorpha quadripuntaria*, named for the Roman numeral IV on their black, brown, white and red wings) flock here, attracted by the resin. This is one of their two breeding grounds in the world, and in recent years their numbers have declined because of tourists clapping their hands to see their wings: every flight weakens them, so resist the urge.

You can follow the trail up the valley to the monastery of the **Panagía Kalópetra**, built in 1782 by Alexander Ypsilántis, grandfather of the two brothers who wanted to be kings at the start of the 1821 Greek War of Independence (and gave their name to the town in Michigan). It's a tranquil place, well worth the uphill trek, with wonderful views and picnic tables in the grounds. From here another wooded trail leads to the **Monastery of Ag. Soúlas**, just off the road down to **Soroní**. Here they have a giant festival on 30 July with donkey races and folk dancing made famous in *Reflections on a Marine Venus*.

✆ (0246–)   ***Where to Stay and Eating Out***

In Monólithos, try the little **Thomas**, ✆ 61 291, 🖷 28 834 (*D; inexp*). *Open all year.* Kámiros Skála is popular for fresh fish, especially at weekends, with several tavernas overlooking the sea: **Loukas** at the harbourside is good and a jolly place to wait for the Chálki ferry. By the sea on the old Kámiros road, the **Taverna New Kamiros** isn't much to look at but serves good seafood and meat dishes. To escape from the sun-and-fun crowds, head for the hills and Sálakos, home of Rhodes' new natural spring water, where the **Nymfi** ✆ 22 206/346 (*B; exp*) is a real oasis with four traditional rooms, the perfect island hideaway. *Open all year.* Favourites, especially for a cool, shady prolonged Sunday lunch, are near Arthípoli: **Psinthos** is one, **Pigi Fasouli** under the plane trees another, or **Artemida**, with charcoal grills and good house wines. **Taverna Oasis** at Eleoussa is another fine choice, lost in the trees.

A Day Trip to Marmaris

The Carians were quick to appreciate the beautiful natural harbour of Marmaris, or Fyskos as it was then, and used it as a base for terrorizing the Phoenicians or Rhodes. After the eclipse of the Carians at the hands of Alexander, the town was passed around, from the Egyptians to Romans and Byzantines before becoming part of the Ottoman empire in 1425. It remained an almost forgotten outpost for a century, until Suleiman the Magnificent followed the Carian example and used Fyskos as his base to besiege Rhodes. When the Knights surrendered, Suleiman was so pleased with the result that he ordered a castle to be built in the town. The result was quaint, almost cute, affording a lovely view of the coast. However, Suleiman didn't like it. '*Mimar as*,' he allegedly grumbled when he saw it—'Hang the architect.' Hence the town's name. Or so they say.

Set in the lovely pine-clad Bay of Marmaris, the town of Marmaris itself was devastated in an earthquake in 1958, and little of architectural interest remains apart from Suleiman's castle. Nevertheless, its lovely setting on the deeply indented coast, its access to the bay's beaches, and its fjord-like scenery have made it one of Turkey's premier pleasure ports and one of the country's most popular resorts. Superficially it looks a lot like Bodrum, down to its **Castle of St Peter**, built by the Knights of St John, although this is a smaller version (*open daily 8–12 and 3–7*), restored to house an ethnographic museum with a collection of kilims, daggers and so on. The castle is reached through a convoluted series of back streets that offer hints of Marmaris as it was, when like Kálymnos and Sými it derived its income from that most hazardous of occupations, sponge-diving. The statue of the woman and child by the harbour commemorates all those who waited in vain for the return of their men.

Behind the statue begins the town's **bazaar**, one of the more pleasing touristic bazaars, all bustling and cheerful. From here the town's spacious beach is a short walk away to the west. East of town, over a wooden bridge, **Günnücek Park** is a favourite picnic spot in a grove of frankincense trees. You can swim off a small platform here, or for better swimming catch an excursion boat to the islet of **Sedir** on the other side of the peninsula in Gökova Bay. The islet is only half a mile long but very popular, thanks to its unusual snow-white sand with perfectly round grains, shipped in from the Red Sea some 2000 years ago for Cleopatra. Then, a city called Cedrea occupied the islet; the ruins of walls and a theatre remain.

CHALKI

The Islands

Astypálaia (ΑΣΤΥΠΑΛΑΙΑ)

Butterfly-shaped Astypálaia is the most westerly of the Dodecanese, halfway between Amorgós and Kos, and it would be perfectly at home in the Cycladic archipelago, with its austere rocky geography and dazzling sugar-cube houses spilling from the citadel on the hill. Yet there's more here than meets the eye: the island nurtures a rich, fertile, definitely Dodecanesian valley called Livádia in its bosom, which led Homer to call it 'the Table of the Gods', and equally fertile fishing in the sheltered nooks and crannies of its wildly indented coastline—in antiquity Astypálaia was called Ichthyoessa, 'fishy island'. Besides the lure of seafood, Astypálaia's relative inaccessibility makes it a good place to escape the worst of the summer crowds. It now has a tiny airport, offering the chance to skip the long ferry slog from Piraeus or hops from Kos. Most of all, although it gets busy in August, it remains a friendly, jovial, relaxed island that moseys along at its own pace.

History

The name Astypálaia may mean 'old city', but mythology claims that the name is derived from a sister of Europa, the mother of King Minos. Early on, its inhabitants may have founded another Astypálaia, the ancient capital of Kos. In Classical times the island was most famous for its lack of snakes and a tragically short-tempered boxer named Kleomedes, who, when competing in the Olympics, killed his opponent, which even then was enough to get you disqualified. Kleomedes returned to Astypálaia and took his disappointment out on the local school, knocking it down and killing all the pupils. Pliny says the island's snails have curative powers.

Getting There and Around

By sea: beware that weather can easily upset schedules, especially the hydrofoils. There are links 3 or 4 times a week with Kos, Kálymnos, Amorgós, the Back Islands, Náxos and Piraeus; once a week with Sýros, Sými, Rhodes, Níssyros, Páros and Tílos.

Excursion boats from Skála to the south coast beaches Ag. Konstantínos, Vatsés and Kaminiakia, and to the islets Ag. Kyriáki and Koutsomíti. **Port authority**: ✆ 61 208.

By air: six flights a week from Athens (four in the winter) on a 19-seater, so book early in season. **Airport**: ✆ 61 665.

By road: there are four **buses** a day between Skála, Chóra, Livádia and Maltézana. **Taxis** are also available at reasonable rates; fares are posted.

Tourist Police

The **Municipal Tourist Office**, run by helpful, English Daphne Petrinoli, has a booth that opens when ferries arrive, and otherwise may be found

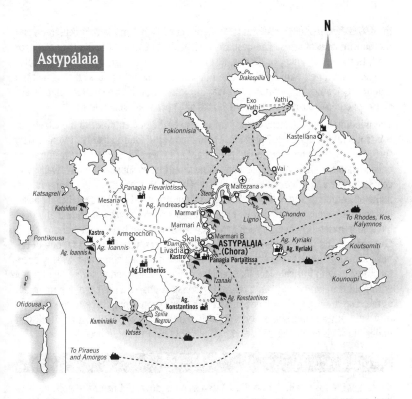

Astypálaia

from June to mid-September in the windmill at Chóra, ℗ (0243) 61 412. She has a list of rooms if you get stuck.

Festivals

21 May, Ag. Konstantínos; **20 July**, Profítis Ilías; **27 July**, Ag. Pantelémonos; **15 August**, Panagía Portaïtíssa in Chóra.

Skála and Chóra

The capital and main port of the island, **Skála Astypálaia** or **Perigialós** (ΠΕΡΙ-ΓΙΑΛΟΣ), curls gracefully down from the Venetian castle to a sandy beach. In the morning or evening you'll see the fishermen's mascots, a pair of pelicans currently named Iannis and Carlos, although those hoping for romance think Carlos is really a Jenny. Skála has everything you need if you don't want to go any further, including an antique shop selling foreign papers and a new ATM machine. Just above the bus stop, the new **Archaeology Museum** (*open Mon–Fri 8–2.30, Sat 10–2.30*) contains finds from Kástro as well as four Mycenaean chamber tombs discovered in the 1970s by shepherds, classical steles, a 6th-century Byzantine chancel screen and the Quirini coat of arms. The best architecture, however, is up flights of steps (or road) in the upper town, or **Chóra**, just above by a file of eight restored windmills. The lanes are lined with Cubist white houses, many sporting Turkish-style painted wooden balconies or *poúndia*. Halfway up, nine little barrel-vaulted chapels are stuck together in a row and hold the bones of Chóra's oldest families.

The winding lanes and steps eventually lead up to the one entrance to the citadel, or **Kástro**, built between 1207 and 1522 by the powerful Quirini family of Venice who ruled the island as the Counts of Stampalia. On either side of the narrow entrance, once locked tight every evening, a pair of new buttresses support the high walls; you can see what a tight corset squeezes Astypálaia's middle, and if it's clear you can make out Amorgós and Santoríni on the horizon. Among the ruined medieval houses built into the walls and surviving Quirini coats of arms (a display of pride that would have been much frowned on back in Venice itself) are two bright white churches: **St George**, on the site of an ancient temple, and the **Panagía Portaḯtissa**, one of the most beautiful in the Dodecanese, topped with a white-tiled dome and lavishly decorated inside with intricate lace-like designs and a carved wooden shrine highlighted with gold leaf (*unusually, open late afternoons*). Archaeologists have dug up much of the rest, finding ancient lanes and temple foundations going back to the 6th century BC, with a sophisticated system of drains. Finish your visit with a drink just under the walls at the Kástro bar with a goat skull over the entrance.

Around Astypálaia

Set in a wide lush valley, **Livádia** (ΛΙΒΑΔΙΑ) is downhill from the windmills to the west; its shingly, sandy beach can get busy in high season. Little roads through farms lead back eventually to the barren mountains, where in 1994 EU funds built a dam to create a rather unexpected little **lake**. The first thing the locals did when it was finished was plant little trees around it; bring some bread for the ducks. Follow the coast along to the south and you can cast your clothes to the wind on the unofficial nudist beach at **Tzanáki**, or continue along the track to **Ag. Konstantínos**, one of the best beaches on the island; other sandy strands, at **Vatses** (with a stalactite cave, **Negrou**, just behind) and **Kaminiakia**, can only be reached by boat. An unpaved road starting at the windmills goes to **Ag. Ioánnis** on the west coast, a lush spot with orchards, a whitewashed church, a ruined Byzantine castle and an excellent beach, calling in at the monastery of **Panagía Flevariótissa** en route.

The paved road north of Skála passes a few beaches, all called Mármari. Just over on the north coast, ferries dock at **Ag. Andréas** if the wind is up, and it has a good fish taverna, open evenings only. The road passes over the waist of the butterfly, or Steno (barely 50 metres wide at its narrowest point) and ends up after 9km near the airport at wannabe resort Análypsi or more commonly **Maltezána**, once a lair of Maltese pirates. Here the French Captain Bigot died in 1827 when he set fire to his corvette to avoid capture. The cove next door is popular with nudists. On the fringe of the surrounding olive groves look out for the remains of the **Roman baths** with their well-preserved zodiac floor mosaics. On the far wing the lost lagoon of **Vathí** (ΒΑΘΗΣ) is a favourite if lonely summer yachting port with a taverna and six rooms to rent, attainable only by sea, with a tiny fishing hamlet and excellent fish taverna heading a deep, fjord-like bay. From here it's possible to visit the stalagmite caves of **Drákospilia** by boat, but take a torch; a path leads south to **Kastéllana**, built by the Italians between the wars.

Astypálaia ✉ *61207,* ✆ *(0243–)*   **Where to Stay**

New hotels are going up like crazy around the harbour in Perigialós, and bargains are easy to find outside mid-July and August. **Astynea**, ✆ 61 040 (*C; mod*) is recently renovated and right on the port; or **Vivamare**, ✆ 61 292 (*C; mod*), smartly appointed, inland from the harbour. You can't beat Gina at **Chrysanthemo** for sheer hostess with the mostest, ✆ 61 429 (winter ✆ (01) 428 4849; *mod–inexp*) with little studios and a big veranda, tucked just behind the beach. **Australia**, ✆ 61 275 (*inexp*) is basic and friendly with a restaurant and flower-filled terrace. Across the bay, **Paradissos**, ✆ 61 224 (*D; inexp*) is right on the harbour. For a traditional house or studio up in Chóra, contact **Vaikoussis**, which has rooms just under the citadel, ✆ 61 430, or **Titika**, ✆ 61 667 (winter Athens ✆ (01) 771 1540). **Camping Astypalaia**, ✆ 61 338, is just out of town near Mármari. A minibus usually meets ferries; otherwise follow the signs.

Astypálaia ✆ *(0243–)*   **Eating Out**

Good tavernas include **Monaxia** (or **Vicki's**) in a small street back from where the ferry docks, with excellent home cooking, and **Akroyiali**, a tourist favourite on the beach at Perigialós, with lovely views up to Chóra after dark when the Kástro is bathed in golden light. **Kiki's Corner** offers good value. Up by the windmills, **Pizzeria Aeolos** does all the pizza favourites well plus 'Lenten Pizza' without meat or cheese (only in Greece!); nearby **Dionysos** serves *soutsoukákia*, piquant meatballs from Anatolia, and *tiganópsomo*, bread filled with feta and fried, only in the evening but open until 6am. Livádia has several waterfront eateries which tend to change hands every so often, but **Kalamia** and **Stefanida** are cheap and reliable, or try one of the rustic *ouzeries* in the hinterland. In Maltezána, **Porto Stampalia** is the best place to dine, and the **Glykazytiko** is famous island-wide for its pastries.

Chálki (ΧΑΛΚΗ)

With its neoclassical houses in pastel shades overlooking a gentle horseshoe harbour, Chálki is a miniature version of Sými, topped by a fairytale Crusader castle on a pointed peak. It is arid, barren and rocky, and water may run short in summer. But traditional island life still ambles on, fishing and goat-herding providing most of the income, as well as small-scale tourism. Chálki is famous for keeping its old music traditions alive, and on occasion you'll hear singers improvise *mantinádes*, impromptu songs with 15-syllable verses. Pronounce their island 'Chalky' at your own risk. The name actually comes from *chalkí*, 'copper', which used to be mined here.

Chálki was designated the 'Island of Peace and Friendship of Young People of All Nations' in 1983 under a joint UNESCO and Greek government scheme. The idea was to launch an international youth centre with annual conferences, and there was an allied municipal project to renovate the houses that had been left after the mass exodus earlier this century, when the local sponge beds fell prey to rot. A *Xenía* hotel was built to serve the visiting groups and bureaucrats, but in the end the scheme went sour as youths and bureaucrats alike abused the little island's hospitality. Peace and friendship between Chálki and UNESCO are at a definite end.

In 1987 a British package holiday company set up a small programme using the restored houses. Since then tourism has slowly grown and owners have returned to convert their ruined family homes into studios and apartments. Although there is the odd hydrofoil excursion from Rhodes, Chálki doesn't suffer from surfeits of day-trippers like Sými. There are no newspapers, 300 inhabitants and a few pick-up trucks and bikes which head up the grandly named Boulevard Tarpon Springs (paid for by island sponge fishermen who now ply their trade in Florida).

Chálki ✆ (0241–) **Getting There**

By sea: 3 times a week with Rhodes; once a week with Kárpathos, Kássos, Sitía (Crete), Ag. Nikólaos (Crete), Sými, Santoríni, Páros, Íos and Piraeus. Daily boat from **Kámiros Skála**, Rhodes, connecting with the 1.30 bus from Rhodes town. In summer **hydrofoil** connections to Rhodes and Tílos. You can also hire a **caique**: ✆ 45 309 or 45 266. **Port authority:** ✆ 45 220.

Chálki ✆ (0241–) **Tourist Information**

Regular police: ✆ 45 213. Also try Halki Tours, ✆ 45 281.

Festivals

5 August, Ag. Sotíris; **15 August**, Panagía; **29 August**, Ag. Ioánnis Pródromos, John the Baptist; **14 September**, Ag. Stávros.

The main claim to fame of **Emborió** is that its church of Ag. Nikólaos has the tallest campanile in the Dodecanese. It also has a magnificent pebble mosaic (*choklákia*) courtyard. There's the usual Italianate customs house and police station, a row of ruined windmills and a small army barracks. Sleepy by day, with fishermen mending their nets, the harbour buzzes with the traditional stroll (*vólta*) in the evening.

From Emborió a 15-minute walk along 'Boulevard Tarpon Springs', just wide enough for a donkey train and single delivery van, takes you to sandy **Póndamos Beach**, a strand constantly being enlarged by the locals. There are loungers and sunshades and Nick's Taverna just a few steps from the sea. The rocky coves a bit further on make for rather more secluded sunbathing and snorkelling. Determined sightseers should continue walking uphill another hour for **Chorió**, the ghost-town capital of Chálki, abandoned in 1950, although cement mixers suggest it might not stay empty for ever. Here the Knights of St John built a castle on the earlier acropolis and recycled most of the ancient building stone. Chorió's church of the **Panagía** has a few Byzantine frescoes and is the centre for the festival on 15 August. On a very clear day there are stunning views down to Kárpathos and Crete from the castle.

A new road runs from Póndamos over the hill past the cemetery and barracks to the Xalki Hotel, and another makes the once-gruelling cross-island trek to the

Monastery of Ag. Ioánnis Pródromos less of a slog. It can still take from three to five hours depending on your pace and time of day: best to go at dawn, or in the evening and stay overnight in one of the cells (a family there is in charge).

Chálki is perfect for serious walkers: take the track off the Póndamos road, right past the water tank on the hill and head for the pebbly cove of **Kánia** with its shady fig trees and little Garden of Eden. Unfortunately the locals have plonked a filling station at the end of the track and there are strong whiffs of petrol at times.

Fishing is still the main way of life but now some of the fishermen are getting into the swing of tourism with trips round the island. The new high-speed launch *Yiánnis Express* with brothers Michaelis and Vassílis Pátros can whisk you to quiet swimming coves—

Aréta, Kánia, Giáli and Trachiá are among the best. Other traditional caiques like the *Meltémi* also offer trips.

The most scenic excursion, however, is to the green isle of Alimniá, which has another Crusader castle and a deep harbour where Italian submarines hid during the Second World War. The islanders abandoned it and moved to Chálki after British Special Boat Services commandos sent to scupper the submarines in 1943 were captured by Nazis on the beach, then taken to Rhodes and executed. You can still see the machine-gun strafing on the walls of some of the buildings as well as paintings of submarines done by troops in the ruined village houses. Although it has a better water supply than Chálki the islanders pledged never to return, leaving Alimniá to grazing sheep, barbecuing holidaymakers and the occasional yacht, all in all a beautifully tranquil place in which to laze about, swim and picnic.

Chálki ✉ 85110, ☎ (0241–)   *Where to Stay*

Most accommodation is taken up by the holiday companies. There's the small but welcoming **Captain's House**, ☎ 45 201 (*mod*), a turn-of-the-century mansion with three lovely rooms with shared external bathrooms, run with nautical precision by Alex Sakellarídes, ex-Greek Royal Navy, and his English wife Christine. There's even a crow's nest. Breakfast or drinks are available on the terrace beneath the trees, often with classical music. **Xalki**, ☎ 45 390, 📠 45 208 (*C; inexp*), the former scheme hotel and converted olive factory to the left of the harbour, offers a sun terrace, snack bar/restaurant, and swimming off the rocks. **Kleanthi**, ☎ 45 334 (*B; mod*) has rooms and studios in a traditional stone house newly restored near the school; little **Roula** is similar. **Markos** offers newer furnished flats, ☎ 45 347, and **Manos** has six rooms (*mod*) in the ex-sponge factory. **Argyrenia**, ☎ 45 205 (*inexp*) has self-contained chalets in shady gardens on the way to the beach. **Nick Pondomos**, ☎ 45 295 (*inexp*) has rooms overlooking the bay.

Chálki ☎ (0241–)   *Eating Out*

Pondomos Taverna is the popular lunchtime haunt, a step from the sands with a tasty menu. Greek oven dishes appear at **Ouzerie Maria** where Maria and her triplet daughters also do good *souvláki*. **Omonia** is the place for fresh fish, seafood and grills, but **O Houvardas**, once arguably one of the best tavernas in the Dodecanese, has never quite been the same under the new management. It's still a good eaterie, popular with yacht people, but the standard depends on who's in the kitchen. If you are self-catering there are three small general stores—Petros has everything—and a good bakery specializing in cheese and spinach pies and honey pancakes.

Nightlife on Chálki tends to be spontaneous, with outbreaks of traditional dancing in the bars like Nikola's **To Steki**. Some of the young people are learning the old instruments like the *lýra* and have even put out a Chálki cassette. Otherwise enjoy a drink at café-bars like **Areti's**, the old favourite **Kostas**, or **Vokolia**, who also do delicious cakes. Easter and festivals are times for determined merrymaking, with live music and dancing, sometimes in traditional costume.

Kálymnos (ΚΑΛΥΜΝΟΣ)

Sailing into Kálymnos from Kos as the sun sets on one side and the moon rises on the other is a stunning experience. Even if you aren't lucky enough to sail in at the proper twilight hour, you may want to breathe at least a sigh of relief when you get to the port and capital Pothiá—for, unlike Kos, this is the Real Greece. Although the massively bustling waterfront has all the usual paraphernalia of tourism, venture one street back and you'll find yourself in the thick of a busy, exceptionally friendly Greek town going about its daily life, winter or summer. Carpenters, tailors and bakers hammer, stitch and bake away; grocers have the old spicy Greek smell of coffee and herbs. Just as it finds an attractive balance between tourism and carrying on its everyday business, Kálymnos also strikes a harmonious geographical equilibrium, with fertile emerald valleys wedged into its dry, rocky face and high peaks (the loftiest, Mount Profítis Ilías, is the driest spot in all the Dodecanese) sweeping down to almost Scottish lochs. The inhabitants are known for being friendly and down to earth, and like to tell the story of Aristotle Onassis' visit to an island school. 'I'll give three million drachmae to any child who can tell me what I'm worth,' announced the shipping magnate to the class. The guesses went higher and higher until one little girl stood up and said: 'Mr Onassis, at the end of the day you're worth a six-foot hole in the ground.' Onassis could only agree and poneyed up.

Economics dictated that many Kalymniots emigrate to Australia or America, but now they've begun to return: you're likely to hear plenty of accents from Down Under or the States, especially in hotels, bars and taxis—new family businesses set up with their savings. On a more traditional note, even the most fleeting visitor can't help but notice that this island is preoccupied with sponges: Kálymnos has Greece's last fleet of sponge-divers, employing 400 people.

History

In mythology Ouranos (Heaven) angrily flung Kalydnos, one of his sons by Gaia (Earth), into the sea, but he landed on some bits of his mother that rose up to become the Kalydna islands. The name Kalydna is either derived from *kalos* (good),

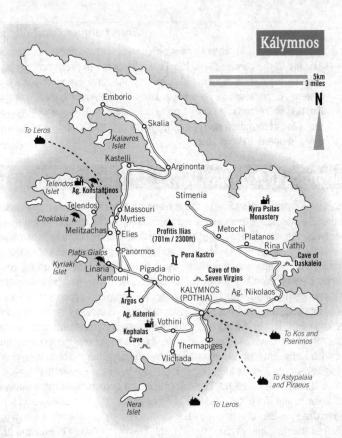

Kálymnos

and *hydna* (truffle), or it means well-watered (from *kalos* and a derivative of *hydor*, water). Others say it comes from *Kalydneon* (ancient).

Homer mentions the Kalydnai participation in the Trojan War and it wasn't until the 4th century BC that the largest island came to be known as Kálymnos or Kálymna. The first Kalymniots lived in a Neolithic settlement at Vothíni and worshipped Zeus in the cave shrine of Kefalos. Argos sent Mycenaean colonists to the island, who named their capital after their mother city; the Dorians who followed had their city just northeast of Pothiá, at Dímos.

Kálymnos next enters history in the 11th century, when Seljik Turks launched a sudden attack on the island and killed almost everyone. The few survivors fled to fortified positions at Kastélli and the virtually impregnable Kástro, which by necessity became the capital of the island. The Vinioli of Genoa occupied Kálymnos, but later sold it to the Knights of St John, who strengthened the fortress of Kástro. In

1522 the Knights abandoned it to succour Rhodes, leaving the Turks to take their place. During the Italian occupation, attempts to bring the Orthodox church in line with the Fascist regime and close down the Greek schools resulted in fierce opposition; prominent citizens were jailed or exiled. The women of Kálymnos, who over the centuries had become fiercely independent with their menfolk away at sea for so long (they had a feminist movement from the early days of the century), held a protest march in Pothiá. There was a violent clash with the troops and a shepherd boy, Kozónis, who was helping the women, was shot dead. Other riots erupted during the occupation and in a show of defiance the islanders painted everything in sight the blue and white of Greece as a sign of solidarity with the motherland.

Recently Kálymniot patriotism nearly landed Greece in the soup with Turkey over two tiny uninhabited islets to the east near Bodrum, called Ímia by the Greeks and Kardak by the Turks. In 1995 Papandréou's government had made it their policy to make a tighter Greek claim on the disputed territorial waters by colonizing these fly specks on the map, promising to subsidize all the basics of life and long leases to anyone, Greek or foreign, who would live there. While Ímia/Kardak awaited their Greek *Mayflower*, the mayor of Kálymnos duly erected the Greek flag on the island; in January 1996 two Turkish journalists helicoptered in and changed it to the Turkish flag. Greece replaced it and sent a permanent flag guard. Warships and aircraft from both sides moved in; a Greek helicopter crashed, killing three. Prime Minister Simitis had just taken office and, under intense American diplomatic pressure, agreed with Turkey to remove the flags and withdraw forces pending future negotiations. At the time the Greek press widely accused Simitis of giving in, although clearer heads now admit it may not have been an issue to die for.

To Sponge, or Not to Sponge

When fresh from the sea, sponges are foul, smelly and black, and have to be stamped, squeezed and soaked until their skeletons (the part you use in the bathtub) are clean. Many are then chemically bleached in a bath of vitriol, acid and permanganate to achieve the familiar yellow colour—but if you're out to buy, opt for the natural brown versions, which are much stronger; look for the ones with the densest texture, the smallest holes. Whole ones last longer than cut sponges. The seller should have a bucket of water on hand so you can feel and squeeze your potential purchase.

Diving for these primitive plant-like porifers is a difficult and dangerous art. In ancient times the divers strapped heavy stones to their chests to bear them down to the sea bed, where they speared the sponges with tridents then at a signal were raised to the surface by a lifeline. As modern equipment permitted divers to plunge to new depths, cases of the 'bends' were frequent;

old-timers on Kálymnos remember when, not so long ago, it was common to see sponge-divers crippled, paralysed or made deaf, a problem now greatly alleviated by decompression chambers.

These days divers wear oxygen tanks and attack the sponges with axes, going down to a depth of 90m. Politics limiting access to sponge beds (especially Libya's), sponge blight, oversponging and synthetic substitutes have undermined Kálymnos' traditional livelihood. In the last century, many divers emigrated to Florida to exploit sponge beds off Tarpon Springs. Many of the cheaper sponges you see are the big holey kind that they've shipped back from the Caribbean; they feel synthetic and crumbly and never last very long.

In the past Kálymnos' sponge fleet left home for seven months of the year to work off the coast of North Africa. Today only a few boats depart for a four-month tour, sticking mostly to Aegean and Cretan waters. On Kálymnos, the week before the fleet sets out (traditionally the week after Orthodox Easter, but it varies with the weather) is known as the Iprogrós or Sponge Week, devoted to giving the sponge-divers a rousing send-off, with plenty of food, free drinks, traditional costumes and dances—including Kálymnos' traditional dance, *mechanikós*, which mirrors the divers' often tragic lives. The last night of Sponge Week is tenderly known as *O Ípnos tis Agápis*, the 'Sleep of Love'. It ends with the pealing of church bells, calling the divers to their boats for another dangerous four months at sea. They circle the harbour three times in farewell and wave their caps as their loved ones wave back from the shore.

Kálymnos ☎ (0243–)   **Getting There and Around**

Kálymnos may have an airport some day, if they can level the runways.

By sea: daily to Piraeus, Rhodes, Kos, Léros, and Pátmos; 4–5 a week with Sámos and Lipsí; frequently with other Dodecanese, even Kastellórizo, thanks to the island's own boat, the *Kalymnos*; twice a week to Bodrum (Turkey; *see* p.188), Ikária and Fourní; once a week to Mýkonos, Sýros, Náxos and Páros. Frequent summer **hydrofoil** connections with Kos, Rhodes, Sými, Níssyros, Léros, Lipsí, Pátmos, Ikaría and Sámos. Daily **boats** to Psérimos, Platí and Vathí; daily **caique** from Myrtiés to Xirókambos, Léros; 3 **ferries** a day from Mastichári, Kos; local caiques from Myrtiés to Télendos and Emboriós; excursions to Pátmos, Lipsí, and Léros. **Port authority:** ☎ 24 444.

By road: the station in Pothiá is next to the domed Dimarcheion. **Buses** every hour to Myrtiés, Massoúri, 5 times a day to Vlichádia, 3–4 to Vathí,

Árgos, Platís Giolos and Emborió. **Taxi** prices are posted (the main rank is up Venizélou street, in Plateía Kýprou) but they may make you wait until the car is full before setting off; other drivers offer guided tours of the island, ✆ 29 555 and 24 222.

Kálymnos ✆ *(0243–)*   ***Tourist Information***

Information booth open April–Oct, Mon–Fri 7–2.30 next to Olympic Hotel on Pothiá's waterfront ✆ 29 310. (Note the sign advertising an excursion to Turkey: 'Come to the beautiful town of Bordum [*sic*] and view the unspoiled lovely bitches.') At Myrtiés Deborah Faulkner of Premier Travel is especially helpful, ✆ 47 830, ✉ 48 035.

Festivals

Ear-splitting **Easter**, in Pothiá; a **week after Easter**, the Iprogrós (Sponge Week). Other celebrations are held when the divers return, although each boat arrives at a different time and celebrations are not as general as at the Iprogrós. **27 July**, Ag. Panteleímon at Brostá; **15 August**, Panagía at Télendos, Kyrá Psilí and Galatianí at Arginónta; **14 September**, Ag. Stávros on Névgra islet.

Pothiá (Kálymnos Town)

Brightly coloured **Pothiá** (ΠΟΘΙΑ), third largest city in the Dodecanese, encompasses the harbour and much of the island's largest valley, stretching right back to the old capital Chório. Pines close off one end, white churches hang on to cliffs as dry as biscuits. More spread out than the typical tightly knotted island town, Pothiá has many lovely old mansions along its back streets, walled orchards, and some fine views from the town's upper level. By the waterfront you can see the first two of the 43 bronzes that local sculptors Michail Kókkinos and his daughter Irene have made to decorate their island: a *Poseidon* by the Olympic Hotel and the waterfront *Winged Victory*, with the history of sponge-diving in relief. The police occupy the former governor's house, a domed pink Italianate villa on the sea, one of Kálymnos' most fanciful confections, rivalled only by the silver domes of 18th-century cathedral **Chrístos Sotíros**, full of works by local painters. Pothiá's oldest quarter is just behind here, while by the Italian administration buildings you'll find the old stone **sponge-diving school**. Being born to such a risky career has made the Kalymniots tough hombres used to living dangerously. They illegally fish with dynamite and can regale you with stories of friends who blew themselves to smithereens; at Easter Pothiá is like a war zone as rival gangs celebrate the Resurrection with dynamite and home-made bombs to see who can make the most noise. Some of the crosses you see in town are in memory of the reckless who blew themselves up. Think twice, too, before accepting a ride on their omnipresent motorbikes.

Perhaps not surprisingly, Pothiá has an excellent hospital as well as one of Greece's rarer institutions—an orphanage. Until recently many Orthodox priests came here to choose a dowryless bride before they were ordained. On the waterfront, culture gets a say in **The Muses Reading Room**, with its Corinthian columns and bronze reliefs, founded in 1904 as a club to further Greek education and preserve national identity during the Turkish occupation. The Italians destroyed all the Greek books and artworks and turned it into the Café Italia, which in turn was damaged in the bombing. The club started up again in 1946, and in 1978 the building was restored to house their collection of local historical documents and books, including some in English. A five-minute walk up from the waterfront—allow fifteen for getting lost in Pothiá's higgledy-piggledy lanes—the **Archaeological Museum**, © 23 113 (*open Tues–Sun, 10–2*) is housed in a lovely neoclassical mansion, former home of the Vouválís family, the first merchants to export sponges overseas, in 1896; the 'Victorian' furnishings, portraits, and panoramas of Constantinople tend to stick in the mind more than the miscellany of prehistoric finds.

At night Pothiá's hilltop landmark is a huge illuminated cement cross looking down over the harbour from the 'sacred wood' and monastery of All Saints, **Ag. Pánton**. Here lie the remains of Ag. Sávvas, a monk who ran the secret school during the Turkish occupation and was later canonized. Sávvas is the local answer to fertility drugs: his reliquary has a fine collection of wax effigies of babies granted to hopeful mothers. Recently an icon of the Panagía in the school by the monastery dripped blood, but it's not Kálymnos' only miracle in the past few years: an X-ray of a man's lung distinctly showed the face of Christ.

There is a small **beach** near the yacht club, and beyond that a sanitarium at **Thérma** with natural thermal baths, for rheumatism, arthritis and digestive and kidney disorders. Around the headland, the beach at **Vlicháda** is one of the island's nicest spots, popular with the locals. From Pothiá caiques sail south of Kálymnos to **Néra** islet, with a monastery and small taverna, and to **Képhalas Cave**, a 30-minute walk from the sea (the latter also accessible by taxi as far as the **Monastery of Ag. Kateríni**, followed by a 2km path). Discovered in 1961, the cave has six chambers full of colourful stalactites and stalagmites, one of which had been a sanctuary of Zeus; a huge stalagmite in the main chamber looks like Zeus enthroned.

Up to Chorió and Árgos

Inland, just behind Pothiá, is a suburb called **Mýli**, with three monumental derelict windmills looming over the road as its landmark. On a hill to the left stands the ruined Castle of the Knights, or **Kástro Chryssochéria** ('Golden-handed') after the church of the Virgin built within its walls, over an ancient temple of the Dioscuri. Treasure was once supposedly discovered there, and the area has been thoroughly combed on the off-chance of more.

Mýli blends imperceptibly into the pretty white town of **Chorió**, the old capital of Kálymnos. It grew up around **Péra Kástro**, the citadel that served as a place of refuge during the Middle Ages; on a gloomy day it looks more Transylvanian than Greek. The walls were repaired by the Knights but the ruined village inside, inhabited from the 11th to the 18th centuries, predates them. The only intact buildings are nine chapels kept freshly whitewashed by the faithful women of Chorió; the views from the top are well worth the trouble of climbing up. The **Shelter of the Nymphs** or **Cave of the Seven Virgins**, at the foot of Mount Flaská near Chorió's hospital, has never been thoroughly explored, but take a torch and you can see traces of ancient worship: holes in the rock where supplicants poured libations to the nymphs. Legend has it that seven maidens took refuge there during a pirate raid and were never seen again, lost in the bottomless the depths of the cave.

The island's old cathedral, **Panagía tis Kechaitoméni**, contains columns from a Hellenistic temple of Apollo. Traces of the temple remain just beyond Chorió and the Árgos crossroads: most of its other stone went into the 6th-century church of **Christós tis Ierúsalim**, built by the Byzantine Emperor Arkadios in gratitude for his shelter at Kálymnos during a terrible storm; now only part of the apse and the mosaic floor survive. There are many rock-cut Mycenaean tombs in the area, not too surprising as **Árgos** is just to the west. Although some ruins have been found, scholars doubt whether the ancient city stood precisely here.

Pothiá ✉ *85200,* ✆ *(0243–)* **Where to Stay**

A few strides from the ferry will bring you to the **Olympic**, ✆ 28 801 (*C; mod–inexp*), comfy but nothing special. Others are in the back streets above: **Panorama**, ✆ 23 138 (*C; mod*) has lovely décor, and all rooms have balconies with magnificent views. **Greek House**, ✆ 23 752 (*inexp*), near the sponge factory, is friendly with cosy wood-panelled rooms. **Katerina**, ✆ 22 186 (*inexp*) is also a good bet further up with self-catering facilities; **Patmos**, ✆ 22 750 (*inexp*) in a relatively quiet side street by the tourist office is similar.

Also try **Johnny's Studios** above the port which have commanding views over Pothiá. **Themelina**, ✆ 22 682 (*mod*), a lovely old 19th-century villa with shady gardens and swimming pool by the Archaeological Museum, has traditionally furnished rooms. It's probably the best in town but your only chance of a room is in the off season because it's block-booked from May to October.

Most of the restaurants are on 'Octopus Row' at the far end of the quay beyond the administration buildings, and specialize in octopus *keftédes*: **Minore** is the favourite here. **Vouvali's** is decorated with nautical bric-a-brac and has seawater tanks from which you can choose your own lobster or fish—otherwise try their excellent fish casseroles. Locals recommend the **Xefteries**, in a back street near the Metropolis church, in the same family for over 85 years. Sit in the garden and enjoy the fresh fish and roast lamb, or *dolmádes* and *stifádo*; prices can be a bit of a shock. **Goofy's**, behind the National Bank, is good in spite of its name but again a bit pricey. On the waterfront **Ouzerie Athinas** serves up large portions of fresh shrimp at a kind price; the nearby **Apollo** is a popular local hangout. In Árgos you'll find authentic Kalymniot food at the **Argos** taverna; try the *moorí*, lamb cooked overnight in a ceramic pot. The waterfront bars, especially **Apollo**, are popular after dark; you may find live music at **Apothiki** near the cathedral, or **Nea Afrikaner**, a traditional bouzouki club.

West Coast Beaches and North Kálymnos

North of Chorió the tree-lined road dips down to the island's beaches—which with all the goodwill in the world are nothing to write home about. Kálymnos' resort strip starts with **Kantoúni**, with a sandy beach enclosed by hills, and **Panórmos**, running into **Eliés**, named after its olive groves, although these are fast becoming playgrounds for the big package-tour companies. As beaches go they're only just adequate—small fringes of grey shingly sand shaded with tamarisk trees—but the deep blue coves offer excellent swimming. **Linária** is the next resort, with a small square with a few bars and tavernas and a path down to a small harbour and sea-weedy bay. A little further along, beyond the giant rock on the coastline, the beaches at **Platís Giálos** and **Melitzáchas** are quieter and a bit more upmarket.

The road plunges down to **Myrtiés** (ΜΥΡΤΙΕΣ), the heart of the island's tourist strip, where the blood-red sunset over the islet of Télendos is one of Greece's most famous. Myrtiés blends into **Massoúri** and the two villages have become a surprisingly loud Golden Mile with neon-sign bars belting out conflicting music and local lads racing up and down on motorbikes. Some tavernas have gone the way of Kos with brash fast-food photo menus outsides; supermarkets, jewellery shops and 'English breakfasts' are in full expansion. Yet the far end of Massoúri towards **Arméos** is less frenetic: you can still hear the goatbells from the rocks above and see the local women doing their crochet as they mind their souvenir shops.

From Myrtiés jetty, a good half-hour walk from Massoúri (buses hourly from Pothiá), frequent caiques make the short trip to the islet of **Télendos** (ΤΕΛΕΝΔΟΣ), which broke off from Kálymnos in a 6th century AD earthquake. Facing the strait are the derelict monastery of Ag. Vassílios and a fort, both medieval. Up a narrow lane from the harbour you'll find the pretty church of the Panagía. There are ruins of Roman houses and, high above the beaches, the Byzantine Monastery of Ag. Konstantínos. Several small pebble beaches have loungers: Chokláka (through the village and down steep steps in the cliff) is the most popular, while the shingly coves reached from the track beyond the waterside tavernas towards Pothiá are nudist haunts. Most of the islanders are fishermen and, apart from its daytime visitors, Télendos is a perfect island if you need to get away from it all: it has a handful of excellent seafood tavernas, rooms to rent, and a few new holiday villa developments.

North of Massoúri, **Kastélli** was the refuge of survivors of the terrible 11th-century Turkish massacre and overlooks the sea in a wild region of rocky cave-mouths full of fangs. There are steps down to the church of the Panagía below. From here, see if you can trace the profile of the sleeping or marble princess in the left-hand side of the pointed peak of Télendos. She's looking out to her lover, the prince of Kastélli. The legend goes that the prince was supposed to send her a lighted candle to prove his love. But it blew out en route and she killed herself.

The coast road is spectacular, overlooking fish farms in the bay on its way to the fjord-like inlet at **Arginónta**. The hamlet lends its name to the entire northern peninsula, a perfect place for strenuous, isolated treks in the quiet hills. The small beach is pebbly and peaceful with a couple of eateries—the small Sea Breeze Taverna is perfect for lunch—and sunbeds and rooms to rent. The northernmost village on Kálymnos, **Emborió** (ΕΜΠΟΡΙΟΣ), is a pretty fishing hamlet with a small beach (bus twice a day from Pothiá, caiques from Myrtiés), within walking distance of some exceptional countryside and terraced hills. The **Kolonóstilo Cave** (or Cyclops Cave) is nearby, sheltering vast curtains of stalactites resembling columns; unfortunately treasure-hunters have damaged it with dynamite. The remains of a **Venetian castle** and a tower are close by. The tower is believed to have been a Neolithic temple; a sacrificial altar was found in the vicinity.

Vathí: the Fjord of Kálymnos

Nothing on the island properly prepares you for the sudden vision of 'the Deep', **Vathí** (ΒΑΘΥΣ), the beauty spot of Kálymnos: a volcanic valley containing three charming, lush villages, Rína, Plátanos and Metóchi, superbly situated at the mouth of a magnificent fjord. Fragrant groves of mandarins and lemons provide the valley's income, and houses and white-walled roads fill in the gaps between the trees. **Rína**, named after St Irene, is where the boats dock. Although the original village was destroyed by pirates in the 15th century, it's a pretty harbour with a few tavernas, hotels and rooms, and a working boatyard. The middle village, **Plátanos**, named for its enormous plane tree, has **Cyclopean walls**; Rina has a mysterious 'throne' carved in the rock. North of Vathí you can walk to the **Monastery of Kyrá Psilí**, the 'Tall Lady'. Near the mouth of the fjord is the **Cave of Daskaleío**, accessible only by sea. A trove of Neolithic to Bronze Age items was found in its inner stalactite chamber.

Kálymnos ✉ *85200,* ✆ *(0243–)*   ***Where to Stay and Eating Out***

Kantoúni/Pánormos

Kaldyna Island, set back a bit from the sea, ✆ 47 880 (*B; mod*) has a swimming pool and sea sports. **Elies**, near Panórmos, ✆ 48 146 (*B; mod*) has a restaurant, two bars and a swimming pool. **Taverna Marinos** in Eliés specializes in roast stuffed lamb in the evenings and has an inventive and reasonably priced menu.

Myrtiés

Delfini, ✆ 47 514 (*C; mod*) and **Myrties**, ✆ 47 512 (*D; inexp*) are centrally placed; the latter is open all year. **Hermes**, ✆ 47 693, 🖷 48 097 (*C; mod*) is also a good bet. If you're sick of Greek food try **Nectar** with a wide international menu; **Babis Bar** in the square does good snacks and breakfast and is the perfect place to wait for buses, taxis and the boat to Télendos.

Massoúri

Studios Tatsis, ✆ 47 887 (*C; mod*) are stylish with great views over Télendos. **Niki's Pension**, ✆ 47 201 (*mod*) between the two resorts also has great views but is set up steps over rough terrain. The Arméos area is more peaceful with the **Plaza**, ✆ 47 134 (*B; mod*) perched high over the bay with a swimming pool and fine views. Massoúri has many eating places from fast-food joints to good tavernas which look like tacky take-aways, like **To Iliovasilima** ('The Sunset'), owned by the local butcher. **Mathaios** does all the Greek favourites well, as does family-run **Barba Iannis**. **Kokkinidis** looks pretty but gets very mixed reviews. Locals recommend **Ouzerie Psaras** and **Sopiarkos** on the way to Kastélli.

Télendos Island

Pension Rita, ✆ 47 914 (*inexp*) has rooms located over the friendly cafeteria that bakes cakes. **Pension Uncle George's**, ✆ 47 502 (*inexp*) is above the excellent restaurant. Further along, the **Café Festaria**, ✆ 47 401 (*inexp*) has decent doubles with en suite bathrooms. **Dimitrios Harinos**, ✆ 47 916 (*inexp*) also has village rooms set back in a pretty garden. All the tavernas are good value; **Ta Dalinas** has Greek music on Wednesdays and Saturdays.

Emborió

Xaris Apartments, ✆ 47 434, are the most comfortable; Harry's Pension/Taverna Paradise, ✆ 47 483 (*C; mod*) has lovely secluded gardens, and Themis, ✆ 47 277 (*C; inexp*) inland is also good.

Vathí

Galini, in Rína, ✆ 31 241 (*C; inexp*) has immaculate rooms and home-baked bread, served on a restful terrace overlooking the fjord-like harbour; inexpensive rooms and a good spot for lunch, too. Pension Manolis, ✆ 31 300 (*inexp*), higher up to the right, has a communal kitchen and nice garden. Manólis is an official guide and mine of information. The Harbour Taverna is excellent for seafood, lunch or dinner.

Entertainment and Nightlife

There are numerous bars in the resorts from the Domus Bar to the Rock and Blues Pub at Kantoúni to Babis Bar at Myrtiés for a cocktail or game of backgammon. Massoúri is for night owls and occasionally lager louts with the Smile Pub, NoName Pub, Paradise Bar, Ambience (the current 'in' choice), Rebel Saloon, and Look disco near Kastélli.

Kárpathos (ΚΑΡΠΑΘΟΣ)

Halfway between Crete and Rhodes, on the same latitude as Malta and Casablanca, Kárpathos has for decades been an island-hopper's best-kept secret: hard to reach, with a number of beauty spots and a very distinct character, most strongly marked by the affection it inspires in its inhabitants; although many have been forced to go abroad to make a living they come back as often as possible, and ship their bodies home to be buried on the island if fate decrees they die elsewhere. They have the money: Kárpathos' sons and daughters have one of the highest rates of university education in Europe. And the climate gets a gold star too, for people suffering from respiratory diseases.

Kárpathos offers two islands for the price of one: long, thin, austere and ruggedly mountainous in the north, and fertile, softer, beach-fringed and 'European' in the south, the two linked by a giant's spine of cliffs which culminates in two wild mountains over 1000m in height. These two distinct geographical personalities extend to the population; the northerners and southerners may have originally belonged to different ancient races. For long generations the little contact they had with one another was by caique. The centuries of isolation of the north left it a goldmine of traditions lost a century ago in the rest of Greece. Even today songs, dances and celebrations like Easter remain unchanged; in the village Ólympos women still bake their bread in outdoor ovens and dress every day in their striking traditional costumes—among the most beautiful in Greece. A rough road connecting the south to Ólympos was finished in 1979. Once limited to jeeps, now taxis ply it, and sadly buses too, and every year they somehow find more 'handicrafts' to sell to tourists.

History

One ancient name of Kárpathos was Porfiris, 'Red', after a red dye once manufactured on the island and used to colour the clothes of kings; another was Tetrapolis, describing its four ancient cities of Vrykous, Possidion, Arkessia and Nissyros. In Homer the island is called Kárpathos, some believe from *Arpaktos* or 'robbery', from the earliest days of piracy when Vróntis Bay hid pirate ships that darted out to plunder passing vessels. The Venetians slurred it into 'Scarpanto', a name you may occasionally see on maps.

Off the coasts, the prized *scarus* (or parrot fish, which, as Aristotle noted, ruminates its food) was so abundant that the Roman emperors hired special fleets to bring them back for the imperial table. Any signs of prosperity, however, had long ended by the time the

Kárpathos

pirates made the island their headquarters and one town, Arkássa, their chief slave market. Things were so rough that even the Turks didn't really want Kárpathos, and sent only a *cadi*, or judge, to the island a few times a year; he never stayed longer than a few days, and depended entirely on the Greeks to protect him. The bays at Vróntis and Arkássa are said to be riddled with sunken treasure, although if any has been found it's been kept very hush-hush. In the last war 6000 Italians were based on Kárpathos, which they used as a base to attack Egypt.

Kárpathos has a strong tradition of delicately lyrical poetry of its very own, and people like to compete in impromptu singing contests of *mantinades*, or 15-syllable couplets. Two Austrians, Rudolph Maria Brandl and Diether Reinsch, spent ten years on the island studying its songs and wrote the monumental *Die Volksmusik der Insel Karpathos* (Edition Re 1992), in several volumes with transcribed songs and cassettes. One of the prettiest old songs was collected in the 19th century:

> *A little bird was singing high up on the rough hillside,*
> *And a king's daughter listened from her window,*
> *'Ah, bird, that I had thy beauty, and would I had thy song,*
> *And would I had such golden plumes for hair upon my head!'*
>
> *'Why dost thou crave my beauty? why dost thou crave my song?*
> *Why dost thou crave my golden plumes for hair upon thy head?*
> *For thou hast cakes to feed on, as many as thou wilt,*
> *I eat my scanty portion from herbage in the fields;*
> *Thou sleepest on a lofty couch, with sheets of thread of gold,*
> *But I lie out in solitude among the dews and snows;*
> *And when thou drinkest water thou hast a gleaming cup,*
> *But I must drink my water from the spring thou bathest in;*
> *Thou waitest for the priest to come thy way to bless thee,*
> *But I await the huntsman, who comes to shoot me down.'*

Kárpathos ✆ (0245–) **Getting There and Around**

By air: 4 flights daily with Rhodes, several times a week with Athens, Santoríni and Kássos (the world's shortest scheduled flight—5 mins) and once with Sitía (Crete); also charters—no longer from the UK, but from Slovenia! The **Olympic office** in town is run by helpful Kostis Frangos, 25 Martiou, ✆ 22 150. **Airport information**: ✆ 22 058. **Taxis** to the airport around 3500dr.

By sea: 4 times a week with Rhodes, 3 times a week with Kássos, Piraeus, Santoríni, Heráklion, Ag. Nikólaos, Sitía (Crete) and Mílos, once a week with Páros, Síkinos, Folégandros and Sífnos. Some **ships** call at both island ports, Diafáni and Pigádia. Small **boats** daily in the summer connect the two, leaving Pigádia at 8.30am. At weekends there's a **caique** from Finíki to Kássos. A pair of excursion boats make beach and picnic outings to Kýra Panagía, Apélla, Acháta, and Kató Lata. **Port authority:** ✆ 22 227.

By road: not always easy. The often appalling state of the roads makes car and motorbike hire dear, the only petrol pumps are in Pigádia, and the bus service seems like an afterthought. One a day runs from Pigádia to Ammopí, and one to Pilés by way of Apéri, Voláda and Óthos, and one or two go on to Finíki and Arkássa and Lefkós.

Kárpathos ✆ *(0245–)*   **Tourist Police**

See regular police on the waterfront, Pigádia, ✆ 22 222. Also check out the island's homepage at *www.karpathos.com*.

Festivals

25 March, Evangelismós at Pigádia; **Easter** at Ólympos, one of the most ancient in Greece; **1 July**, Ag. Marínas near Menetés; **15 August**, at Apéri and Menetés; **22–23 August**, Kyrá Panagía and Myrtónas; **27–29 August**, Ag. Ioánnis at Vourgounda; **6 September**, Larniotisa at Pigádia; **8 September**, Panagías at Messóchorio.

Kárpathos Town (Pigádia)

The island capital and southern port, Kárpathos or more properly **Pigádia** (ΠΥΓΑΔΙΑ) is attractively sheltered in that old pirate cove, mountain-ringed Vróntis Bay. Once the ancient city of Possidion, it was abandoned in the Byzantine era, and all that remains of its predecessor is a clutch of Mycenaean tombs and a few stones of a temple to Lindian Athena on the rocky outcrop to the east. The modern town is just that—modern, and ungainly, but it's no accident that the local National Bank branch has such an air of prosperity: Kárpathos receives more money from its emigrants than any other island in Greece. New hotels and apartments are mushrooming up in Pigádia and along the sands outside town, and although German and Scandinavian holiday companies seem to be thriving the town still has a relaxed, friendly feel to it; with all those bucks in the bank the islanders don't have to be obsequious towards tourists.

Beyond the pretty Mussolini port authority building it's a short walk to the 3km stretch of fairly good beach that rims **Vróntis Bay**, lined with trees and a few new hotels, and dotted with pleasant tavernas specializing in grilled fish. Within an enclosure on the sands several columns have been re-erected of a 5th-century basilica, **Ag. Fotiní**. Across the bay stands the chapel of **Ag. Nikólaos**, the saint who replaced Poseidon as the protector of sailors; nearby a once-sacred cave called Poseidona has sweet water. On the south side of Vróntis Bay, another ancient site,

Ag. Kiriakí (the track is signposted from the road) had a 7th century BC Geometric-era sanctuary dedicated to Demeter; a few years back one of the tombs hewn in the rock yielded a golden statuette.

Around the South and up the West Coast

South of Pigádia, the land is flat and desolate, vegetation is sparse and the few trees are bent over from the wind. The wild coast softens 7km south of Pigádia at **Ammopí**, two sandy coves decorated with great rocks, a popular family resort. Further south a forlorn ship that ran aground in 1985 is like an advertisement for Kárpathos' windblasted windsurfing 'paradise', **Afiárti**, with rentals and accommodation springing up; Homer, after all, called the island, Anemoussa, the 'windy one.' The airport is further south, by the desolate site of the ancient city of Thaetho.

Colourful **Menetés** (ΜΕΝΕΤΕΣ), set in gardens on the flanks of Mount Profítis Ilías above Ammopí, has a small ethnographic museum and a church in a dramatic setting. Beyond, the road continues down to the west coast and **Arkássa** (ΑΡΚΑΣΑ), with its little beaches and big hotels in a picturesque setting at the mouth of a jagged ravine, cliffs riddled with caves that once sheltered shepherds. A paved road will take you south in a few minutes to the ruins of its predecessor, ancient **Arkessia**, where the Mycenaean acropolis with Cyclopean walls stands on a rocky headland of Paleokástro. The city was inhabited into late Byzantine times; the coloured geometric mosaic floor of a 5th-century church, **Ag. Anastásia**, is just under the fine layer of weeds and dirt; the best sections have been moved to Rhodes.

Just north, **Finíki** is a bijou little fishing harbour with a good, inexpensive restaurant and sandy beach nearby; the sponge divers of Kálymnos call here, and caiques depart for Kássos if the sea isn't too rough. Although the asphalt peters out, the road north passes several tempting strands and mini-fjords far, far below in the pines (one spot, **Adia**, has an excellent taverna) en route to **Lefkós** (ΛΕΥΚΟΣ), the nicest beach on the west coast—there's one bus a day from Pigádia. Tucked in the rocks, Lefkós has white sandy beaches, a wealth of pine trees and a scattering of antiquities, including a large stone that resembles a menhir. Lefkós is being developed, but so far nothing too drastic; there are a few small pensions, tavernas and villas owned by the Karpathiots. A short walk away are the ruins of a medieval fort; there was another on the offshore islet of **Sokástro**.

Inland Villages and the East Coast

The beautiful road north of Pigádia rises first to opulent **Apéri** (ΑΠΕΡΙ). The capital of Kárpathos up to 1896, it is reputed to be the richest village in Greece per capita; nearly everyone (90 of whom are said to be doctors) has lived in New Jersey, including the family that gave the world the late Telly 'Kojak' Savalas. One *kafeneío* still proudly displays a picture of Roosevelt. In the new cathedral built over the Byzantine cemetery you can pay your respects to Kárpathos' miracle-working icon, and if you have a chance to peek in a house don't miss it; unlike most Greek islanders the Karpathiots have lavish tastes, and traditionally appoint their homes with colourful carpets, lace, mirrors, portraits, antiques from around the world and elevated carved wood beds, or *souphas*; if you don't get inside, you can glean an idea from the exquisitely tended gardens.

The other central villages are just as houseproud. Delightful whitewashed **Voláda** has pretty lanes, and a ruined castle built by the Cornaros of Venice, who owned the island until 1538. From here the road climbs to **Óthos**, at 650m the highest village of Kárpathos, and one of the oldest, its houses decorated with carved wooden balconies. Although you may need a pullover, even in summer, it produces a fine local red wine, *othitikó krasí*. A 150-year-old house has been opened as a small **ethnographic museum**, run by the excellent Ioannis T. Hapsis, ex-barber, ex-shoemaker and *lýra* player who now paints pictures which he sells for 2000–20,000dr, solely by the size. To the west coast the pretty village of ΠΥΛΕΣ, whose name in Roman letters unfortunately reads **Pilés**, has fine views over Kássos, with the profile of Crete as a backdrop.

Caiques from Pigádia call at the east coast beaches, although you can brave some of them by road. A steep zigzag from Apéri leads down to **Acháta**, a lovely, empty white pebbly beach with fresh water, enclosed in a rocky amphitheatre. The unpaved road north of Apéri (currently being improved) takes in the increasingly majestic coast, with a steep, dangerous by-road winding down to **Kyrá Panagía**, a lovely wide beach, varying from fine white sand to large pebbles and with a pretty red-domed church for a landmark. Rooms and tavernas are sprouting apace and fill up in the summer; an easier way to get there is by a 45-minute walk down through the lush greenery and trees from the mountain village of **Myrtónas**. Another rotten road descends from Myrtónas to **Apélla**, the most beautiful, a crescent of fine sand, turquoise water and dramatic scenery, set in boulders and rocks furiously riven, ravaged and rolled in the Clash of the Titans. Caiques from Pigádia make excursions to the beaches; Myrtónas is the place to be on 22 August, when it hosts the best *panegýri* on the island with music and folk-dancing lasting into the following day. The east coast road ends at **Spóa**, at the crossroads of the road to Ólympos; massive forest fires in 1980s have left large patches between Spóa and Diafáni denuded and melancholy. A track from Spóa descends to the beach of **Ag. Nikólaos**, with too much new building, and in summer too many people.

An unpaved, narrow road from Spóa circles Kárpathos' tallest mountain, **Kalílimni** (1188m), the highest point in the Dodecanese. Continuing anticlockwise from Spóa, the road descends on a corniche to **Messochóri**, set in an amphitheatre facing the sea, with the pretty 17th-century church of Ag. Ioánnis, with a carved iconostasis and well-preserved frescoes. From here a road descends to Lefkós (*see* above).

Out of season a few room-owners meet ferries; if you get stuck ring the **Association of Hotel Owners**, ✆ 22 483.

Kárpathos Town (Pigádia)

Possirama Bay, ✆ 22 511, ✉ 22 929 (*A; exp*) is 400m from the town centre, on the sandy beach of Affoti, offering air-conditioned apartments for 2–4 people, and large balconies overlooking the sea. In the same area **Miramare Bay**, ✆ 22 345, ✉ 22 631 (*B; exp*) is also new, with swimming pool, sea views and good breakfast included. **Romantica**, ✆ 22 460, ✉ 22 461(*C; mod*) is the most charming place to stay, with 32 studios half-hidden in a grove of citrus trees, and a short walk from the beach; it serves a delicious breakfast. Up in town, the **Pavillion**, ✆ 22 059, is a favourite of Americans, with cocktails on the roof garden. **Artemis Pension**, ✆ 22 724, has self-catering facilities. New, moderate-sized **Oasis**, ✆ 22 915 (*C; mod*) has flowery and welcoming studios. **Blue Bay**, by the beach, ✆ 22 479, ✉ 22 391 (*C; mod*) has rooms (some with disabled access), a pool, bar and children's playground. Older cheaper choices **Kárpathos**, ✆ 22 347, and **Annessis**, ✆ 22 100 (*both D; inexp*) both stay open all year. There are quite a few rooms for rent: **Fotoula Georgiadou's**, ✆ 22 519, up at the top of town are among the cheapest and quietest.

Kárpathos' restaurants are beginning to revive traditional recipes and serve wine from Othos—although it's rare to find it in bottles. Old favourites like **Mike's** in a narrow lane in the centre and **Kali Kardia** (for fish) towards the beach aren't expensive. **Oraia Karpathos** on the waterfront serves the best *makarounes* (handmade pasta with fried onions and cheese) south of Ólympos. New places include **Aeraki**, on the waterfront, which serves island specialities—pumpkin fritters, stuffed mushrooms, onion pies, chicken stuffed with feta and bacon, local sausages and mild *manouli* cheese; the same owners run **Anemoussa** upstairs, with good Italian dishes. **Archontiko** occupies a neoclassical house and serves a wide variety of well-prepared dishes on its terraces. Little old **Café Karpathos**, ✆ 22 701, just off the waterfront towards the ferry, is a good cheap place for breakfast or a snack, and **Elias** and **Argyro** offer a warm welcome.

Ammopí

New on the beach scene are **Argo**, ✆ 22 589, and **Helios**, ✆ 22 448, ✉ 22 171 (*both C; mod*). **Long Beach**, ✆ 23 076, ✉ 22 095 (*C; mod*) has a pool and tennis. **Ammopi Beach**, ✆ 22 723 (*inexp*) has simple rooms—help yourself to figs. For windsurfers, there's the traditional styled **Poseidon**, south of Ammopí, ☎/🖷 22 020 (*C; mod*) with a lovely garden terrace.

Arkássa

Dimitrios, ☎ 61 255, and the brand new **Arkesia**, 61 290 (*both B; mod*) are the plush choices here, at the end of the village; or for something cheaper try **Johnny's**, ☎ 61 310.

Finíki/Lefkós

Fay's Paradise, ☎ 61 308 (*inexp*) has lovely rooms near the harbour. There are three or four good fish tavernas, and the **Cuckoo's Nest** *ouzerie* with an all-blue interior for pre-dinner imbibing. North in Adia, eat at the **Pine Tree**, with great pasta, chick pea soup and fresh-baked bread. In Lefkós, **Studios Lefkosia**, ☎ 71 288, is simple but okay, and the **Small Paradise** serves good food.

Kýra Panagía

Book to have a chance at any of these. Since 1976, **Sofia's Paradise Taverna**, ☎ 31 300, 🖷 31 099 (run by a former New Yorker) has offered good home cooking, cheap fish, and figs drowned in raki to go with your coffee; also pleasant rooms with bath and breakfast; she also has a boat for private or group outings. If you want to go upscale, there's the new **Kyra Panagia Studios**, ☎ 31 473 (*exp*) with a bar and the popular **Studios Acropolis**, ☎ 31 503 (*mod*) with lovely views. Up in Voláda, the **Klimateria** has traditional good taverna food under a pergola.

Entertainment and Nightlife

There's live impromptu Karpathian *lýra* of variable quality on summer nights under the pergola at the **Kafenion**, on Apodi Kárpathos street. On the town waterfront, **Symposeio** is a popular music bar, or there's the **Yuppy** bar near the church, in the skeleton of an unfinished building playing a mix of Greek and rave. **Filagri**, between Pigádia and Ammopí, is where locals and returned Karpathians dance the summer nights away. Every Wednesday night the locals get together and play traditional music in the *kafeneíon* in **Finíki**. In Apéri, the popular **Platania Bar** is in a restored old house and plays Greek music and international hits.

Ólympos and Northern Kárpathos

The easiest and least expensive way to reach Ólympos (ΟΛΥΜΠΟΣ) from Kárpathos is by caique to **Diafáni**, the village's laid-back little port, from where a minibus makes the connection to Ólympos. The harbour improvements enable big ferries to dock, so there's currently a lot of concrete about and plans to build a big hotel. There's a beach with flat rocks nearby and several others within walking distance; boats make excursions to others.

Ólympos, one of the most striking villages on the Greek islands, is draped over a stark mountain ridge with a long line of ruined windmills running like teeth along the top. To the west are magnificent views of mountains plunging headlong into the sea. Decorative painted balconies, many incorporating two-headed Byzantine eagles (one head Rome, one Constantinople), adorn the houses which in many places are literally stacked one on another and opened with wooden locks and keys that Homer himself might have recognized. The frescoes and recently cleaned iconostasis in the church date back to the 18th century.

As the ability of the Byzantines to defend the seas declined, Ólympos became the refuge for all those fleeing the abandoned coastal towns in the north, themselves isolated for so long that linguists were amazed to find people here using pronunciations and expressions that could be traced back to ancient Doric and Phrygian dialects. Women are more visible than men because of emigration: an eldest son inherits all of his father's property, leaving the younger ones no choice. Many of those who remain are noted musicians, playing the *lýra* (smaller and narrower than the Cretan version) with a bell-covered bow, the *laoúto*, and goatskin bagpipes, *tsamboúna*. Likewise, a mother's property all goes to the eldest daughter, the *kanakára*; if you're lucky enough to be in Ólympos during a *panegýri* or wedding you can recognize a *kanakára* by the gold coins she wears on chains—coins that her forefathers will have earned while working abroad. Twenty years ago all the women wore their traditional costumes every day (these days it's mostly those working in the tourist trade): black scarves printed with flowers, baggy white trousers, a dark skirt and apron, a loose embroidered chemise, and fine goatskin boots for special protection (snakes hate the smell of goat). One cobbler still makes them for around 50,000dr a pair, but they last a lifetime. Women bake bread in outdoor ovens, even using wheat and barley ground in the two remaining working windmills out of 40 that turned a few decades ago.

Ólympos, pop. 1800 in 1951, is down to 581 today, but where even 20 years ago visitors were so few that they had no effect on the village's traditional life, tens of thousands a year are another story. To see Ólympos as it was, stay overnight or come in the off-season. On weekend evenings the *kafeneíons* still fill with live music. One *kafeneíon* displays a certificate from the Governor of Alabama, thanking him for his service in the state militia.

From Ólympos you can drive most of the way to **Avlóna**, a village that wouldn't look too out of place in Tibet, inhabited only during the harvest season by farmers from Ólympos, who work the surrounding valley; some of the tools they use are more commonly seen in museums. From Avlóna it is a rough walk down to **Vrykoús**, the ancient Phrygian city of Vourkóunda, remembered today by a stair, a breakwater, rock-cut burial chambers and walls; a tiny chapel sits out on the rocks. In a cavern in Vrykoús the chapel of **Ag. Ioánnis** hosts the largest *panegýri* in north Kárpathos, a two-day event where everyone sleeps out, roasts meat over an open fire and dances to the haunting music. Another two hours north of Avlóna, in the bay of the 'three-mouthed' **Tristomo**, are the submerged remains of the ancient city of Níssyros, colonized by the island of Níssyros to exploit the iron and silver mines at Assimovorni; according to the inscriptions, there was a temple of Apollo here. Boats from Diafáni sail to **Sariá**, the islet that dots the 'i' of long, narrow Kárpathos. The ruins known as **Ta Palátia** (the palaces), are actually a post-Byzantine pirate base, with dolmus-style houses under barrel-vaulted roofs. It is a good walk up from the landing place, so wear sturdy shoes.

Kárpathos ✉ *84700,* ✆ *(0245–)*   **Where to Stay and Eating Out**

Diafáni

Chryssi Akti, ✆ 51 215 (*E; inexp*) opposite the quay, is clean and basic; **Mayflower**, ✆ 51 228, is similar, and **Delfini**, ✆ 51 391, a bit further back, is quieter. There is a slightly crazed unofficial campsite at Vanánda Beach.

Ólympos

Taverna Olympos, ✆ 51 252 (*inexp*) has three traditional rooms with en suite baths and is highly recommended, also with great views. **Aphrodite**, ✆ 51307, too has lovely views; if they're full try **Mike's**, ✆ 51 304 or **Astro**, ✆ 51 378 (*all inexp*). The windmill has a restaurant that serves good pasta stuffed with cheese and spinach.

Kássos (ΚΑΣΣΟΣ)

The southernmost Dodecanese island and one of the most remote of all islands, Kássos (pop. 1500) is a barren rock with steep coasts, ravines and sea grottoes, with the odd beach or two between. Practically untouched by tourism, it can be the ideal place if you're seeking the simple, friendly atmosphere of pre-mass-tourism Greece. The port, Fri, is small, and if the sea is rough simply landing can be a big headache.

History

Homer mentions Kássos in the *Iliad* for the ships it sent to Troy to aid the Achaeans. The ancient city stood at the site of the present village of Póli, and at Hellenokamára cave there are Mycenaean walls. During the Turkish occupation

Kássos retained a good deal of its autonomy, especially with regard to its fleet, which it quickly put at the disposal of the Greek cause when the War of Independence was declared. For the first three years of the war the Greeks, who were better sailors, generally came out ahead in the struggle, but the Sultan, angered by his setbacks, prepared a powerful counter-attack through his ally Ibrahim Pasha, son of Ali Pasha, the Ottoman Empire's governor of Egypt. In June 1824 Ibrahim left Egypt with a massive fleet to crush the Greek rebellion. His first stop, on the 7th, was Kássos, which he obliterated, slaying all the men and taking the women and children as slaves. The few who managed to escape went either to Sýros or the islet of Gramboúsa off the northwestern coast of Crete, where they turned to piracy for survival, defiantly flying the Greek flag in Turkish waters. But Capodístria and his allies put a stop to their activities, and their refuge, Gramboúsa, was returned to Turkish rule. In spite of the massacre, thousands of Kassiots later emigrated to Egypt to work on the Suez Canal. Most now prefer America.

Kássos ✆ *(0245–)*   **Getting There and Around**

By air: 5 flights a week to and from Rhodes, one a week to Sitía and 4 times to Kárpathos.

By sea: twice weekly with Piraeus, Crete, Mílos, Kárpathos and Rhodes, once a week with Chálki, Sými, Santoríni, Mílos, Náxos and Páros; weekend **caique** from Finíki, Kárpathos. All are likely to skip Kássos if the wind's up. **Port authority**: ✆ 41 288.

By road: three taxis and an irregular bus service in the summer are all you get; there are motorbikes to rent, and occasional boat excursions.

Kássos ✆ *(0245–)*   **Tourist Information**

Try the **Maritre Tourist Agency**, ✆ 41 232. **Police**: ✆ 41 222.

Festivals

23 April, Ag. Geórgios; **7 June**, Fri; **17 July**, Ag. Marína; **14 August**, at Panagía.

Around Kássos

There are five villages on Kássos and small, charmingly woebegone **Fri** (ΦΡΥ) is their capital, where the main occupation, fishing, is much in evidence in the little port of Boúka. Every year on 7 June a ceremony is held there in memory of the massacre of 1824, and many people from Kárpathos also attend, coming on the special boats. Swimming at Fri isn't brilliant but boats make the excursion out to the **Armathiá**, an islet just north of Kássos, with a choice of five decent beaches; a long stretch of sand dignifies the other islet, **Makrá**.

Outside a few dwarf olives, trees on Kássos never recovered after Ibrahim Pasha set the island ablaze, but many lighthouses, testimony to the tricky seas, stick out above the rocky terrain. A road and the one bus link Fri with Kássos' four other dinky villages, a 6km circuit. There's **Emborió**, another fishing hamlet where an old commercial port is packed up with silt, and above it **Panagía**, where proud ship captains' houses erode a bit more every year; the 18th-century church that gave the village its name is the oldest on Kássos. **Póli** is built on the island's acropolis, and has a crumbling Byzantine castle and church with inscriptions. At **Ag. Marína**, near the air strip and Kássos' most accessible if mediocre beach at **Ammoúa**, there is a lovely stalactite cave called **Hellenokamára**, where signs of worship go back to Mycenaean and Hellenistic times. From Ag. Marína or **Arvanitochóri** you can spend a day walking across Kássos, the lonely track passing the usually empty monastery of Ag. Giórgios where you can find water, to **Chelathrós bay**, with a sand and pebble beach.

Kássos ✉ *85800,* ☎ *(0245–)*   ### Where to Stay

In Fri the seaside **Anagennissis**, ☎ 41 323, 🖷 41 036 (*C; mod–inexp*) is comfortable and run by an engaging Kassiot-American. You'll pay more for the rooms facing the sea, less for those in the back; **Anessis**, ☎ 41 201 (*C; mod–inexp*) is similar but a bit less. *Both open all year.*

If you prefer self-catering there are the **Borgianoula Apartment**s, ☎ 41 495, 🖷 41 036 (*mod, open April–Oct*) and **Manouses Apartments**, ☎ 41 047 (*mod*).

Kássos ☎ *(0245–)*   ### Eating Out

There are a handful of tavernas in Fri; the **Oraia Bouka** overlooking the port is as good as it looks, and the simple **Kassos** by the town hall has cheap and filling souvlákia. There are also a couple of tavernas in Emborió.

Kastellórizo/Mégisti (ΜΕΓΙΣΤΗ)

The easternmost point of Greece, oddball Kastellórizo is six hours—110km—east of Rhodes, within spitting distance of Turkey. It is the smallest inhabited island of the Dodecanese, 3 by 6km, yet the mother hen of its own small clutch of islets; hence its official name, Mégisti, 'the largest'. They say the Turks know it as Meis Ada, 'eyeland', for one nautical mile away is their town of Kaş ('eyebrow'), but the most common name is Kastellórizo, in memory of the days when the Neapolitans called it the 'Red Castle'. Dry, depopulated, more than half ruined, its once very lonely 170–200 permanent inhabitants now have an airport to bring them in closer contact with the rest of Greece, and Athens as a parent; the city has officially adopted the island and sends it contributions and gifts, including recently 20 council houses. Its success as a film set has given the economy, based on government stipends and fishing, a new life as a tourist resort, as swarms of Italians now come to Kastellórizo; landladies cry '*Stanza? Stanza?*' as the ferry arrives. Some of the old houses are being repaired, mostly by returned Australian emigrants. However it remains a quirky backwater surrounded by a crystal sea brimming with marine life—including oysters, a rarity on Greek islands. And while there aren't any sandy strands, the locals will never fail to tell you that there are plenty of rocks on which to catch some rays.

History

Tradition says the island was named for its first settler, King Meges of Echinada. Neolithic finds suggest an early arrival for Meges, and Mycenaean graves coincide with Homer's mention of the island's ships at Troy. Later the Dorians built two forts on the island, the Kástro by the present town and one on the mountain, called Palaeokástro—the ancient acropolis, where Apollo and the Dioscuri were the chief deities. Dionysos was another favourite: recently 42 rock *patitíria* or grape-trampling presses were discovered, linked to conduits that fed the juice into underground reservoirs. The island had a great fleet of ships based in its sheltered harbour and traded with Lycia on the mainland, transporting its timber to Africa and the Middle East. From 350 to 300 BC Kastellórizo was ruled by Rhodes, and in Roman times Cassius' pirates used it as their hideout. The island was converted to Christianity from the time of St Paul, who preached along the coast of Asia Minor at Myra.

The Byzantines repaired Kastellórizo's fortifications, and their work was continued by the Knights of St John after the fall of Jerusalem. They named the island after the red rock of the castle, which they used to imprison knights who misbehaved on Rhodes. The Sultan of Egypt captured Kastellórizo in 1440 but ten years later the King of Naples, Alfonso I of Aragon, took it back. Although Kastellórizo belonged to the Ottoman Empire by 1512, the Venetians later occupied it twice, in 1570 and in 1659. Despite all the see-sawing to and fro, Kastellórizo was doing all right for itself; at the beginning of the 19th century it had a population of 15,000 who lived either from the sea or off their extensive holdings along the coast of Asia Minor.

Things began to go seriously wrong when the Greek War of Independence broke out. The islanders were the first in the Dodecanese to join the cause, and, taking matters into their own hands, seized their island's two fortresses from the Turks. The Great Powers forced them to give them back in 1833. In 1913 Kastellórizo revolted again only to be put down by the French, who used the island as a base for their war in Syria—hence drawing bombardments from the Turkish coast. In 1927 an earthquake caused extensive damage but the Italians, then in charge, refused to do any repairs, as Kastellórizo had not cooperated with their programme of de-Hellenization. Another revolt in 1933 was crushed by soldiers from Rhodes. In spite of its port serving as a refuelling station for long-distance sea planes from France and Italy, Kastellórizo was in sharp decline—in 1941 only 1500 inhabitants remained.

But the saga of Kastellórizo's misfortunes only continues. During the Second World War the isolated Italian garrison was captured by the Germans. When the Allies shipped the entire Greek population for their safety to refugee camps in the Gaza Strip, occupying British officers pillaged the empty houses. To hide their looting, the British (or, the British claim, Greek pirates doing some looting of their own) ignited the fuel dump as they pulled out, leading to a conflagration that destroyed more than 1500 homes and nearly all the islanders' boats. As if this was not enough, the ship carrying the refugees home after the war sank. The survivors who returned to Kastellórizo discovered that, although they had finally achieved Greek citizenship, they had lost everything else, and there was nothing to do but emigrate, some to Athens but most to Australia, where an estimated 12,000 to 15,000 'Kazzies' now live. The immediately postwar population was reduced to five families, who owed their survival to the Turks in Kaş who sent over food parcels. British compensation for wartime damages came in the 1980s, but there are still bad feelings over the way it was distributed; none actually went to the people who stuck it out on the island.

The rare Greek-Turkish friendship and cooperation continues. In 1992, all the Kastellorizans were invited over to spend Christmas in Kaş hotels, were taken on excursions and given a two-day feast and party. It was Kaş' way of thanking Kastellórizo for its role in the underground railroad that brought Kurds over to Kaş, and thence to Kastellórizo and a large refugee camp near Athens. Since the demise of Papandréou the relationship has improved again. Almost all the Greeks, however, are more than half ready to leave, and the only reason they stay is to keep the island firmly Greek. The government has built a desalination plant, and has bent over backwards to bring television and an airport to the island.

Kastellórizo ✆ (0241–)   ***Getting There***

By air: 4 or more a week from Rhodes. **Airport:** ✆ 49 241. A bus meets planes.

By sea: 'Europe begins here' proclaims the sign by the quay. Twice a week from Rhodes, up to 4 times in high summer; once a week the Kálymnos carries on directly to Kos, Kálymnos, Sými and Tílos. Also an overpriced, unofficial (as Kastellórizo is not an official port of entry) boat to Kaş (*see* p.174). **Port authority:** ✆ 49 270.

Kastellórizo ✆ (0241–)   ***Tourist Police***

See regular police in the harbour by the post office, ✆ 49 333.

23 **April**, Ag. Geórgios; **21 May**, Ag. Konstantínos; **20 July**, Profítis Ilías.

Kastellórizo Town

There is only one town on the island, also called Kastellórizo, full of ruined houses and mansions, burnt, or crumbling from earthquakes or bombing. One can see how wealthy some inhabitants once were from the remaining elegant coffered ceilings and lovely carved balustrades. Some are being restored, others are inhabited by cats, chickens and geese. Small tavernas line the waterfront, in high season packed with Italians and yachties. A hotel occupies one lip of the harbour mouth, while on the other sits the **fort** (*kástro*), last repaired by the eighth Grand Master of the Knights of St John, Juan Fernando Heredia, whose red coat of arms is another possible explanation for the island's name. The ladder to the top leads to a fine view of the sea and Turkish coast; every day an islander climbs up to raise the Greek and EU flags here at the easternmost extremity of both. A Doric inscription discovered at the fort suggests the existence of an ancient castle on the same site. A tomb nearby yielded a golden crown, and in the castle keep the small **museum** (*open Tues–Sun, 7.30–2.30*) has photographs of the prosperous town before everything went wrong, a few frescoes, folk costumes and items found in the harbour—including Byzantine tableware.

The walking path along the shore leads up to a **Lycian tomb** cut into the living rock and decorated with Doric columns; the whole southwest or Lycian coast of modern Turkey is dotted with similar tombs (*see* Kaş, below) but this is the only one in modern Greece. The **Cathedral of Ag. Konstantínos and Heléni** reuses granite columns lifted from a temple of Apollo in Patara. From the town a steep path with steps leads up to four white churches, a monastery and **Palaeokástro**, the Doric fortress and acropolis. On the gate there is a Doric inscription from the 3rd century BC referring to Mégisti; walls, a tower and cisterns also remain.

Kastellórizo's Grotto Azzurro

There are no beaches on Kastellórizo, but the sea is clean and ideal for snorkelling. There are a multitude of tiny islets to swim out to, and a million sea urchins waiting for you to step on them. The excursion not to miss is to the **Blue Cave** or **Perásta**, an hour by caique from the town. The effects are best in the morning when some light filters in, for the entrance is so low you'll have to transfer to a raft. As in the famous Blue Grotto of Capri, the reflections of the water inside dye the cavern walls and stalactites an uncanny blue; wear your swimming gear. The same excursion boats often go to **Rho**, a hunk of rock with a beach, a hundred goats and a flagpole, where a cranky old lady became a nationalist heroine by daily raising the Greek flag just to show those Turks what was what; she died in 1982 and was buried on Rho, but her flag is still raised every day by a caretaker paid by the Greek government.

Kastellórizo ✉ 85111, ☎ (0241–) **Where to Stay**

The islands has 400 beds, but if you want one in August, book. **Megisti**, ☎ 49 272, 📠 49 221 (*C; exp–mod*) overlooking the harbour is the most comfortable place to stay. *Open all year.* **The Blue and White Pension**, book via Taverna International, ☎ 49 348 (*mod–inexp*) to the west of the bay was featured in *Mediterraneo*. The **Mavrothalassitis** family's pension, ☎ 49 202 (*inexp*) is simple with en suite facilities. **Castelo** (*mod–inexp*) behind Plateía Australías has family apartments, ask at Taverna Mavros; also try **Polos**, ☎ 49 302 and **Paradeisos**, ☎ 49 074 (*inexp*); **Barbara**, ☎ 49 295 (*inexp but known to fluctuate*) is a last resort.

Kastellórizo ☎ (0241–) **Eating Out**

Most eateries are in the harbour clustered round the Plateía Ethelontón Kastellórizon. Prices, always dear because of transport charges, have rocketed and fish is expensive, although it's fresh and the only thing that doesn't have to be shipped in. **Mikro Parisi**, 'Little Paris', is still the place for affordable fish, although concentrating on yachties; **Evtychia** is also reasonably priced and the **Oraia Mégisti** opposite another good choice. For more ethnic fare and local ambience head to **O Meyisteas** behind the market building arches for good meat and *mezédes*, while **Platania** up the hill on Choráfia Square is also unpretentious with tasty island dishes.

A Day Trip to Kaş

Fifteen years ago the delightful fishing village of Kaş, huddled shyly under the lower peaks of 9802ft Mt Akdağ, offered perhaps the ultimate in sunny Mediterranean languor. Of course it was too good to last—even then Saudi Arabian interests were plotting the biggest resort complex in the world here, with 10,000 rooms. Fortunately the scheme fell through, but Kaş has been more than overbuilt ever since. Nevertheless it somehow manages to be a happy, relaxed place and still maintains more of its village character than most larger resorts in Turkey.

Kaş was Antiphellos to the Greeks and Habesa to the Lycians, a native Anatolian people who according to Homer fought in the Trojan War on Troy's side under Sarpedon, the brother of King Minos of Crete. Isolated by the rugged nature of the surrounding terrain, Lycia stayed out of history for the most part, and gradually became Hellenized in spite of its Persian satraps—a process completed when Alexander the Great grabbed the coast. The Lycians adopted not only the Greek alphabet but also the architecture, and bits and pieces from the past survive here and there—west of the harbour are the ruins of a temple and a 1st-century BC theatre with 25 rows of seats. Behind the town, several tombs are cut into the almost vertical cliff face. These tombs were a Lycian speciality—elaborate, perfectly cut niches with Greek temple façades. Elsewhere the Lycians made sarcophagi and tombs in the form of miniature stone houses, often set on platforms topped with barrel roofs. One of these survives in the centre of Kaş, a tall, lovely tomb, with inscriptions in ancient Lycian; the hole in its side was made centuries ago by looters. Another stands at the harbour, and another on the hill just to the west on a narrow peninsula. All except the one at the harbour (which the town relocated), and all the other Lycian tombs in the vicinity of Kaş, face Kastellórizo. Archaeologists and anthropologists alike are totally baffled as to why.

Kos (ΚΩΣ)

Dolphin-shaped Kos, with its wealth of fascinating antiquities, flowers and orchards, sandy beaches and comfortable climate, is Rhodes' major Dodecanese rival in the tourist industry. In other words, don't come here looking for anything very Greek—the *kafeneíon* and *ouzerie* serving octopus sizzling from the grill have long been replaced with fast-food joints and tourist-trap cafés. The streets are packed with T-shirt and tatty gift shops; where garlanded donkeys once carried their patrons home from the fields, swarms of rent-a-bikes rev. In high season English, German and Swedish tourists fill the island's myriad big, self-contained resort hotels. Even the architecture isn't particularly Greek, partly owing to an earthquake in 1933: the Italian occupation contributed some attractive buildings, and the pair of minarets rising from the mosques add an aura of elegance and *cosmopolitana* to the capital. Inland, Kos in summer looks uncannily like a mini California: sweeping golden hills, with a few vineyards, groves and orchards, grazing cattle and steep, pale cliffs, but otherwise empty, contrasting with rashes of buildings crowding the countless sandy coves that ruffle the coasts.

History

Evidence in Áspri Pétra cave suggests people have been living on Kos since 3500 BC. A Minoan colony flourished on the site of the modern city; the Mycenaeans who came later traded extensively throughout the Mediterranean. The island went through a number of name changes: Meropis, after its mythical king; Karis, for its shrimp shape; Nymphaeon, for its numerous nymphs; Kos, which finally won out, is either from a princess named Koon or a crab, an early symbol. In the 11th century the Dorians invaded and made Astypálaia their capital, and in 700 BC they joined the Dorian Hexapolis, although they seem to have been the most insignificant member.

Fertile and poised between East and West (Turkey is just over the channel), Kos flourished with the trade of precious goods—and revolutionary ideas.

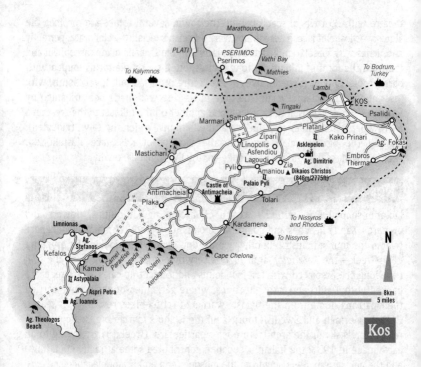

Kos

Halicarnassus was the birthplace of Herodotus, the 'father of history', the first to attempt to distinguish legend from fact, and in the 5th century BC Kos produced an innovating papa of its own, Hippocrates, father of medicine (*see* p.60). His school on Kos, where he taught a wholesome medicine based on waters, special diets, herbal remedies and relaxation, was renowned throughout the ancient world. When Hippocrates died an Asklepeion (dedicated to Asklepios, the healing god) was founded, and people from all over the Mediterranean came to be cured in its hospital-sanctuary.

In 411 BC, during the Peloponnesian War, the Spartans played a nasty trick on the island; pretending to be friends, they entered the capital Astypálaia and sacked it. In 366 BC the survivors refounded the old Minoan/Mycenaean city of Kos, conveniently near the now flourishing Asklepeion. The next few centuries were good ones; besides physicians, Kos produced a school of bucolic poetry led by Theocritus, a native of Sicily (319–250 BC) and the most charming of all ancient Greek poets; his *Harvest Time in Kos*, evoking a walk across the island to drink wine by Demeter's altar, meeting a poetic goatherd on the way, is one of his masterpieces that gave English the word 'idyllic'. Apelles, the greatest painter during the lifetime of Alexander, was a native of Kos, as was Philetas, inventor of the Alexandrine and teacher of another native, Ptolemy II Philadelphos, who went on to become king of Egypt; many subsequent Ptolemies were sent over to Kos for their education. The Romans were later to prize Kos for its translucent purple silks, wines and perfumes and gave it a special autonomy because of the Asklepeion. St Paul called in and began the island's conversion to Christianity; so far 21 early basilicas have been discovered.

Kos' wealth and strategic position made it a prize for invading Persians, Saracens, pirates and Crusaders. The gods themselves, it seems, were jealous, and earthquakes in AD 142, 469 and 554 levelled most of the island's buildings. In 1315 the Knights of St John took control and in 1391 began fortifications using the ancient city as a quarry, incorporating even marble statues from the Asklepeion in their walls. In 1457 and 1477 the Turks besieged Kos without success, but they gained the fortress by treaty after the fall of Rhodes.

Kos ✆ (0242–)   **Getting There and Around**

By air: charters direct from London and other European cities, 3 daily with Athens, and 3 a week with Rhodes. Olympic's office is at Leof. Vass. Pávlou 22, ✆ 28 331; the airport is 26km from town. Olympic airport buses from Kos town depart 2 hours before each flight, or there are public buses (the stop is outside the airport gate—ask for Taverna Panorama) to Kos town, Mastichári, Kardámena and Kéfalos. **Airport**: ✆ 51 255.

By sea: daily to Piraeus, Rhodes, Kálymnos, Léros and Pátmos; frequently to Lipsí, Sámos, Ikaría, Fourni, Sými, Tílos and Chálki; once a week to Amorgós, Astypálaia, Kárpathos, Kássos, Lésbos, Mýkonos, Páros, Kastellórizo, Chíos, Límnos, Alexandroúpolis, Sitía (Crete) and Thessaloníki. Daily **excursions** sail to Bodrum (Turkey), Níssyros, Psérimos, Platí, Lipsí, Léros and Kálymnos from Kos Town as well as Mastichári and Kardaména. **Hydrofoil**: daily in season to nearby Dodecanese and Sámos (Pythagório and Vathí) and Ikaría. **Port authority**: ✆ 26 594.

By road: flat Kos town is especially suited to bicycles and several shops hire them out. The city **bus** runs every 20 minutes from the centre of the waterfront (7 Akti Koundouriotou, ✆ 26 276) to Ag. Fokas and Lampi; roughly every hour to the Asklepeion, and 7 times a day to Marmari (buy tickets in the office before boarding). Buses to other points on Kos, ✆ 22 292, leave from the terminal behind the Olympic Airways office, but they get packed so get there early. Otherwise you'll find yourself at the wrong end of a long queue waiting for a taxi. In theory at least you can summon a **radio cab**, ✆ 23 333 or 27 777. Keep a close eye on the meter.

Helpful **municipal tourist office** in the Albergo Gelsomino on Vass. Georgíou just before the hydrofoil berth, ✆ 26 585 or 28 724, 📠 21 111 (*open 7.30 am–9pm and weekends 8.30–3*). **EOT**, ✆ 28 710, 📠 28150, and the **tourist police**, ✆ 26 666, share the yellow edifice with the clocktower opposite the main harbour with the regular **police**, ✆ 22 222. **British Consulate**: 8 An. Laoumtzi St, ✆ 26 203.

Festivals

25 March, Evangelismós at Asfendíou; **23 April**, Ag. Geórgios at Pylí; **24 June**, Ag. Ioánnis, bonfires everywhere; **29 June**, Ag. Apóstoli at Antimácheia; **29 August**, Ag. Ioánnis at Kéfalos. In **August** the *Hippocratia* features art exhibitions, concerts, theatre and films. **8 September**, Panagías at Kardaména; **21 November**, Isódia tis Panagías at Ziá; **6 December**, Ag. Nikólaos at Kos.

Kos Town

Bustling **Kos**, capital city and main port, is roughly in the region of the dolphin's eye. As you sail into the harbour it looks magical, especially at twilight, the port still guarded by a medieval castle, the silhouettes of mountains behind, with its lush garden setting, the multitude of flowers and stately palm trees and the fragrant scent of jasmine in the air; opposite, the coast of Turkey fills the horizon. Close up, the town doesn't quite live up to the promise. Most of it postdates the 1933 earthquake, although this means it has more Art Deco buildings than the average Greek island town. Another side-effect of the quake: when the rubble was cleared away several ancient sites were revealed, leaving a serene Greek and Roman oasis of antiquities peppered among throbbing holiday bedlam—Greece has only two licensed tattoo artists, and one of them is here. Declared 'European City of 1995' for its self-improvements, a new water treatment system guarantees pristine beaches, the monuments are being restored and new pedestrian areas and a one-way system have been established to cut down on some of the cacophony. But the tourist fleshpots have not lost any of their garishness: no lack of fast food, touts, T-shirt shops, and even a hard sell from the excursion boats all lit up along the front.

One block up from the harbour, the city's main square **Plateía Eleftherías** has been freed of cars, leaving it eerie and empty, like a Pirandello character in search of a play. Here you'll find the 18th-century **Defterdar Mosque** (*still used by the 50 or so Muslim families on the island, not open to the public*) and two Italian Art Deco buildings. One, laid out like a Roman house, holds the **Archaeology Museum** (✆ 28 326, *open Tues–Sun, 8.30–3; adm*). The prize exhibit is a 4th-

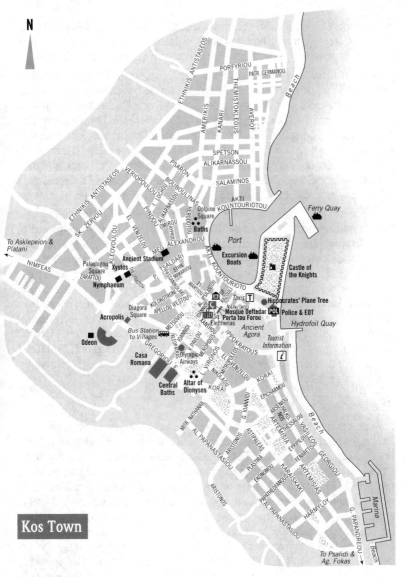

N

To Asklepeion & Platani

NIMFEAS

ETHNIKIS ANTISTASEOS

SK. ZERVOU

ELEVOULOU

VERIOPOULOU

PINDOU

EL. VENIZELOU

OMIROU

AMERIKIS

KANARI

AVEROF

PORFYRIOU

PATR. GERMANOU

THEMISTOKLEOUS

Beach

AKTI KOUNTOURIOTOU

Ferry Quay

ETHNIKIS ANTISTASEOS

PSARON

BOUBOULINAS

LOCHOU

SIMARNASSOU

HERODOTOU

SPETSON

ALIKARNASSOU

SALAMINOS

Dolpine Square

Baths

Port

Excursion Boats

MEG. ALEXANDROU

TSALDARI

P. TSALDARI

ETHN. MAKARIOU

MARTIOU

25

Castle of the Knights

Ancient Stadium

Paleologou Square

ZARAFTOU

Xystos

Nymphaeum

KOLOKOTRONI

APELLOU

IFESTOU

METSOVOU

ALIKARNASSOU

KOLOKOTRONI

Hippocrates' Plane Tree

Taxis

Mosque Defterdar

Porta tou Forou

Sq. Eleftherias

NAFKLIROU

Police & EOT

POL

Hydrofoil Quay

Acropolis

Diagora Square

Ancient Agora

Tourist Information

Bus Station to Villages

GREGORIOU

IOANNIDI

PINDOU

ALEKRATOUS

IPPOKRATOUS

Odeon

Casa Romana

Olympic Airways

Central Baths

Altar of Dionysos

NIKOLAOU

KORAI

KORAI

MITROP. VENIZELOU

VIRONOS

EL. VENIZELOU

NEOFYTOU

AKROPOLIS

MITR. NATHANAIL

AL. PAPANASTASIOU

ARISTONOS

PLASTIRA

ASTIPALEAS

EKONOMOU

PAPATHEOFANOUS

KARAISKAKI

ARTEMISIAS

KORAI

EPICHARMOU

ARSENIOU

ARTEMISIA

EVRIPILOU

VASILEOS GEORGIOU

FENAREIOS

HARMYLOU

G. PAPANDREOU

Marina

Beach

To Psalidi & Ag. Fokas

Kos Town

century BC statue of Hippocrates with a noble, compassionate expression; other items include an intriguing fragment of an archaic Symposium, a 2nd-century AD seated Hermes, with a little pet ram and red thumb, a statuette of a pugilist with enormous boxing gloves, and another of Hygeia, the goddess of health, feeding an egg to a snake. There are also fine mosaics, of a fish and of the god Asklepios with his snake, stepping from a boat and being welcomed by Hippocrates. The upper floor and its collection of Geometric–Roman era ceramics may reopen in 1999.

Plateía Eleftherías also has the city's **market**—walk through it to Ag. Paraskévi square with its shady cafés, and don't miss the superb bougainvillaea arching over the back of the market. Buying and selling is old hat here; Plateía Eleftherías also has the entrance into the ancient **Agora** by way of the **Pórta tou Foroú**, draped with another massive bougainvillaea. This was where the Knights of St John built their town and *auberges*, just as in Rhodes (*see* p.116). When these collapsed in the earthquake, they revealed not only the market, with the re-erected columns of its *stoa*, but the harbour quarter of the ancient city, a temple of Aphrodite Pandemos, and a 5th-century Christian basilica. While wandering round, you'll probably stumble across trails of dried cat food scattered by the Kos Animal Protection League.

On the northern end of the Agora, Plateía Platánou is almost entirely filled by **Hippocrates' plane tree**, its trunk 52ft in diameter, its huge boughs now supported by an intricate metal scaffolding instead of the marble columns that once kept the venerable tree from disaster. At an estimated 700 years old it could easily be the most senior plane tree in Europe. Hippocrates may well have taught under its great-grandmother, for he believed, as do modern Greeks, that of all the trees the shade of the plane is the most salubrious (*see* p.72). The Turks loved the old plane just as much and built a fountain under it with a sarcophagus for a basin, and overlooking it constructed the lovely **Mosque of the Loggia** (1786). On 1 September the citizens of Kos pluck a leaf from the tree to include in their harvest wreaths as a symbol of abundance.

The Castle of the Knights

A stone bridge off Plateía Platánou takes you over the former moat (now the Finilon, or palm grove) to the entrance of the **Castle of the Knights of St John**, (© 28 326, *open Tues–Sun, 8.30–3*). Combined with their fortress across the strait in Bodrum, this was the premier outer defence of Rhodes. After an earthquake in 1495, Grand Master Pierre d'Aubusson rebuilt the walls and added the outer enceinte, and the tower overlooking the harbour bears his name and coat of arms. Since d'Aubusson mostly used stones from the Agora, the masonry is a curious patchwork quilt of ancient inscriptions and reliefs of the knights' coats of arms. Some have been removed to the castle's **antiquarium**, to join other stacks of defunct columns and marble that nobody seems to know what to do with. The castle's dishevelled weeds and wildflowers and the stillness of the noonday sun attracted director Werner Herzog, who set his first black and white film *Signs of Life* (1966) partly within its walls, although the elaborate cockroach traps and hypnotized chickens that played a major role are no longer in evidence.

Roman Kos

From Plateía Eleftherías, Vass. Pávlou leads to Kos' other main archaeological sites. In the quarter called the Seraglio, Minoan and Mycenaean houses were found as well as later structures. Opposite the Olympic Airways office stands a ramped Hellenistic **Altar of Dionysos**, and across Grigoríou Street, the ruins of **Central Baths** (site of the Vourina spring praised by Theocritus) and the **Casa Romana** (✆ 23 234; *open Tues–Sun, 8.30–3; adm*), both victims of the earthquake of AD 554, and excavated and reconstructed in grim concrete shell by the Italians in 1940 (currently the reconstructions are being reconstructed). The house, begun in the Hellenistic era, has well-preserved mosaics and offers a fair idea of the spacious elegance the wealthy could aspire to; even on the hottest days it remains cool inside. To the west along Grigoríou Street the **Roman Odeon** or concert hall has its rows of white marble seats, partially restored by the Italians; the statue of Hippocrates was discovered under its arches. Besides this the city had three other theatres and a music school. Strabo wrote of it: 'The city of the Koans is not large, but one lives better here than in others, and it appears beautiful to all who pass it by in their ships'.

Some of this good living is evident in **Western Excavations** just opposite. On one side of the main path rise the great Hellenistic walls built around the **acropolis** (now studded with a minaret); on the other side you can pick out the marble paved *Cardo* and *Decumanus*, the main arteries of Roman Kos, lined with ruined houses. Although the Italians took many of the best mosaics off to Rhodes, some good bits remain (often under a protective layer of sand), especially the **House of Europa**, on the *Decumanus*. Just north of this, lining the *Cardo*, is an elegant 3rd-century BC **Nymphaeum** or fountain house which supplied running water to the nearby **public toilets** with marble seats. The gymnasium has a **Xystos**, a running track covered by a marble colonnade, used in the winter months—a rare ancient luxury that even Kos' most luxurious beach hotels lack. The Romans also had a heated pool near the brick **baths** (the *thermae* still survive). Part of this was transformed into a Christian basilica in the 5th century; the lintel has been rebuilt and the baptistry has a well-preserved font. At the north end, an unidentified 3rd-century BC building contains mosaics of battling bulls, bears and boars. The **Stadium** is a block north along Tsaldári Street; only a few of the seats have been excavated, but on the far side near the church is a well-preserved *aphesis* or starting gate.

Beaches near Kos Town

Since the advent of the water treatment plant these have won blue flags for cleanliness, but that's about the nicest thing you can say about them. The sandy and pebbly beaches are packed with rows of sunbeds and umbrellas edge-to-edge; in places along Vassiléos Georgíou the smell of gallons of sun lotion is overpowering. The city bus will take you in a few minutes to better, less crowded beaches to the north of town at **Lambí** (ΛΑΜΠΙ), now occupied by package tourists rather than the military; the closest strands to the south are at **Psalídi** (ΨΑΛΙΔΙ), 3km away, and **Ag. Fokás** (8km), both sporting fancy hotel complexes. For something more remote, get your own transport to continue to **Embrós Thermá** (13km), where volcanic black sands and thermal springs make the bathing a little warmer; a new spa is currently planned to replace the old hot pit where the water oozes out.

Sports

Learn to **dive** from certified instructors at the Kos Diving Center, 6 Koritsas Sq, ℰ 20 269/22 782; if you can already, try Dolphin Divers, whose boat is moored with the excursion craft. The proximity of Turkey and other islands makes for lovely **sailing**: Sunsail, 3 Artemisias, ℰ 27 547, or Kavos Moorings, 7 Themistokleous, ℰ 27 115. Go **riding** in Mármari (*see* below).

Kos Town ✉ *85300,* ℰ *(0242–)*   **Where to Stay**

In days of yore, ill visitors would stay in the Asklepeion and sacrifice a chicken to the gods. These days beds can be so scarce in high season that you still might need that chicken. Book, or if you get offered a room as you get off the ferry, take it. If you want to stay in the centre *and* get a good night's sleep, buy earplugs. Package companies block book everything in the moderate range, so splurge or slum.

expensive

These are all A class and out in Psalídi. **Hippocrates Palace Hotel**, ℰ 24 401, ℬ 24 410, has Olympic Health Centre spa, indoor and outdoor pools, tennis. *Open Mar–Nov.* The new **Kipriotis Village**, ℰ 27 640, ℬ 23 590, is huge and packed with amenities: two pools, one Olympic-sized; hammam, tennis, jacuzzi, gym, etc. Also rooms for the disabled. **Dimitra Beach**, ℰ 28 581, is another beachside complex; or there's the neo-Venetian, air-conditioned **Platanista**, ℰ 27 551, ℬ 25 029, with tennis and pool. **Ramira Beach**, ℰ 28 489, is cheaper than the others.

inexpensive

Afendoulis, 1 Evripílou ℰ 25 321/797, is a friendly pension with jasmine-filled terrace in a quiet road near the sea, run by Ippokrátis and brother Aléxis Zíkas of the **Pension Alexis**, 9 Irodótou, ℰ 28 798 (*E*), the Mecca for back-packers and young budget travellers. **Acropol**, Tsaldári 4, ℰ 22 244 (*C*), has OK rooms in an old house with lush garden. **Hara**, 6 Halkonos, ℰ 22 500 (*D*), is a pleasant small hotel near the Chinese restaurant. **Kos Camping**, ℰ 23 910, 3km from the port is a well-run site with a wide range of facilities from laundry to bike hire. A minibus meets the ferries.

Eating out in town is like playing Russian roulette if you want real food. Avoid the harbour front, where waiters aggressively *kamáki* or 'harpoon' punters in. By far the loveliest place to dine is the **Anatolia Hamam,** 3 Diagora Square, ✆ 28 323, in the sumptuously restored Turkish bath, with a garden terrace; the food has an appropriate Anatolian touch. By the beach, at Vass. Georgíou, **Miramare** serves good Greek dishes at normal prices. One of the most authentic and reasonably priced tavernas, hidden way in the back streets (you'll have to ask half a dozen times to find it, but it's worth it), **Kouros** on G. Papandreaou by the marina has fancy international dishes in a romantic garden setting. **Barba George** near Omírou is good and does an excellent *exohikó* or country-style spit roast; in contrast the chic **Bristol**, on Vass. Giorgíou, ✆ 22 865, offers some Chinese dishes. On the same street the sparkling **Chevalier**, ✆ 23 053, has a French menu, with prices to match. The **Kástro**, near the ancient Agora on 15 Hippocratous, ✆ 23 692, belongs in the same league except the setting is much more alluring. Atmospheric **Platanos**, next to Hippocrates' tree, combines OK international and traditional dishes, cakes, live music and tables on the roof garden. For a real neighbourhood taverna with good food, big portions and low prices,try **Antonis** at Koutarys St, behind Hotel Anna on Megalos Alexandros St, or for even better food go out to **Taverna Ambavri**, a ten-minute walk south of the Casa Romana. *Ouzeries* are reappearing: **Kohili**, 9 Arlikannassou and Amerikis has the finest *mezédes* but they don't come cheap.

On the way to Psalídi near the Ramira Beach Hotel, **Syntrivani** still retains a Greek ambience and traditional food; ditto **Nestoras** near the campsite.

Entertainment and Nightlife

Kos is one big party at night. The ancient Agora is alive with the thumping sound of house music from the 'Disco Alley' on pedestrian Navklírou Street where every establishment is a bar pumping out conflicting sounds. Discos go in and out of fashion season by season but **Playboy**, Kanári 2, has a laser show and **Kalua** and **Heaven**, both at Lámbi, also have a watery backyard and garden. For Greek music and rembetika, there's **Happy Club**, Navarinou 1. **Jazz Opera**, 5 Arseniou, plays jazz, funk, reggae and the blues. If you want to catch a film **Orpheus** has an indoor screen in Plateía Eleftherías and an outdoor screen along Vass. Georgiou St, ✆ 25 713. For anyone homesick for football, rugby, cricket or just about any other sport, **Taurus Bar**, 9 Mandilara St, keeps up with all the scores and events and shows many matches live.

The Asklepeion

City bus to Plátani or a short bike climb will take you up to the **Asklepeion** (ΑΣΚΛΕΠΕΙΟΝ; ✆ 28 763; *open Tues–Sun, 8.30–3; adm*), 4km west of the city. This was one of the ancient world's most important shrines to the healing god Asklepios, served by the Asklepiada, a secret order of priests, who found that good water and air and relaxing in beautiful surroundings did much to remedy the ills of body and soul. The cult symbol was the snake, the ancestor of that on the modern medical symbol, twining itself around the caduceus. Snakes, sacred intermediaries between the living and the dead (they were often found in holes in cemeteries, eating mice fattened on grave offerings), were believed to have a knack for seeking out healing herbs and transmitting dreams, which were part of the therapy—the Asklepiada made good use of hallucinogens and the power of suggestions. The sanctuary on Kos was built after the death of Hippocrates, who left a whole school of disciples behind him, but most of the buildings date from the Hellenistic age, when the earthquake-damaged Asklepeion was last reconstructed. Many of the structures were cannibalized by the Knights, who found it too convenient a quarry.

After the 16th century, however, the site was covered by the dust of centuries and forgotten. In 1896 a French archaeologist named Payet searched in vain for the Asklepeion; in 1899 the German Herzog, a keen student of the history of Kos, came to the island and, believing he could succeed where Payet failed, got permission from the Turks to dig for it in 1902. Believing that he was following Strabo's description he dug in Marmarato and found only tombs. He did, however, meet an enthusiastic Koan named Iakovos Zaraftis who told him that he was digging in the wrong place and should turn his spade on a place the Turks called Kanza Baxese, the 'village garden'. Herzog refused at first, but Zaraftis insisted, and even offered to pay the wages of 20 labourers if they failed to unearth the Asklepeion. Herzog, laughing, gave in, and Zaraftis and his crew began to dig, growing increasingly angry as the German laughed at their efforts—until, of course, they found it. Herzog at once rushed over to the telegraph office in Bodrum to notify the world of his great discovery, without a word of credit for Zaraftis. Herzog finished excavating the site in 1904, and smuggled out many of its finest antiquities. The Asklepeion was partially restored by the Italians during their tenure.

The Site

Set on a hillside, the Asklepeion is built in a series of terraces sliced by a grand stair. On the lowest level are Roman baths, built in the 3rd century AD. The next level, once surrounded by a huge portico, has the main entrance and another large bath; here were the medical school and the museum of anatomy and pathology, with descriptions of cures and votive offerings from grateful patients. Near the stair are the remains of a temple dedicated by the Kos-born physician G. Stertinius

Xenophon, who served as the Emperor Claudius' personal doctor and murdered his patient by sticking a poisoned feather down his throat before retiring on Kos as a hero (so much for the Hippocratic Oath!). On this level, too, was the sacred spring of the god Pan, used in the cures. On the next terrace is the altar of Asklepios, and Ionic temples dedicated to Apollo and Asklepios (a few of the columns have been reconstructed by the Italians); on the top stood a Doric temple of Asklepios from the 2nd century BC, the grandest and most sacred of all, and enjoying a view that in itself might shake away the blues. In August, for the *Hippocratia*, the teenagers of Kos get off their motorbikes for a day to don ancient chitons and wreaths to re-enact the old rituals and recite the Hippocratic oath.

Just up the road, the modern **International Hippocrates Foundation** is dedicated to medical research. In 1996 several Nobel Prize winners and other leading lights attended the first 'International Medical Olympiad' here, and no, they didn't hold brain surgery races, but gave out awards and held conferences. Plans are to hold similar Olympiads every five years, in a 'City of Hippocrates' to be built around the foundation. Here the five rings of the Olympic symbol are used to sum up Hippocratic philosophy: 'Life is short. Science is long. Opportunity is elusive. Experiment is dangerous. Judgement is difficult.'

Platáni

On the way back to Kos town, downhill all the way along the cool cypress-lined avenue, stop for refreshments in Platáni, Kos' main Turkish settlement, although tension since the Cyprus troubles has decreased population by two-thirds. The Greeks hang out at the *kafeneíon* while the Muslim majority frequent the cafés at the crossroads. A little out of Platáni, on the road back to the harbour, the **Jewish Cemetery** stands in a pine grove near the Muslim graveyard. The inscriptions on its headstones end abruptly after 1940. Without any parishioners, the pretty synagogue back in Kos Town (4 Alexándrou Diákou, by the ancient Agora) has been converted into the civic cultural centre.

Eating Out

They're busy and a bit touristy, like everything on Kos, but Turkish food in Platáni's tavernas is excellent and relatively cheap; the best of the bunch is the **Arap**, offering excellent aubergine with yoghurt, borek, grilled kebabs and chicken. If you want a more peaceful setting, try the taverna on the way down the hill.

Around Kos

The northeast of Kos is flat and very fertile, with fields of watermelons and tomatoes. Beyond Lambí and the reach of the town bus, **Tingáki** (ΤΙΓΚΑΚΙ) is a smart little resort overlooking the island of Psérimos and still has a village feel, especially when the day-trippers have gone. In March and April the nearby salt-pans, Alikes, are a favourite port of call for flamingoes and numerous migratory birds, while the sandy coast and estuary are a loggerhead turtle nesting area. On the far end of the wet lands, **Marmári** (ΜΑΡΜΑΡΙ) has a generous sandy beach and a chance to explore on horseback at the **Marmari Riding Centre**, ✆ 41 783. Just inland, two ruined Byzantine basilicas (Ag. Pávlos and Ag. Ioánnis) lie on the outskirts of **Zipári**; above, Kos' spinal ridge has a bumpy, curiously one-dimensional profile.

From Zipári the road ascends to **Asfendíou**, a cluster of five peaceful hamlets set in the woods, with whitewashed houses and flower-filled gardens, many now being turned into holiday homes. The highest of the five hamlets, **Ziá**, is a pretty place of fresh springs, fruit and walnut groves—the bucolic Pryioton described by Theocritus—now converted into a 'traditional village' for package tours, receiving busloads every evening for the spectacular sunsets and a Disneylandish Greek Night out in the schlocky tavernas; but there are others, such as the excellent Olympiada, minus dancing 'oopa oopa' waiters. Kos' ancient sculptors came up here to quarry marble from Kos' highest peak **Díkaios Christós**, 'Justice of Christ' (846m), the summit of which can be reached without too much difficulty in about three hours from Ziá, and well worth it for the god-like views of Dodecanese and Turkey.

From the Asfendíou a road runs across country to **Lagoúdi** and continues from there to **Amaníou**, where there's a turn off to **Palaío Pýli**, a Byzantine capital of Kos, a ghost town on a crag surrounded by concentric walls camouflaged in the rocks. Within its walls is the church of Panagía Ypapandí, built in the 11th century by the Blessed Christódoulos before he made a trade for land on Pátmos; it and two others, Ag. Antonio and Ag. Nikólaos, have 14th-century frescoes. Another side lane, just west of Amaníou, leads to the **Charmyleion**, an ancient *herioön*, hero's tomb in the shape of a tholos, with twelve little vaults, reused as a church crypt. The modern grotty village of **Pýli** below is a major agriculture centre, although the upper part of town has a great place to stop for lunch, in the taverna by a handsome spring-fed fountain or *pygí*, built in 1592. On 23 April, for the feast of St George, Pýli holds a horse race, with an Easter egg as prize, cracked on the forehead of the winning horse—a custom going back to remotest antiquity. Further west, in a wild setting and enjoying more great sunset views, the **Castle of Antimácheia** was built by the Knights as a prison in the mid-14th century. Within its great battle-mented triangular walls are two churches (one with a fresco of St Christopher carrying baby Jesus), a few surviving cisterns and, over the gateway, the arms of Pierre d'Aubusson. The sprawling village of **Antimácheia**, near the airport, has the island's last operational windmill as its landmark, wheat grinder and museum, along with some traditional stone houses; even better, head up to **Pláka** on a paved road from the airport, a green oasis and favourite picnic ground with more sunsets.

There are beaches on either coast: on the south coast, the sand stretches between **Tolíri** and **Kardaména** (ΚΑΡΔΑΜΑΙΝΑ), once a charming fishing village famous for its ceramics and now a heaving resort. Commercialized to Costa Brava proportions, it's very much the Brit and Scandinavian family package destination, complete with pubs, chips and smorgasbord. But there is also golden sand, boats to Níssyros, and watersports and entertainment for all ages. On the north coast, **Mastichári** (ΜΑΣΤΙΧΑΡΙ) is quieter, and has frequent boats for Kálymnos and Psérimos, and, a 20-minute walk beyond the Kanari Beach hotel, the ruins of a 5th-century **basilica of Ag. Ioánnes** with a fine mosaic floor.

There are more mosaics (again, under a layer of sand), Ionian columns and remains of an atrium and baptistries, the extensive ruins of the lovely twin 5th-century basilicas of **Ag. Stéfanos** near the beach at **Kamári**. In the bay you can see the islet of **Kastri**, a natural volcanic bulwark, often surrounded by windsurfers skimming over the blue sheet, with a Club Med complex as a foreground. A long fringe of sand runs under the cliffs to the east with a few access roads; the steepest descent is to pretty **Camel Beach** by picturesque rocks and the easiest to **Paradise Beach**, or 'Bubble Beach' for the bubbles that rise to the surface through the clear waters at one end of the bay; it's perfect for children, although they'll have to fight their way through the sunbeds and umbrellas to get to the water. Further along the headland to the left, the beaches **Lagáda** (or Banana; generally considered the most beautiful with its dunes), **Sunny**, **Poléni** (or Magic) and **Xerokambos** are much quieter although still offering their share of sunbeds, parasols and little cantinas.

The road twists up to **Kéfalos** (ΚΕΦΑΛΟΣ) to the west, high up on the headland of the dolphin's tail. It's where the bus terminates, and when the hotels are bursting-full elsewhere you just may find a room here. Another Knights' castle stands looking over Kamári and isn't particularly impressive, although it inspired many travellers' tales in the Middle Ages, all involving a dragon; Mandeville in his *Travels* claims the serpent was none other than Hippocrates' daughter, enchanted by Artemis and awaiting a knight brave enough to kiss her to transform her back into a maiden. South, just off the road, there's a Byzantine chapel of the Panagía built out of a temple that once belonged to the ancient capital of Kos, **Astypálaia** (signposted Palatia), the birthplace of Hippocrates. A few bits of the ancient city remain, including a theatre. Isthmioton, another ancient city on the peninsula, was important enough in the past to send its own delegation to Délos, but not a trace of it remains. A track descends to **Ag. Theológos** beach, offering some of the island's most secluded swimming (but often big waves) and a nice taverna. Neolithic remains from 3500 BC were found in the **Áspri Pétra cave** just south, reached by an unmarked path. The road passes through dramatic scenery, sheer cliffs and a telecommunications tower, then ends at the charming **Monastery Ag. Ioánnis Thimianós,** 6km from Kéfalos.

Tingáki/Marmári ✉ 85300

In Tingáki, **Park Lane**, 150m back from the beach, ✆ 69
651 (*B; exp–mod*) is a fine family hotel, with pool and
playground and friendly staff. **Meni Beach**, ✆ 69 217
(*C; mod*) is close to the sea, or try **Paxinos**, ✆ 69 306
(*C; inexp*). In Marmári, the **Caravia Beach**, ✆ 41 291, 📠 41 215 (*lux*), is
a super club hotel set in beautiful grounds a little out of town with a vast
range of facilities. *Open April–Oct.*

Mastichári ✉ 85301

Mastichari Bay, ✆ 59 300, 📠 59 307 (*A; exp*) is good for families, with
lots of activities, floodlit tennis, open air theatre and satellite TV.
Mastichari Beach, ✆ 51 371 (*C; mod*) is near the harbour; the **Arant**,
✆ 51 167 (*C; mod–inexp*) and the cheerful **Zevgas**, ✆ 51 622, 📠 22 059
(*E; inexp*) with en suite bathrooms are also good bets. The long-established
Taverna Makis is just off the waterside and reliably good.

Kardaména ✉ 85302

Kardaména has scores of hotels, but unless you go on a package you may
only find rooms on the edges of the season. **Porto Bello Beach**, ✆ 91 217
(*B; exp*) has a luxurious setting with views of Níssyros. **Lakitira** between
Kardaména and Kéfalos, ✆ 91 537 📠 91 541 (*A; exp*), has a vast range of
facilities and an endless amount of sports from aerobics to 'Crazy Banana',
and teachers to show you how do them. **Restaurant Andreas** refuses to
pander to tourists and has a nice ethnic range of dishes; Kardaména lives it
up with happy hours and has something for night owls of all ages.

Kéfalos ✉ 85301

Panorama, overlooking Kastri island, ✆/📠 71 524, has apartments that
live up to its name and a garden; breakfast available. Down by the sea,
there's **Kokkalikis Beach** ✆ 71 466 (*C; mod*) with a pool and **Kordistos**,
✆ 71 251 (*C; mod*) with a decent restaurant. In the hill village **Esmeralda**
does quails and liver as well as more usual Greek fare; **Kastro** has OK food
and a good view of the bay; **Stamata** by the sea has a wide selection of fish,
including 'dogs' teeth' for adventurous diners.

A Day Trip to Bodrum

Bodrum, set in a sunny region of spectacular scenery, is the most sophisticated
resort on Turkey's Aegean coast (even though its name means 'dungeon' in

Turkish). It occupies the site of ancient Halicarnassus, a Carian city colonized by the Dorians and later part of the Hexapolis. In the 6th century the other five members gave Halicarnassus the boot: it was too ambitious and too susceptible to Ionian free-thinking. Although the city soon came under direct Persian rule, the spirit of enquiry survived to inspire Herodotus (485–420 BC), 'the father of history': after being exiled from Halicarnassus in 457 BC for conspiring against the Persians he travelled extensively around the Mediterranean before settling in a Greek colony in southern Italy, from where in his *History* he offered the first account of people, customs and events (in particular the Persian Wars) without resorting to the gods for an explanation, in the same spirit as Hippocrates.

Halicarnassus' most glorious period came under the Hellenophile satrap Mausolus, who made himself king of a powerful, independent Caria from 377 to 353 BC. He was so pleased with himself that he began the Mausoleum to his glory, which his widow (and sister) Artemisia II finished as a tomb to beat all tombs, one of the Seven Wonders of the World. Artemisia baited the Greeks so much that they put a price on her head 'thinking it a matter of great shame for a woman to make war on Athens.' It was her younger sister, Queen Ada of Alinda, who became a good buddy of Alexander and encouraged him to attack Halicarnassus in 334 BC; for Ada's sake Alexander spared the Mausoleum but little else.

When the Knights of St John lost their castle in Smyrna to Tamerlane in 1402 they came here; finding the Mausoleum toppled by an earthquake, they used it as a quarry to build their Castle of St Peter. It was one of their key fortresses, along with Kos and Rhodes. One of their most interesting visitors was the Ottoman Great Pretender, Cem Sultan, younger brother of Beyazit II. Cem thought the Knights would assist him in his frequent attempts to depose his brother, but the Knights, paid off handsomely by Beyazit, had other ideas, and kept him as a hostage. They handed him over to Pope Alexander VI, the Borgia pope, who made a small fortune on the ransom before poisoning Cem.

The Town

Bodrum follows the classic Turkish resort plan closely: castle in the middle next to a port lined with seafood restaurants and full of excursion boats waiting to take you on cruises around the peninsula. Farmers bring in camels for the tourist to ride. Just north of the castle is the frenetic **bazaar district**, where mountains of gold and hecatombs of leather await tourists. Shopkeepers keep a sharp eye on the arcades, ready to pounce on anyone who stops to look in the window. At the centre, with some of the swankiest shops, is the restored 18th-century **Hacimolla Hani**.

The castle of St Peter, on its tiny neck of land, neatly divides the harbour into two parts. Dreadnoughts of the wealthy tie up at the yacht marina in the West Harbour, but the action is to the east, along pedestrianized **Dr Alim Bey Caddesi/**

Cumhiriyet Caddesi. Here the real tourist inferno begins—a rather jolly one, as tourist infernos go, with more food and carpets and jewellery lurching out at you from every shop window, perused by cosmopolitan crowds of happy campers.

The Castle of St Peter

The Knights' castle (*open daily exc Mon; adm*), standing high on a small rocky peninsula over the original Carian settlement, now houses a superb museum—the world's largest—of underwater archaeology, thanks to state-of-the-art expeditions financed by *National Geographic* and other benefactors. It also offers a well preserved example of the Knights' fortifications—it was never captured and was only surrendered by the Knights after Suleiman's taking of Rhodes. Because they ruled the seas, they concentrated their defences on the landward side. Near the first of seven gates you'll see some of their 250 coats of arms embedded in the walls, as well as reliefs and other architectural fragments reused from the Mausoleum. A wooden bridge replaces the old drawbridge leading into the outer citadel, where a small **Gothic chapel** contains a Bronze Age collection, much of it brought up from the sea—the oldest and in many ways most fascinating wreck in the museum is a Mycenaean vessel, salvaged and reconstructed; other wrecks, a 4th-century BC ship and a 7th-century AD Byzantine galley, have also yielded rich finds. They have proved invaluable in dating artefacts found around the Mediterranean: a ship, after all, sinks with its cargo at a definite time; a city slowly disappears under the dust.

One of the towers, the **Snake Tower** (named for the relief over the door), contains a theatre of amphorae. Each city state had its own trademark amphorae that guaranteed the quality of the contents to clients, although just like today producers of mediocre wine or oil were not above copying the more successful exporters and selling their products in counterfeit amphorae, a few of which are on display in the courtyard. Four towers of the different 'tongues' survive: the **German Tower**, near the hammam, built for prisoners when the castle served as a state prison; the **Italian Tower** and the **French Tower**, the tallest of all, offer wonderful views of Bodrum and its two harbours on either side of the peninsula. The **English Tower**, done up to replicate the life and times of the Knights, complete with Turks dressed as knights and ladies serving glasses of wine, has the arms of Edward Plantagenet on the west wall. Inside the marble window sills, note the names and dates carved during long hours of idleness. Perhaps they were secretly relieved when England was expelled from the Order upon Henry VIII's divorce from Catherine of Aragon.

Further chambers in the castle have been arranged to display collections of ancient and medieval glass, coins, and jewellery; best of all is the **Hall of the Carian Princess**. In 1989 a sarcophagus was discovered in Bodrum, belonging to a woman who was probably a member of the same dynasty as King Mausolus, sometime in the 4th century BC. Besides rich jewellery and furnishings, enough of the body and clothing remained for a medical team from the University of Manchester to attempt a reconstruction of the poor girl in clay. They've got her standing in a niche, wearing a rich ball gown and looking for all the world like Imelda Marcos.

The Mausoleum

What little remains of the legendary **Mausoleum of Halicarnassus** is a bit outside the bustling trendy centre of Bodrum on Turgutreis Caddesi. Designed by the great Ionian architect Pytheos, only the massive foundations remain, capable of supporting a 200ft pile. Models on the site tentatively reconstruct it, and there are a few copies of its reliefs, most of which were carted off to the British Museum.

The Mausoleum was the biggest tomb ever built by the ancient Greeks, and not just its name has come down to us: it has been imitated ever since (as in the Masonic Temple in Washington DC, a full-size copy). The only ancient monument of Halicarnassus to survive is the restored amphitheatre, with an original seating capacity of 10,000, north of the Mausoleum on Göktepe.

Psérimos (ΨΕΡΙΜΟΣ)

Psérimos, wedged between Kos and Kálymnos, has a beautiful sandy beach which its 70 residents have come to regard as a curse, as day in and day out it becomes invisible under rows of day-trippers like well-oiled sardines during high season. Even in September excursion boats from Kos town, Mastichári and Kálymnos queue up to dock, the tavernas are thronged and the islanders short-tempered. It becomes even more crowded on 15 August, when hundreds of pilgrims attend the *panegýri* at its monastery, Grafiótissa. If you are staying any length of time (when the day boats have gone the people become quite friendly), you'll probably want to take to the interior by day or hunt up one of the smaller pebbly strands on the east coasts; the main beach can be murder. Some boats now head instead to the adjacent islet of **Platí**, with another sandy beach, and make a day of it by stopping for lunch in Kálymnos.

Psérimos ℮ (0243–)   **Where to Stay and Eating Out**

The seaside **Tripolitis**, ℮ 23 196, is pleasant, located over Mr Saroukos's taverna; the **Pension Niki-Ross** is also worth a try (Ross is Australian Greek). The **monastery** has simple accommodation for up to 10 people. There are a few rooms to be had in the village; try **Katerina Xiloura**, ℮ 23 497, or **Glynatsis** on ℮ 23 596. If not you can sleep out on one of the island's more distant beaches, a kilometre from the village. Most of the tavernas on the main beach are packed, and the service in them surly at lunchtime. The unnamed one with the garden area does excellent and reasonably priced fresh *kalamári*.

Léros (ΛΕΡΟΣ)

With its serrated coastline like an intricate jigsaw puzzle piece, sweeping hills, tree-fringed beaches and unspoiled villages, Léros is a beautiful, underrated and much misunderstood island. Few places have had such a bad press, both as an isle of exile and home to Greece's most notorious mental institutions. Yet the people are welcoming and friendly, and visitors who discover the island's charms are often hooked.

Léros has long been the butt of ignorant jokes in Greece, where its name evokes the same reaction as 'Bedlam' in Britain; to make matters worse, Léros sounds like *léra*, 'filth' or 'rogue'. The 1989 Channel 4 documentary exposing the grim conditions in the hospitals was another blow, but it prodded the authorities to get their act together. Dutch medical teams have been working to improve conditions; a care-in-the-community scheme was set up and you might see patients in the villages. But they are not intrusive, and, to be frank, you're likely to see more lost souls wandering the streets back home.

Léros is not a dreary or downbeat island. Green and pretty, it offers little strands of shingly sand, very clear waters, excellent fish tavernas and a lively but very Greek nightlife. It is an exceptionally musical place, home of the famous Hajiadákis dynasty whose folk songs have influenced Greece's leading composers; it's not at all rare to hear the *santoúri* or the *tsamboúna*, as well as the more usual instruments playing dances such as the Soústa, Passoumáki and the ancient Dance of the Broom. The ancient island of Artemis, Léros has a special atmosphere you either love or hate. The bad press shields the island from the masses and might help preserve its charm.

History

On the death of the hero Meleager (of Chalydonian boar hunt fame), his sisters mourned him so passionately that Artemis turned them into guinea fowl and put them in her temple at Léros. This worship of the goddess of the chase and the guinea fowl might be traced back to Ionians from Miletus who colonized Léros; Robert Graves notes that, because of their religious conservatism and refusal to adopt the patriarchal state religion of Olympos, the Greeks called the Leriots 'evil-livers' (an epigram went, 'The Lerians are all bad, not merely some Lerians, but every one of them—all except Prokles, and of course he is a Lerian too'). Fittingly for an island dedicated to Artemis, property has been passed down through the female line, to the extent that most of Léros is owned at least on paper by women.

Homer included Léros with Kálymnos as the 'Kalydian isles' in his *Catalogue of Ships*. The island sided with Sparta in the Peloponnesian War, despite its Ionian ancestry. Under the Romans pirates preyed among the islets that surround Léros; some nabbed a young lawyer named Julius Caesar on his way back to Rome from Bithynia, where according to rumour he had a dissolute affair with the governor;

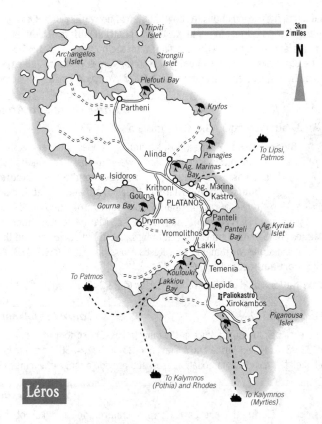

Léros

released after a month when his ransom was paid, Caesar later got his revenge by capturing and crucifying every brigand around Léros. Under the Byzantines the island was controlled by Sámos, but in 1316 it was sold to the Knights of St John and governed by the Duke of Náxos as part of the monastic state of Pátmos.

Léros paid a high price for its excellent anchorages in the Second World War. After 1912 the occupying Italians built their main air and naval ordnance bases at Lépida. Their Eastern Mediterranean fleet was based in Lakkí Bay; when Churchill sent the British to occupy the island after the Italian surrender in 1943, Hitler sent in an overwhelming force of paratroopers to take it back, causing a good deal of damage in the Battle of Léros (November 12–16). The Allies in turn bombed the German fleet at Lakkí, and for three years after the War the British fleet took its place. When the junta took power in 1967 Communist dissidents were imprisoned in the notorious camp in Panthéni; during the later Cyprus dispute the Greek government dismantled its military installations to show that it had no warlike intentions against Turkey. One of the brightest lights in Australian poetry, Dimítris Tsaloúmas, was born on Léros and emigrated with his family to Melbourne in 1952; his work explores the bittersweet feelings of emigrants in the Greek diaspora and explains why so many hotels, bars and restaurants are named *Nostos*, a longing for home.

Léros ℂ (0247–)   *Getting There and Around*

By air: daily from Athens, information ℂ 22 277.

By sea: daily to Pátmos, Kos, Kálymnos, Rhodes; 2 a week with Lipsí and Agathónissi; once or twice a week to Níssyros, Chálki, Tílos, Sými, Kássos, Kárpathos, Páros, Náxos and Sýros. **Excursion boats** from Ag. Marína to Lipsí, Arki and Marathi; **caique** twice a day in high season from Xirókambos to Myrtiés, Kálymnos. **Hydrofoil**: daily from Ag. Marína to Kálymnos, Kos, Pátmos and Sámos; 4 times a week to Lipsí, Agathónissi, Fourní and Ikaría. Check schedules with main agent Kastis Travel in Lakkí, ℂ 22 872, ◉ 29 125. **Port authority**: Lakkí ℂ 22 234.

Taxi ranks: Lakkí ℂ 22 550, Ag. Marína ℂ 23 340, Plátanos ℂ 23 070.

Léros ℂ (0247–)   *Tourist Information*

There's a helpful tourist office at the quay in Lakkí next door to the cafeteria, ℂ 22 937. In Ag. Marína DRM Travel, ℂ 23 502 ◉ 24 303, are exceptionally helpful, have accommodation to let and provide a range of excursions.

Festivals

During the **pre-Lent** Carnival children don monks' robes and visit the homes of the newly married, reciting verses made up by their elders; **16–17 July**, Ag. Marínas at Ag. Marína; **first ten days of August** at Alínda, the Alintia regatta run since 1907 with sailing races; **6 August**, Sotíris at Plátanos; **15 August**, Panagías at the Kástro; **20 August**, foreign tourist day at Alínda; **24–25 September**, Ag. Ioánnis Theológos at Lakkí. Starting on **26 September**, three days of memorial services for those who lost their lives on the *Queen Olga*; Greek naval vessels always attend ; **20 October**, Ag. Kýras at Parthéni.

Lakkí and South Léros

Arriving at **Lakkí** (ΛΑΚΚΙ) by ferry, usually at night, is quite an experience, its extraordinary *Fascisti* Art Deco buildings reflected in the gulf. If Fellini had been

Greek Lakkí would have been one of his favourite sets. The streets are perfectly paved and wide enough to accommodate several lanes of traffic, although they're usually empty except for a few lone bikers rumbling through, while what remains of Mussolini's dream town, a tribute to Italian Rationalism and the International Style, crumbles away, forlorn, dilapidated but still weirdly compelling, a proper De Chirico ghost town. The grandiose cinema and school are defunct, as is the old Hotel Roma, later the **Leros Palace** (where this writer was once led down a mile of huge white halls, hypnotically lit by swaying bare bulbs, to a room the size of a bus station, completely untouched since its last clients pounded a flock of mosquitoes into the walls. The son of the owner, seeing my reluctant glances at the rumpled bed, rolled his eyes and exclaimed in disgust, 'Oh, and I suppose you want clean sheets, too!'). Now it's stuffed with litter. Lakkí's style was dubbed 'Ignored Internationalism' by Greek scholars when the Lerians decided to abandon the town and make the more convivial Plátanos the capital. Many islanders commute to Lakkí to work in the three mental hospitals, set up during the Italian occupation across the bay. These days the park around the institutions is open to visitors; one building here was intended to host Mussolini—the Duce's summer retreat.

Near the waterfront there's a monument to the many who perished in 1943 when a Greek ship, the *Queen Olga*, was bombed by German planes and sank in Lakkí's harbour. A path leading up from the jetty goes to the nearest beach at **Kouloúki**, with a taverna and unofficial camping under the pines. At **Lépida**, across the harbour, the **Moní Panagía** is built on the ruins of an old lighthouse, and further south, overlooking **Xirókambos** (ΞΗΡΟΚΑΜΠΟΣ), is the fort **Paliokástro**, built near an older fortification dating back to the 3rd century BC. The church inside has mosaics and Xirókambos itself, a simple fishing village, has a pleasant sandy beach to the west. In summer the caique goes over to Myrtiés on Kálymnos twice a day. There are also secluded pebbly coves accessible from a track beside the chapel.

Pantéli, Plátanos, and Ag. Marína

Up the tree-lined hill from Lakkí it's only 3km to the very popular coarse sandy beach of **Vromólithos** ('Dirty Rock'), with sunbeds and tavernas, prettily closed in by deeply wooded hills. There are more places to stay just around the bay at **Pantéli** (ΠΑΝΤΕΛΙ), a working fishing village by day with its little harbour full of caiques and passing yachts, and by night the rendezvous of Léros' seafood-lovers, with tables spilling on to the small, tree-fringed beach.

Uphill, the capital **Plátanos** (ΠΛΑΤΑΝΟΣ) is as near the centre of Léros as possible. With a few neoclassical houses mixed in with more traditional ones, it's a pretty place, especially at night, with stunning views over Pantéli below; the main square is the focus of local hubbub and transport. Overhead the ancient acropolis is occupied by the **Kástro**, a Byzantine fortress renovated by the Venetians, the Knights and the

Greek military, who have recently upped sticks for another hill. A winding, rough asphalt road rises to the top, but the alternative 370 steps, lined by houses with fragrant flower gardens, will make you feel more righteous. From the top the 'four seas' of Léros are spread at your feet: the bays of Pantéli, Ag. Marína, Gournás and Lakkí. Within the walls, the church of the **Megalóchari Kyrás Kástrou** (open 8.30–12.30 and Wed, Sat and Sun 4–8) houses a miraculous icon of the Virgin and small display of religious relics. The story goes that during the Turkish occupation the icon set sail from Constantinople on board a boat lit by a sacred candle and turned up on Léros. The inhabitants, led by the bishop, carried it in great procession to the cathedral. The next day, however, the icon had vanished and the Turkish captain of the Kástro found it, candle dangerously blazing, in the gunpowder store, even though the door had been firmly locked. The icon was taken back to the cathedral, but on the following nights it decamped to the arsenal again and again, until the Turkish governor was convinced it was a miracle and gave the powder storeroom to the Christians. They cleaned it up, and the wilful icon has stayed put ever since.

Ag. Marína (ΑΓ. ΜΑΡΙΝΑ), the seaside extension of Plátanos, is easily reached by the main street, Ódos Xarami, but if you want to avoid the motorbike Grand Prix take the quiet lane that runs parallel down to the pottery. Ag. Marína is a windswept harbour, again full of fishermen at work and excursion boats from Lípsi and Pátmos; there are plenty of tavernas, and accommodation up the road by the beach and coves at **Krithóni**.

Álinda and the North

Álinda (ΑΛΙΝΤΑ), once the old commercial port of Léros on the north end of the same bay, is the island's oldest resort and principal package holiday destination, although still low-key by Kos standards. There's a long sandy beach, with water sports, and plenty of seafront cafés and tavernas. The pretty mosaics of an Early Christian basilica, **Panagía Galatiani**, may be seen in the forecourt of the town hospice, while nearby the immaculate **British War Cemetery** looks out over the crystal bay, where 183 servicemen lie at rest—next to a motorbike rental shop, where lads the age that they died are known as the *kamikazi*. Léros has strong links with Egypt as many notables fled to Cairo in the twenties. Álinda's folly, the **Bellini Tower**, was built by one of them, Paríssis Bellínis, and now houses a more interesting than average **Historic and Folk Museum** (open daily, 9–12 and 6–9). North of Alínda, a track leads to the secluded beaches at **Panagíes** and sandy **Kryfós**, where you can skinny-dip. There's a large sandy beach just over the isthmus at **Gourná**, although it tends to be windblown; you're better off seeking out one of the small coves leading to Léros' answer to Corfu's Mouse Island, **Ag. Isidóros**, a white chapel perched on an islet reached by a causeway. If you fancy a long walk off the road there are sandy beaches at **Ag. Nikólaos** further along the coast.

From Alínda there's a road lined with eucalyptus trees north to **Parthéni** ('the Virgins'), former centre of guinea fowl worship, now a military base, used in the 1960s as a detention centre for political dissidents. Above, only a few ruins remain of the **Temple of Artemis** (near the present church of Ag. Kyrás) but they still enjoy a superb setting; linger under a sacred myrtle tree and look at the nearby airport. Further north there's a family beach and taverna at **Plefoúti**, in a lake-like bay, while over the headland at **Kioúra** there are quiet pebble coves reached via the chapel gates. You can easily do a round-island trip by car past **Drymónas** with lovely coves and an oleander gorge, then over the mountain back to Lakkí.

Léros ✉ *85400,* ✆ *(0247–)*   **Where to Stay and Eating Out**

The lushness of Léros translates into an extra airborne division of Lilliputian vampires by night so bring big bug-goo, especially if you sleep under the stars.

Lakkí/Xirókambos

Katikiés, ✆ 23 624, 📧 24 645 (*A; exp*) has lovely studios and apartments, sleeping up to six. **Miramare**, ✆ 22 053, 📧 22 469 (*D; inexp*) is central and comfortable; **Katerina**, ✆ 22 460, 📧 23 038 (*E; inexp*) is fine if you've just staggered off the ferry, but a little out of town the **Xenon Angelou**, ✆ 22 514, 📧 24 403 (*C; mod*) is a beautiful old pink farmhouse tastefully converted into a B & B.

Food is generally limited to fast food and pizza, an exception being **Sostos** taverna behind the defunct Léros Palace Hotel, serving excellent local fare. In Xirókambos, **Villa Maria**, ✆ 22 827 (*mod*) is the best place to stay. **Camping Leros**, ✆ 23 372, is up the road.

Vromólithos/Pantéli

Tony's Beach, ✆ 27 742 (*mod*) often has rooms in Vromólithos, although the rest tends to be block-booked. Slap on the beach, **Frangos** is legendary for traditional food, while the **Taverna Paradisos** also has a good menu but slow service in high season. Several good inexpensive pensions overlook the picture-postcard harbour at Pentéli including the simple **Rosa**, ✆ 22 798, and the nicer **Kavos**, ✆ 23 247 (the same family also owns Pension Anastasios, in Vromólithos). Up the lane back towards Plátanos, **Rena** near the church has a lovely shady garden; neighbouring **Aphroditi**, ✆ 23 477 (*mod*) and **Aegean Sky Apartments**, ✆ 24 722, are also good.

At the bottom of the hill, upmarket **Faliro** has excellent seafood and courteous service plus a bizarre grotto housing a fishtank. **Zorba's** off the square gets packed; **Drossia**, opposite Pension Rosa, is less touristy than some, with fish almost leaping from the family nets; **Taverna Maria** with a terrace at the water's edge is the best for atmosphere and popular with the local fishermen. Gold-toothed Maria will rustle you up a huge dish of small whitebait-style *marídes* or *kalamári* fresh from their caiques.

Plátanos/Ag. Marína/Krithóni

In Plátanos, the pleasant and quiet **Eleftheria**, ✆ 23 550 (*C; mod*) has family apartments as well as nice doubles, owned by Antónis Kanáris of the local Laskarina Travel agency, confusingly unconnected with the British holiday company. Food choices here run the gamut from **Funny Bunny Fast Food** to the ancient *ouzerie*, **Leriako Lexi**.

Down in Ag. Marína **Ta Kamakia** is one of the best places to eat, with excellent *yígantes*, and **Taverna Ag. Marina** is is also good for lunch and watching the world go by. If you've OD'd on Greek salads then head for **Garbo's Restaurant** where Kath and Frank offer relief in the form of steak and kidney pie and curries that attract locals as well as visitors. Further up the bay in Krithóni the swish **Krithoni Paradise,** ✆ 25 120 (*exp*) with a pool and piano bar has just opened. **Nefeli Apartments**, ✆ 24 611, is another tasteful, upmarket new complex designed by a woman architect.

Álinda

Set in a cool, flowery garden, **Archonitkó Angelou**, ✆ 22 749, ✆ 24 403 (*C; mod*), built in 1895, was lovingly restored by the same family as the Xenon in Lakkí. **Boulafendis Bungalows**, ✆ 23 515, ✆ 24 533 (*C; exp–mod*) is an interesting studio development around a traditional mansion. **Chryssoula**, ✆ 22 451 (*mod*) has bright white studios overlooking a pool and the sea, 300m away; **Ara**, set up high with views of both 'seas', ✆ 24 140, ✆ 24 194 (*exp–mod*) has studios and apartments, and a restaurant and a pool; **Marileen**, ✆ 24 100, is similar, with a convenient market and TVs in the rooms. **Papa Fotis**, ✆ 22 247 (*inexp*) is good for travellers on a tight budget. Amongst the tavernas, seaside **Finikas** is an old favourite and **To Steki** does tasty grills.

Entertainment and Nightlife

There are a number of cultural events during the summer, including performances by the **Léros Theatre Group** and **Artemis**, a society dedicated to the revival of the island dances in traditional costume. There is a **bouzouki club** on the way to Plefoútis; otherwise Pantéli has a disco and the cool **Savanna** bar at the end of the harbour; **Nectar** and **Café Continent** are also decent watering-holes. In Ag. Marína, **La Playa Bar** is the happening place and the **Faros** plays great world music.

In the great war between gods and giants one of the casualties was the fiery Titan Polyvotis, who so incurred Poseidon's wrath that the sea god ripped off a chunk of Kos and hurled it on top of him. This became the island of Níssyros, and the miserable Polyvotis, pinned underneath, sighs and fumes, unable to escape.

The story is geologically sound: Níssyros was indeed once part of Kos, and one of the craters of its volcano, the only one in the Dodecanese, is named after the giant, still struggling to break free. Níssyros sits on the same volcanic line as Áegina, Páros, Antíparos, Mílos, Santoríni and Kos. Almost circular, the island in ancient times was crowned by a central 1400m peak. When it erupted in 1422 the centre imploded, forming the fertile Lakkí plain, which looks like a moonscape in places with its ashy slag heaps and yellow sulphurous rocks. Dormant these days—the last eruption was in 1933—the volcano dominates the island's character as well as its tourist industry. Its rich soil holds tight to water so Níssyros is lush and green, its terraces thick with olives, figs, citrus groves and almond trees (someone once called it the Polo mint island—green outside, white inside with a hole in the middle). Quarrying the gypsum and harvesting the pumice fields, both on Níssyros and its little sister islet Gialí opposite, keep the economy going year-round. The coast is a jumble of black volcanic boulders and pebbly or grey sandy beaches, and although Gialí is an industrial centre, gradually being chipped away by its miners, it also has some lovely golden sands. Drinking water is a problem on Níssyros; although there is a desalination plant it isn't always working and tap water is pretty ghastly. To provide cheap power to run the plant, and serve Kos, Kálymnos and Léros via undersea cable, the Greek electricity board DEH sunk several geothermal wells but went about it so heavy-handedly, botching up some lovely landscapes in the process, that a local referendum sent them packing.

Níssyros © (0242–)   **Getting There and Around**

By sea: daily **taxi boat** and *Nissiros Express* to Kardaména, Kos; **ferry** several times a week to Kos, Kálymnos, Tílos and Rhodes, and once a week to Astypálaia, Chálki, Léros, Lípsi, Pátmos, Sými, Sýros, Páros, Náxos and Piraeus. **Hydrofoil**: regular but variable services to Kos, Kálymnos, Sými, Tílos and Rhodes. Hire a **caique** from Manolis Melianos, © 41 221, or Manolis Manis, © 41 218. **Port authority**: © 31 222.

By road: there is a regular **bus** service, © 31 204, from the harbour to Páli via White Beach, but buses for the village of Emborió and Nikiá leave early morning and return mid-afternoon only. Níssyros also has two **taxi** firms, Bobby's, © 31 460, and Irene's, © 31 474. A round-island tour will cost about 6000dr; to the volcano 4000dr.

Níssyros © (0242–)   **Tourist Information**

Enetikon Travel, © 31 180, @ 31 168, on the right as you head up from the harbour, are particularly helpful and offer a range of excursions.

Festivals

23 April, Ag. Geórgios; **29 June**, Ag. Apóstoli at Páli; **27 July**, Ag. Panteleímonos at Nikiá; **15 August**, Panagías at Mandráki; **25 September**, Ag. Ioánnis Theológos at Nikiá.

Life revolves around the cafeteria on the quay in **Mandráki** (ΜΑΝΔΡΑΚΙ), the capital and port, where agents sell tickets for trips to the volcano and buses wait to take groups from the excursion boats. A short walk from the quay leads down the narrow road towards the village with its wide choice of seaside tavernas. Despite the boatloads of day-trippers from Kos who come to see the volcano, the centre of Mandráki manages to retain its charm, especially in the higgledy-piggledy **Langadáki** district. The little lanes, cobbled or picked out with pebble mosaic patterns, twist under the wooden balconies of the tall, narrow, brightly painted houses. They were originally designed to confound marauding pirates and there's still an air of being closed to outsiders, especially during siesta time, *mesiméri*, with the shutters pulled over the traditional embroidered curtains. But at night what looked like ordinary houses by day suddenly open up as shops selling drapery and baby clothes.

Seawards the lanes aim for **Plateía Ilikioméni** with its bars, while others weave inland past the public orchard or *kámbo* into a succession of shady squares. Signs point the way to major attractions: up to the ancient **Kástro** (or **Enetikon**), taken over in 1315 by the Knights, and, within its walls, the monastery of 15th-century **Panagía Spilianí**, Our Lady of the Cave (*open daily 10.30–3*). A finely carved iconostasis holds a much-venerated icon of the Virgin, loaded with gold and silver; she apparently chose the site for the church herself, appearing in a vision to early Christian islanders. The church's fame grew after raiding Saracens failed to find its secret trove of silver, worked into the rich collection of Byzantine icons. There are guest rooms in the monastery and fantastic views out over the village at sunset.

On the stairway up to the monastery a small **Historical and Popular Museum** (*open when the owner's around*) houses an assortment of island exhibits and a reconstruction of a traditional kitchen. Higher up, a rough path leads from the Langadáki quarter, crossing fields and olive groves to the 7th century BC Doric **Paliokástro**, a spectacular site with vast Cyclopean walls hewn from volcanic rock. The acropolis of ancient Níssyros, the mighty bastion dates back 2000 years and you can walk along the top of the wide walls from where they used to pour boiling oil on attackers and look out to Gialí and Kos.

Beaches and Hot Springs

There are a few sandy strands along the front, usually packed with trippers. The nearest beach to town is often windswept **Chochláki**, under the monastery cliffs, reached by a daisy-patterned pathway. The beach is covered with blue-black volcanic rocks that give way to shale further along. At one end of the beach there's a wacky beachcomber's house-cum-bar made from driftwood and all kinds of flotsam and jetsam. A 10-minute walk from Mandráki takes you to **Miramare** beach, nicer for fish tavernas than bathing. Further along, **Gialiskári** (alias **White Beach**) is a better bet with its black and white crystals by the thermal spa of **Loutrá** (*open June to October*) where the hot springs ease arthritis and rheumatism.

Further along the coast the pretty fishing village of **Páli** (ΠΑΛΟΙ) has a succession of dark volcanic sandy beaches, some shaded by trees, and some rudimentary early Christian catacombs. Fishing boats in the harbour are often surrounded by masses of bobbing pumice stones—great souvenirs for the bath. Páli has an incongruous central roundabout and a selection of good fish tavernas. Follow the beach road, hung over with fig trees, and you'll come to another spa in throes of construction which looks like an abandoned jail. In August the *meltémi* blows fiercely on Níssyros and the beaches along here can be littered with junk and rutting piglets. About an hour's walk or twenty minutes by moped along the road brings you to the island's best beaches: the bronze sands of **Lýes** with its Oasis cantina and free camping, and **Pachiá Ámmos**, a broad expanse of reddish sands reached via a scramble over the headland. With mining operations for a backdrop, the islets **Gialí** and **Ag. Antónis** have white crystal sand and are great for swimming and snorkelling, with their curious rocks and, on the former, 'Miaoulis' Well' dug by the admiral's sailors in 1821 while hiding out from the Turks.

Into the Volcano

The excursion not to be missed on Níssyros, however, is to the volcano. It has five craters—Polivotis, Alexandros, Logothetis, Achilles and the biggest, Stéfanos, 80ft deep and 1150ft across, the main attraction for the day-trippers. The volcano buses leave the port in succession as the tourist boats arrive; if you want more time and a bit of solitude, take the village bus to **Nikiá** (*see* below) in the morning and walk down. There are wonderful views from the winding road up from Mandráki, where the greenery and neat terraces offer a stunning contrast to the vast plain below, an extra-terrestrial landscape of pale greys and yellows, the smell of sulphur so pungent that you can almost see cartoonish stink lines curling up out of the great crater (you may have to hang out your clothes to air when you get back to keep from smelling like a rotten egg). After passing several geothermal pools, the bus stops near the great fuming heart of **Stéfanos**. A slippery zigzag path descends to the floor of the crater, with bubbling fumeroles all around. You can feel the great heat and turmoil of the gases beneath the crust. Stout shoes are a good idea. In some places the crust is so fragile that your foot could go through, so if you have children in tow make sure they don't stray. After the steam and the stench, you can join the queues to quench your thirst at the café on the rim of the crater.

Emborió and Nikiá

The villages of Emborió and Nikiá cling to the rim of the crater. **Emborió** (ΕΜΠΟΡΕΙΟΣ) above Páli only has a handful of inhabitants who haven't emigrated to Australia or America, but the population rises in the summer as houses are being restored as holiday homes. Many of these old houses come with a free mod con in the basement: natural volcanic saunas. If you want to partake, there's a public sauna in a cave on the outskirts of the village. A ruined Byzantine fort offers memorable views of the crater 1000ft below. An old cobbled pathway also leads down to Páli. In contrast pretty **Nikiá** (NIKAIA) is lively with dazzling blue and white paintwork, bright gardens and views over Tílos as well as the caldera in all its ghostly enormity far below. The village square has a lovely *choklákia* mosaic and there are a couple of *kafeneía* and a taverna, plus a hostel if you want to stay. The path down to the volcano is steep but clearly marked and takes about 40 minutes. On the way watch out for the **Calanna** rock, said to be a witch who was turned to stone; a safer place to rest is the **Monastery of Ag. Ioánnis Theológos**, with shady trees and picnic benches as well as icons and frescoes.

Níssyros ✉ *85303,* ☏ *(0242–)*   **Where to Stay**

It can be very difficult to find a room in July and August and there is no official campsite so it's worth booking. Prices tend to be lower than on the other Dodecanese islands.

In Mandráki harbour **Xenon**, ☏ 31 011 (*mod*) is inviting and handy for ferries; **III Brothers**, ☏ 31 344 (*mod*) is a pleasant place by the sea, with a decent restaurant. Over the road, **Haritos**, ☏ 31 322, ☏ 31 122 (*C; mod*) is a friendly pension with spacious rooms and sea-view balconies. *Open all year.* On the coast road to Páli **Miramare Apartments**, ☏ 31 100, ☏ 31 254 (*mod*) are luxurious by island standards, beautifully appointed with a sea-view terrace. Further in the village opposite the orchard, the most comfortable and well-priced bet is the **Porfyris**, ☏ 31 376 (*C; mod, inc breakfast*) with a swimming pool and views to Gialí; **I Drossia**, ☏ 31 328 (*inexp*) is one of the cheapest in the village, and the waves crash on the black rocks beneath your balcony. At Gialiskári, the ungainly **White Beach**, ☏ 31 497/8, ☏ 31 389 (*C; mod*) is right on the sands; in Páli, the **Hellenis**, ☏ 31 453 (*mod*) has a decent restaurant.

Níssyros ☏ *(0242–)*   **Eating Out**

Níssyros has thirteen tavernas and ten bars at last count, from waterside tavernas to village favourites in Mandráki's Elikioméni Square. Local specialities are *pittiá*, delicious chickpea fritters, and *soumáda*, a non-alcoholic almond drink which tastes like liquid marzipan. **Karava**, next to Enetikon Travel, offers a wide choice of very good food, *soumáda*, and if it's a bit more pricey than the rest, the sea view compensates. Further along the front the **Captain's Taverna** has excellent home-made dishes including mouthwatering *pittiá* and wild caper salad made to Granny's recipe; **Kleanthis** is a popular lunchtime haunt with locals, and don't be put off by **Mike's Tourist Corner**—there's a dab hand in the kitchen. There are some pleasant surprises further inland, too. Old **Taverna Nissyros**, spilling out into a narrow alley, is one of the most popular and authentic with its vine-clad canopy and jolly atmosphere. It gets packed at night, the food is good but portions small. In lively Platéia Elikioméni, the centre of Mandráki nightlife, **Irini** is good value with friendly service and a wide menu from *laderá* to roasts. The **Panorama** gets very busy at night: the food is good but a bit pricey. So is the beer. Just beyond the harbour, the **Ouzerie Paradeisos** is aptly named, set back off the road in a lovely garden, great for an evening aperitif. In Páli make a bee-line for **Angistri** on the far edge of the beach where Mama makes a knock-out moussaka; **Aphroditi** is also excellent with home-made desserts; while the **Hellenis** has music when the owner's husband is playing his *lýra*. At Nikiá the **Taverna Nikia** has great views over the crater and out to Kos.

Pátmos (ΠΑΤΜΟΣ)

Of all the Greek islands, dramatically beautiful Pátmos is the most sacred to Christians, both Orthodox and Western; here St John the Theologian received the vision he described in the *Apocalypse* or *Book of Revelations*; and here, in the 11th century, the Blessed Christodoulos founded a monastery more wealthy and influential than any in Greece except for Mount Áthos. Although by day the harbour is thronged with day-trippers and cruise passengers being hauled up to the monastery, and there are plenty of cafés, restaurants and stylish gift shops to make sure they don't leave thirsty or empty-handed, Pátmos still maintains something of its otherworldly feel, especially in the evening, and outside July and August. But even in high summer it maintains certain standards: there's a law banning 'promiscuity and looseness'; although it may seem appropriate in theory, don't come to the island of the Apocalypse to rave, rave, rave against the dying of the light.

History

Pátmos was inhabited from the 14th century BC, its main settlement near present-day Skála and its acropolis and fortifications at Kastélli. It was subject to Asia Minor and not terribly important. In AD 95 however the island's destiny was forever altered with the arrival of a certain John, according to tradition St John, the beloved apostle of Jesus (known variously as the Theologian, the Evangelist or the Divine). The story goes that after the Crucifixion he spent most of his life in Ephesus as appointed guardian of Mary; after her death (or Assumption), during Emperor Domitian's persecution of Christians, he was taken to Rome and cast into a pot of boiling oil, from which he emerged without a burn, which upset the Romans so much that they

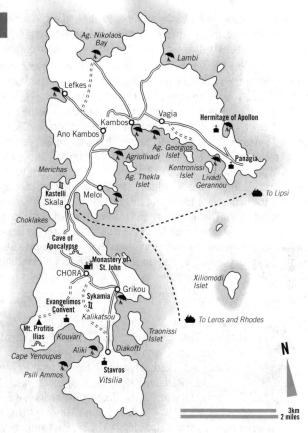

Pátmos

exiled him to desolate Pátmos. While living in a cave, he received his end-of-the-world *Revelations*. He only spent a year or so on Pátmos before returning to Ephesus, but in that time John provided enough material to keep fire-eating preachers and literal-minded cranks going for the next 1900 years (*see* p.63).

Pátmos was abandoned from the 7th century, its barren volcanic rock not worth defending from pirates. Destiny remained on hold until the late 11th century, when in Constantinople things were going badly for Alexius Comnenus—'born to the purple' but so battered by fate and politics he had nothing but the blues. Nevertheless a saintly hermit named Christódoulos predicted his ascent to the throne of Byzantium, and the miserable Alexius promised him that, should it come true, he would grant him any wish in his power. Of course it did, and in 1088

Christódoulos made his wish: the island of Pátmos, to found a monastery on the site of an ancient temple of Artemis. The Emperor provided not only the island but the building funds, as well as tax exemptions and the right to engage in sea trade.

The island remained under absolute control of the monastery for centuries, against poverty, pirates and a thousand other afflictions. The Venetian Dukes of Pátmos, its nominal rulers, were content to leave it as an autonomous monastic state. In the 13th century the village of Chóra was built in the shadow of the monastery's powerful walls, which offered a safe haven in case of attack. Because the Turks respected the monastery's imperial charter Pátmos flourished, particularly from the 16th to the 19th centuries, and its school of theology and liberal arts, founded by deacon Makarios Kalogeras in 1713, was one of the rare institutions of learning able to function in the open. Gradually monastic control lessened as the islanders took over the monks' sea trade, and in 1720 the monks and laymen divided the land between them. The monastery and island prospered to the extent that in the 18th century it established colonies in the Balkans, a prosperity nipped in the bud, however, by the invention of the steamship. To this day the monastery enjoys special privileges and is subject only to the Patriarch in Constantinople, while its modern college of Theology carries on the traditions of the first school of Pátmos.

Pátmos ✆ (0247–)   **Getting There and Around**

By sea: ferries daily to Piraeus, Kálymnos, Léros, Kos and Rhodes; 4 weekly to Sámos, 3 weekly with Ikaría and Agathónissi, 2 a week with Arki, once with Kárpathos, Níssyros, Náxos, Páros, Sýros, Chálki and Kássos. **Hydrofoil:** regular summer services to Léros (Ag. Marína), Kálymnos, Kos, Agathónissi, Sámos' three ports, Lipsí and Ikaría. **Excursion boats** leave Skála for most beaches as well as to Arkí, Maráthi, Sámos (Pythagório) and Lipsí. To hire a **caique** contact Apollon, ✆ 31 724. **Port authority:** ✆ 34 131.

By road: buses depart from the ferry dock in Skála to Chóra, Gríkou and Kámbos. **Taxis:** ✆ 31 225, from rank on central square; to avoid being ripped off, agree on prices before setting out.

Pátmos ✆ (0247–)   **Tourist Information**

The municipal tourist information office in Skála, ✆ 31 666 or 31 158, is very helpful and has a good range of leaflets and timetables.

Festivals

Besides the **Maundy Thursday** Niptíras ceremony, the monastery holds services for St John on **8 May** and **26 September**; **27 July**, Ag. Panteleímonos, on the islet of Xiliomódi; more popular *panegýria* take place **5 August**, Ag. Sotiris at Kámbos; and **15 August**, Panagías, also at Kámbos; **14 September**, Ag. Stávros.

Skála

All boats drop anchor at **Skála** (ΣΚΑΛΑ), the island's main resort, and a smart and upmarket one it is too. Glitzy cafés and trendy shops have been set up to deal with the wealthy tourists disgorged by the cruise ships. One of the first things you'll see is a statue of Protergatis Xanthos Emmanuel, who led an uprising against the Turks in 1821. Skála didn't even exist until that year, so fearsome were the pirate raids. Near the beach, marked by a red buoy, is a reminder of another troublemaker, the evil magician Yenoupas, who at the urging of priests from the temple of Apollo challenged St John to a duel of miracles. Yenoupas' miracle was to dive into the sea and bring back effigies of the dead; John's was to ask God to petrify the submerged magician, which abruptly ended the contest. Even petrified, Yenoupas is a menace to shipping and stinks of sulphur, but all attempts to dislodge him have failed.

Water can be short in high summer. You can hike up to the site of the ancient city, **Kastélli**, in about 20 minutes, a walk rewarded more by stunning views than any archaeological excavations. The remains of a Hellenistic wall and the chapel of **Ag. Konstantínos** are perched on the summit. Go in the evening for a wonderful sunset.

Chóra

From Skála you can see whitewashed **Chóra** (XOPA) clinging to the mighty castle walls of the monastery. Buses and taxis make the ascent in a few minutes, but if you have the time it isn't too strenuous to walk up the old cobbled path to enjoy the panorama below. Chóra is a lovely, almost Cycladic village with a maze of narrow alleyways and masses of chapels and mansions built on the hillside to the north in the 17th and 18th centuries by the owners of Pátmos' merchant fleet. Although from the outside most of the mansions present blank walls screening the courtyard, the decoration limited to a few carvings around doors or windows, many have star-tlingly lavish interiors. One of the most notable is the Simandris House, near the Convent of Zoodóchos Pigi, which combines oriental influences with the western style introduced in the 19th century. Besides these, there are other distinct quarters for a wander: Alotina, west of the monastery, the old quarter of refugees from Constantinople, and Kritika, settled in the 17th century by Cretan refugees.

Monastery of St John the Theologian

© 31 398. Opening times may vary; at the time of writing open May–Nov daily 8–1 and Tues, Thurs, Sun also 4–6. Try to get there first thing in the morning before the cruise passengers. Shorts prohibited; women must wear skirts. Adm for the Treasury.

The usual gauntlet of trinket-vendors marks the entrance to Pátmos' prime attraction; and once you get past them and through the walls that stood up to every invader and marauder for centuries, expect, alas, a grumpy welcome; apparently no one told the monks when they took their vows that dedicating their lives to God meant spending their days as museum guards and dress code enforcers.

The intimate scale and intricate little corridors are delightful but can easily become unbearably crowded. A charming 1698 court incorporates the exonarthex of the church; just inside is the chapel-tomb of the Blessed Christódoulos. The church retains its original marble floor; its icon of St John was a gift from Alexius Comnenus and the high altar is a stone from a temple of Demeter that once stood in Chora. Frescoes cover every surface; those in the 12th-century **Chapel of the Theotókos** are as old as the church; others are in the Refectory, off the inner courtyard.

The **Treasury Museum** displays the original monastery deed—a chrysobul, signed and sealed, from the Emperor, along with his mitre; an inscription from the temple of Artemis, stating that Orestes sought refuge here from the Furies; and some of the many exquisite gifts the monastery has received over the centuries: gold and silver crosses, croziers and stoles; superb icons, including a rare one from the 11th century, brought here by Christódoulos; ships' pendants made of diamonds and emeralds donated by Catherine the Great; the 7lb golden mitre of Patriarch Neophytos VI; and a Cross of Patriarch Gregory V, who was hanged by the Turks when the Greek war of Independence broke out. Like many leading figures belonging to the revolutionary 'Friendly Society' the Patriarch had been an alumnus of the School of Pátmos. The **library** contains hundreds of rare codices and manuscripts, including the 6th-century *Codex Porphyrius*, St Mark's gospel written on purple vellum, but may only be visited with permission from the abbot. Lastly, if it's open, climb up to the roof terrace for a commanding view over the Aegean.

Around Chóra and down to the Monastery of the Apocalypse

After the monastery, you could spend a day finding the 40 or so churches wedged in the narrow lanes of Chóra. Especially good are the **Convent of Zoodóchos Pigí** (1607), the second largest institution on Pátmos, with fine frescoes and icons in its two churches, and lovely flowers in the courtyards (*open mornings and late afternoons*); also the **Convent of the Evangelismos** (follow the signposts west of town, *open mornings*) and 11th-century **Ag. Dimítrios**, contemporary with the monastery, but likely to be locked like many of the others. Nor is hunting out the caretaker particularly easy, as Chóra is one of those very old, silent places where the streets always seem to be deserted, especially once the trippers have gone.

This changes dramatically on Orthodox Maundy Thursday, when Chóra is packed with visitors and even TV crews for the *Niptíras* ceremony, when the abbot re-enacts Christ's washing of his disciples' feet—a rite once performed by the proud emperors of Byzantium. Depending on the weather, it takes place either in Plateía Ag. Leviás or Plateía Lóza. It's a short walk down from Chóra to the **Monastery of the Apocalypse** (*open Mon, Tues, Thurs and Sun, 8–2 and 4–6; other days 8–2*), where a stair covered with pots of flowers leads down to the cave where John lived and dreamed and heard 'a great voice, as of a trumpet' and dictated what he saw to his follower, Próchoros. The cave itself has been converted into a church, where you can see the rock where the good saint rested his head and hand (though he must have been something of a contortionist to manage it) and the massive overhanging roof, split in three sections by the voice of God, symbolizing the Holy Trinity. The iconostasis of the right-hand chapel has icons showing John's visions.If you're walking up from Skála (better for the soul), the cave is marked with signs saying ΑΠΟΚΑΛΥΨΟΣ. Again, be sure to get there on time. The ruined buildings just above the monastery belonged to the original school of Pátmos, and above this are the buildings of its successor, the modern Theological College.

Beaches and Villages around Pátmos

The closest beach to Skála, **Méloi** is a pleasant and tree-shaded area 2km north but tends to get crowded; if you want something more peaceful if less shady, look for the sign to **Agrioliνádi**, a quiet, rocky cove with some sand and a pair of tavernas. Pátmos has great walking country, much of it around the dramatic shore here, with **Áno Kámbos** the centre of the network. Surrounded by Pátmos' most fertile fields, it is the only other real village on the island and the end of the bus line; many long-term residents rent houses in the valley. There are beaches in every direction: one at least will be sheltered from the prevailing winds. **Kámbos** to the east is popular and sandy, with watersports; **Léfkes** to the west is often wild and windswept; to the north **Lámbi**, also reached by excursion boat, is famous for its subtle, multi-coloured pebbles. Further east there are secluded **Vagiá** and **Livádi Gerannoú**, with shade and a cantina. If you need a goal for a stroll, there's the 19th-century **Hermitage of Apollon** near a small mineral spring.

Roads from Skála and Chóra go to Pátmos' principal beach resort, **Gríkou** (ΓΡΙΚΟΥ), overlooking a beautiful lake-like bay, which has windsurfers and water skis for hire. On the south end of the bay, the **Kalikátsou rock** has carved rooms and stairs in rather unlikely places and may have been the 11th-century hermitage mentioned in the writings of Christódoulos. Inland at **Sykamiá** there's an old Roman bath said to have been used by St John to baptize his converts. The south road peters out at the **Stávros** chapel, at Diakofti, where Pátmos is only a few hundred yards across. There's a beach here, but a half-hour's tramp (or caique ride from Skála) will take you to lovely **Psilí Ámmos**, with its fine white sand. West of here, a seaside grotto on **Cape Yenoúpas** was the home of the evil magician (*see* above), and even today it's unpleasantly hot and smelly inside.

Skála

Owners meet the ferries offering *domátia* and on the whole the private rooms are very comfortable and better value than the hotels; although beware, many are out in the boondocks. **Hellinis**, ✆ 31 275 (*C; mod*) has nice en suite rooms right on the waterfront with views of the monastery; the **Skala**, ✆ 31 343, ✆ 31 747 (*B; mod*) is set in attractive gardens with a pool just two minutes from the ferry. The **Blue Bay** , ✆ 31 165 (*C; mod*) enjoys a quiet waterside spot on the road to Gríkou. **Summer**, ✆ 31 769 (*C; mod*) and **Maria**, ✆ 31 201 (*C; mod–inexp*) are both good choices in the Chokhlaká district overlooking the opposite bay. Upmarket **Galini**, ✆ 31 240 (*C; mod*) is also a good bet. **Efi**, at Kastélli, ✆ 32 500, ✆ 32 700 (*C; mod–inexp*) is comfortable. On the edge of Skála, in two traditional mansions, the **Byzance**, ✆ 31 052, ✆ 31663, e-mail: *byzance@hol.gr* (*C; mod–inexp*) has a sauna and roof garden with a snack bar and lovely views over the port: 25 rooms, apartments and studios, all with mini bar, phone and music. **Kasteli**, ✆ 31 361, ✆ 31 656 (*C; mod*) commands fine views from the upper part of town; the friendly **Australis**, ✆ 31 576 (*mod*) is florally decorated and costs slightly less.

Taverna O Vrachos, north of the waterfront, is good for fish; **Grigoris** opposite the ferry dock is tasty, cheap and cheerful with great charcoal-grilled fish and meat. The **Arion café** on the waterfront is a good place to watch the world go by, although **Byblos** is more fashionable.

Chóra

Ask the tourist office about the few rooms up here; if you are numerous, there's **Archontika Irini**, ✆ 32 826, an old stone mansion, with traditional furniture, fireplaces and wood stove, sleeping 6 to 10. *Open all year.* **Vangelis** and **Olympia** in Plateía Ag. Leviás (follow the little signs) both have reasonably priced solid Greek fare, although portions have shrunk a bit at Vangelis. **Aloni** has traditional bouzouki and dancing at evenings.

Méloi

Overlooking the bay, **Porto Scoutari**, ✆ 33124, ✆ 33 175 (*exp*) has pretty apartments, romantic and quiet, with big beds, TVs, and minibus service into civilization. **Rooms and Taverna Méloi**, known to all as Stefanos, ✆ 31 888, is almost on the beach; basic facilities, but serving good, reasonably priced food; there are also unnamed rooms, ✆ 32 382. There's also an excellent **campsite**, ✆ 31 821, with bamboo-shaded pitches, mini-market, cafeteria, cooking and washing facilities.

Kámbos

Traditionally styled **Patmos Paradise**, ✆ 32 624, ✉ 32 740 (*B; exp*) offers the works: an *à la carte* restaurant, American buffet breakfast, swimming pool, squash, tennis courts, sauna and fitness centre. There are also rooms.

Gríkou

Petra Hotel and Apartments, ✆ 31 035, are just back from the beach and have huge panoramic terraces along with minibars and phones. **Panorama Apartments**, ✆ 31 209, ✉ 32 120, are old favourites by the sea; the newly renovated **Joanna Hotel and Apartments**, ✆ 31 031, ✉ 32 031, book in Athens ✆ 981 2246 (*mod*) is a nicely done complex with self-catering, air-conditioned studios and apartments; on the hillside **Athena**, ✆ 31 859, has lovely views from its balconies and isn't block-booked; the **Golden Sun**, ✆ 32 318, ✉ 32 319 (*B; mod*) overlooking the bay, is family-run and friendly. The small, family-run **Flisvos** up on the hill has well-cooked Greek staples and fish at affordable prices and a few rooms; in the middle of the beach, **Stamatis** serves much of the same.

Lipsí/Lipsos (ΛΕΙΨΟΙ)

Lipsí is a little gem of an island, and it's not surprising that Odysseus put off his homecoming for seven years to linger here, beguiled by the charms of the nymph Calypso. If opinions differ on whether Lipsí really is Homer's isle of Ogygia (others believe it's near Corfu or Malta), no one can deny that the island has a certain unworldly magic. For centuries most of the land was owned by the Monastery of St John on Pátmos, and the blue domes of the Cycladic-style churches from that period bubble over a horizon of soft, green hills, while the village houses are painted in wild Fauvist colours.

Lipsí is one of an archipelago of tiny islets and its lovely beaches are a magnet for day excursions, yet once the trippers have gone it quickly regains its tranquillity. Above all, it's a great place to do nothing. The 650 inhabitants are warm and friendly and go about their lives as they have for centuries, fishing and farming. Lipsí is well-known for its sheep's and goat's milk cheese—there are more goats than people and even donkeys and ponies outnumber the wheeled transport.

Lipsí ✆ *(0247–)*　　　　　　　　　　　　　　　**Getting There**

By sea: daily **excursion boats** *Anna Express* and *Rena II* to Ag. Marína, Léros and Skála, Pátmos. **Ferry** connections 3 times a week with Piraeus, Sámos, Pátmos, Léros and Kálymnos; twice a week with Kos, Agathoníssi and Arkí; once a week with Níssyros, Tílos, Sými, Rhodes and Ikaría. **Hydrofoils** from Pythagório, Sámos (closest air connection) Kos, Kálymnos, Léros and Pátmos. Boat excursions around the island and to Arkí, Maráthi and Makrónissi caves. Or hire your own **caique**: try Manolis Melianos, © 41 221. **Port authority**: © 41 240.

Buses: Lipsí's old fleet of pickup trucks-cum-taxis has been replaced with a new municipal bus service in the harbour square, with almost hourly departures in season as far as Platís Gialós beach and Katsadiá beach.

Lipsí © (0247–) **Tourist Information**

At the town hall, © 41 250. Also, friendly Nico and Anna Christodoulou at **Laid Back Holidays**, ©/✉ 41343 are a mine of information, change money at bank rates, sell newspapers and hire out motorbikes and mopeds.

Festivals

Pilgrims pour in for 'the ninth day of the Virgin', 23–24 August (*see* below); a week or so before, the islanders also host a wine festival.

Around Lipsí

Lipsí village greets arrivals with a tidal splash of colour, a smattering of tavernas around the bay and odd front-room cafés which double as shops. Everything is neatly signposted from the harbour, and kept new-pin bright, as if the locals were entering a best-kept island contest. If most of the trippers head straight for the beaches, you may want to follow the Greeks and first visit the famous blue-domed church of **Ag. Ioánnis** to pay your respects to its miraculous icon of the Panagía.

The story goes that a woman prayed to the Virgin to help her son and the Virgin granted her prayer. Being poor, she had nothing to offer in return but a lily, which she humbly placed near the icon. In time the lily withered, but miraculously, on the day of the Virgin's acceptance into Heaven, 24 August, it sprang into full bloom and has flowered on that day ever since. The ancient lily stalk can clearly be seen under the glass of the icon and dutifully in early August it bears small white buds which burst into flower right on time. Dried flowers are also supposed to spring to life on the day at the **Panagía tou Chárou** chapel (Our Lady of Death (!) but actually named after the man who built it) which stands at Lipsí's highest point.

In the Town Hall is the small **Nikoforeion Ecclesiastical Museum** (*open Mon–Fri 9.30–1.30 and 4–8, Sat and Sun 10–2*), an odd collection of motley stuff, from the ridiculous to an interesting letter from Admiral Miaoúlis written on the night of his famous battle. Everything is neatly labelled. There is also a **carpet factory** to visit, one of a score set up across Greece to employ young women in rural areas to work on the traditional looms, but all their handiwork is sold in Athens

Lipsí is a miniature world, only six square miles, so you can walk across it in two hours, taking in its well-tended walled fields and thirty-odd blue and white chapels, as well as views of neighbouring islands Arkí, Maráthi and Agathoníssi. The town beach at **Lendoú** is shaded by trees but gets busy with Greek families in high season. By walking over the dusty headland track to **Kámbos** or beyond to **Kimissí**, you could have the sands to yourself. The buses will deposit you on the island's best-known beach, the white cove of **Platís Gialós** (3km) which has a pretty church and taverna, or take you south to **Katsadiá**, with its succession of sandy coves and a good taverna, Adonis, while on the east coast **Monodéndri** is the unofficial nudie beach. There are vineyards in the valley beyond the town where a good local wine is produced. With a bottle of this, and some octopus grilled at the harbourside, the island casts a gentle spell once the day-trippers have been herded into their boats.

Lipsí ⊠ 85001, ✆ (0247–) **Where to Stay**

All accommodation here is inexpensive, and landladies still meet the boats if they have a free room. There's only one hotel on Lipsí, the harbourside **Kalypso**, ✆ 41 242 (*D*) which also has an information service.

Rena's Rooms, ✆ 41 242, are immaculate and owned by John and Rena, who lived in America and run the *Rena II*. **Glaros Rooms**, ✆ 41 360, are also a good bet, perched high with views over the bay.

Just past Lendoú Beach **Studios Dream**, ✆ 41 271, have kitchenettes and balconies; **Pension Manolis**, ✆ 41 306, overlooks the fishing boats round the harbour to the south. On the far side of the village, a 2-minute walk from the centre, the peaceful **Studios Kalymnos**, ✆ 41 102 or 41 141, are set in a garden and have lovely views over the countryside. There's unofficial camping on the more distant beaches.

Lipsí ✆ (0247–) **Eating Out**

There's little to choose between the waterfront tavernas, all offering reasonable fish and typical oven dishes: among the specialities are *revythokeftédes* and fish croquets in mustard sauce. Places near the day-boats tend to be more touristy. **Kalypso Restaurant** with its shady vines is run by the famous Mr Mungo with dishevelled style; **Taverna O Theologos** specializes in fish and prices won't break the bank; the **Asprakis Ouzerie**, doubling as shop and bar on the corner near the excursion boats, is great for local atmosphere, grilled octopus and ouzo. Towards the ferry dock the **Kali Kardia** is popular, with a lovely terrace and cooking by Vassiléa and family; a few doors along, the restaurant run by **Maria** next to the *ouzerie/*bar **The Rock** is excellent and less frenetic at lunchtime. In the square several *kafeneía* do breakfast; visit the bakery for superb cheese pies and breads.

If you're a party animal, forget it—unless there's a wedding, when the whole island celebrates with a joyous all-night dance marathon. There's a new club at the far end of the harbour that plays Greek music all year round. Otherwise, the action centres on the waterfront, where someone might start gently hammering their *santoúri*.

Arkí (ΑΡΚΟΙ) and Maráthi (ΜΑΡΑΘΙ)

Arkí, a hilly little island just 4km long and 1km wide with 40 inhabitants, sees occasional caiques from Pátmos and Lipsí as well as one or two ferries a week between Agathónissi, Kálymnos, Pátmos, Sámos, Léros and Lipsí. With its few scattered houses, it attracts yachts and adventurous travellers. Facilities are barely minimal—there's no place to change money, and water must be shipped in; a little solar plant provides some electricity. There are some quiet coves and a **Blue Lagoon**—if not a rival to Capri's, just as good for snorkelling and swimming in the vivid waters. The harbour of **Port Augusta** has two tavernas and the **Taverna Asteria** also has inexpensive rooms and the island's one phone, *©* (0247) 32 371.

Even smaller **Maráthi** has a natural harbour popular with fishermen from surrounding islands as well as yachts, but no ferry calls in; once or twice a week excursion boats from Pátmos provide most of the transport and can strand you if the weather turns, so don't wait till the last moment if you have to catch a flight. There's no phone, just a ship-to-shore radio. Maráthi has a long sandy beach and two tavernas with rooms, **Pantelis Marathi Restaurant**, run by Mr Pantelís from Arkí via Australia, who bases himself plus family on Maráthi for the summer, and the **Other Place**. The first has comfortable, very reasonable rooms and serves up tasty dishes. The second is a bit more basic, with its own charm, owing to a Golgotha of goat skulls used for decoration in the trees. Goats leap all over the island and they're often on the menu as well.

Agathónissi (ΑΓΑΘΟΝΗΣΙ)

Northeast of Pátmos, it's 36 nautical miles to steep little Agathónissi (pop. 130). This may be alphabetically the first Greek island but few people have ever heard of it, tucked up as it is next to Turkey. It may be the ticket if you're seeking a very Greek island with a tad of civilization, or quiet sheltered coves to park your yacht.

Agathónissi © (0274–)   **Getting There**

By boat: the **ferry** *Níssos Kálymnos* links Agathónissi with Sámos (Pythagório), Pátmos, Lipsí, Léros, Kálymnos and Kos twice a week. **Hydrofoil**: once a week to Kos, Kálymnos, Léros (Ag Marína), Pátmos and

Sámos (Pythagório); the latter runs **excursion boats** to the island about once a week. **Port authority** (and police) near Megálo Chorió: ✆ 23 770.

Around the Island

Ancient Netousa or Tragea, now literally 'thorny island', Agathónissi has its share of thorn bushes as well as other small trees, but water is scarce and limited to rain-water cisterns: bring enough money for your stay and a bag of fresh fruit. The island has three villages, the port of **Ag. Giórgios**, pleasant **Megálo Chorió**, where most people live, and **Mikró Chorió**, with only about ten inhabitants, linked by a cement road and a rickety three-wheeler or maybe a van. Ag. Giórgios has a pebbly, grotty beach but there's a better one at **Spília**, a sheltered cove to the west. There are boat trips in high season to remote beaches, or else don stout shoes and walk: even paths are something of a luxury.

There are remains of a medieval granary at **Thóli**, and an excellent place to swim. It's worth taking the walk, about 90 minutes, to **Choklakiá**, or to the deserted fishing village of **Kathóliko** either via the **Mikró Chorió** road or over the old goat paths in the hills with great views of Sámos and Turkey. There's a small beach so you can take the plunge on arrival.

Agathónissi ✉ *85001,* ✆ *(0274–)* **Where to Stay and Eating Out**

There are three inexpensive possibilities in Ag. Giórgios: **Maria Kamitsi**, ✆ 23 690, has a nice pension set in a flower-filled garden set back from the waterfront. There are rooms over **George's Taverna**, ✆ 24 385, which also has excellent food and modest prices; otherwise try **Theologia Yiameou**, ✆ 23 692, with use of the kitchen. The rival taverna, **Ioannis**, grills his own fish as well as chicken or lamb. In Megálo Chorió there's **Katsoulieris Pension**, ✆ 24 385, a *kafeneíon*, and the '13 siblings', the **Dekatria Adelfia**, serving good cheap food.

Sými (ΣΥΜΗ)

Inevitably, there's a fusillade of clicking camera shutters and purring of cam-corders when the ferries swing into Sými's main harbour, Gialós, one of the most breathtaking sights in Greece. Few other islands have Sými's crisp brightness and its amphitheatre of imposing neoclassical mansions, in soft ochre or traditional deep shades, stacked one on top of another up the barren hillsides. There are few trees to block the sun, for unlike its neighbour Rhodes Sými is an arid island with insufficient water to support many visitors. Most who do come arrive on daily excursion boats from Rhodes, when pandemonium reigns in several languages as groups are herded along the waterfront or head for the small town beach at Nos. When the boats have sounded their sirens and the invaders departed Sými regains much of its serenity; at night when the lights come on it is pure romance. As its lovely houses are all bought up and immaculately restored, the island has become a very trendy place, with a major cultural festival and fancy restaurants. Sými is very popular with the sailing fraternity, who fill the harbour with yachts, flotillas and jet-set cruisers. Avoid August when the island is heaving, rooms are expensive and tempers frayed in the heat; because it's in a basin and the heat bounces off the rocks Sými sizzles like a cat on a hot tin roof from July to September. On the other hand it stays warm into October and is particularly lovely in spring.

History

According to legend, Sými was a princess, daughter of King Ialysos on Rhodes, who was abducted by the sea-god Glaukos, an eminent sponge-diver and sailor who built the Argo for Jason. He brought her to the island and gave it her name. If such was the case, Princess Sými's descendants inherited Glaukos' shipbuilding skills: throughout history Sými was famous for its ships. Sými was also known as Metapontis, or Aigle, after a daughter of Apollo and mother of the Three Graces. In another myth, Prometheus modelled a man from clay here, angering Zeus so much that he turned the Titan into a monkey for the rest of his natural days on the island. Ever since, the word 'simian' has been connected with apes.

Pelasgian walls in Chorió attest to the prehistoric settlement of Sými. In the *Iliad* Homer tells how the island mustered three ships for the Achaeans at Troy, led by King Nireus. After Achilles, Nireus was the most beautiful of all the Greeks but, as in Achilles' case, beauty proved to be no defence against the Trojans. In historical times Sými was part of the Dorian Hexapolis but dominated by Rhodes. The Romans fortified the acropolis at Chorió; the Byzantines converted it into a fort, which was renovated by the first Grand Master of the Knights of Rhodes, Foulques de Villaret. From Sými's Kástro the Knights could signal to Rhodes, and they favoured swift Sýmiot skiffs or *skafés* for their raiding activities.

Thanks to the Knights Sými prospered through shipbuilding and trade. When Suleiman the Magnificent came to the Dodecanese in 1522 the Sýmiots, known as the most daring divers in the Aegean, avoided being attacked by offering him the most beautiful sponges he had ever seen. In return for a relative degree of independence Sými sent a yearly consignment of sponges to the Sultan's harem. Like the Knights the Turks made use of the swift Symiot ships, this time for relaying messages. In order to keep Sými thriving the Sultan made it a free port and allowed the inhabitants to dive freely for sponges in Turkish waters.

Little Sými thus became the third richest island of the Dodecanese, a position it held from the 17th to the 19th centuries. Large mansions were constructed befitting the islanders' new status; shipbuilders bought forests in Asia Minor. Schools thrived. Even after certain privileges were withdrawn because of its participation in the 1821 revolution, Sými continued to flourish. The Italian occupation and the steamship, however, spelt the end of its luck: the Italians closed the lands of Asia Minor and the steamship killed the demand for wooden sailing

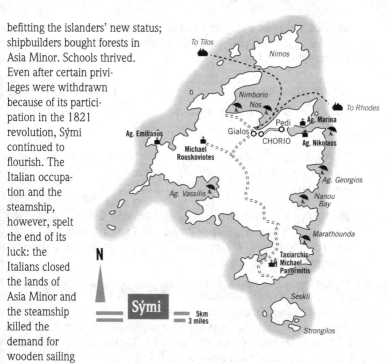

vessels altogether; during the Italian tenure the population of Sými dropped from 23,000 to 600 at the outbreak of the Second World War. At its end the treaty giving the Dodecanese to Greece was signed on Sými on VE Day, 8 May 1945, later ratified on 7 March 1948.

Sými © *(0241–)*   ### Getting There and Around

By boat: the island's own **ferries**, *Symi I* and *Symi II*, leave Mandráki Harbour, Rhodes, daily early evening and return to Rhodes in the early morning. There are at least 3 daily tourist boats from Rhodes, some calling at Panormítis Monastery; a few ferries a week to Rhodes; once or twice a week to Datça (Turkey, *see* below), Tílos, Níssyros, Kos, Kálymnos, Léros, Lipsí, Pátmos, Náxos, Páros, Sýros, Kastellórizo, Astypálaia and Piraeus. Local **excursion boats** visit different beaches, and the islets of Sesklí and Nímos; water taxis go to Nimborió from Gialós and Ag. Nikólaos from Pédi Beach. **Hydrofoil**: daily services to Rhodes, also less frequently to Chálki, Tílos, Níssyros, Kos and Kálymnos. **Port authority**: © 71 205.

By road: the island has 3 **taxis** and the Sými Bus, departing every hour from 8.30am to 10.30pm from Gialós to Pédi via Chorió. There's a place to rent motorbikes nearby.

Sými ✆ (0241–)   **Tourist Information**

Police share the post office building near Clock Tower, Gialós, ✆ 71 111.

Festivals

2 May, Ag. Athanásios; **5 May**, Ag. Iríni; **21 May**, Ag. Konstantínos; **4 June**, Análypsis; **24 June**, Ag. Ioánnis; **July–September**, Sými Festival, with big-name performers, especially music; **17 July**, Ag. Marína on the islet; **20 July**, Profítis Ilías; **6 August**, Nimborió and Panormítis; **15 August**, Panagías; **24 August**, Panagía, Nímos islet, and Panagía Alithiní; **8 November**, Taxiárchis at the monasteries of Panormítis and Roukouniótis.

Gialós and Chorió

Sými divides into down, up and over—Gialós around the harbour, Chorió, the older settlement high above, Kástro even higher, on the site of the ancient acropolis, and Pédi clustered round the bay over the hill. In **Gialós** , arrivals are greeted by the elaborate freestanding bell tower of Ag. Ioánnis, surrounded by *choklákia* pavements and most of Sými's tourist facilities, tavernas and gift shops. Harbour stalls sell sponges and local herbs, filling the air with the pungent scent of oregano and spices. In honour of the island's shipbuilding tradition and the signing of the Treaty of the Dodecanese, a copy of the trireme from Líndos has been carved into the rock with the inscription, 'Today freedom spoke to me secretly; Cease, Twelve Islands, from being pensive. 8th May, 1945'. The treaty was signed in the nearby restaurant Les Katerinettes. Behind the small recreation ground next to the bridge which links the two halves of the harbour, a neoclassical mansion houses the **Nautical Museum** (*open Mon–Sat, 10–3; adm*), with models of Sými's sailing ships, sponge-diving equipment, old photos and a stuffed heron.

At the end of the harbour, behind the clock tower and bronze statue of a boy fishing, the road leads to shingly **Nos Beach** via **Charani Bay**, still a small hive of industry where wooden caiques are being built or repaired while chickens strut about and cats lurk under the beached prows. Heavily bombed during the Second World War, many of the houses here are now being renovated in traditional Sými style with elegant plasterwork in blues, greys, yellows and Venetian red. **Nos**, complete with waterside taverna and sun-loungers, is a small strand popular with families. But it's also the first place the day-trippers hit, so it soon gets packed. It's better to walk further along the coastal path to the flat rocks and small coves popular with nudists on the way to **Nimborió**, a pretty tree-shaded harbour with a good taverna, loungers and a pebbly shore. Sand has been imported further round the bay to make **Zeus Beach** which also has a cantina.

Most of the neoclassical houses in Gialós date from the 19th century, while older architecture dominates in the **Chorió**. The lower part can be reached by road from the port or a slog up the 375 steps of the **Kalí Stráta**, a mansion-lined stairway which starts near the Kaloudoukas agency off Plateía Oekonómou, or Plateía tis Skálas, to reach the maze of narrow lanes of the high town. Worn smooth and slippery over the years, the steps can zap even the fittest in high summer, though local grannies trip up and down like mountain goats. The stairway can be sinister after dark: a torch is a must. In the centre of lower Chorió near the derelict windmills a **stone monument** was erected by the Spartans for their victory over the Athenians off the coast of Sými. On the headland overlooking Pédi Bay are the **Pillars of Sými**, dating from when the island was an important part of the Dorian Hexapolis.

Now mostly restored, the houses in Chorió are crammed together, often forming arches and vaults over the narrow lanes. They're built in the Aegean sugar-cube style, small and asymmetrical, but with neoclassical elements incorporated into their doorways and windows. Many houses have lovely interiors with carved woodwork and Turkish-style *moussándra*, beds on raised platforms or galleries. Among the most interesting buildings are the **19th-century pharmacy**, the fortress-mansion **Chatziagápitos** and the churches of **Ag. Panteleímon** and **Ag. Giórgios** with their pebble mosaics of evil mermaids sinking hapless ships. The island's **museum** (© 71 114, *open Tues–Sun 10–2; follow the signs; adm*) houses icons, coins, pottery, a reconstructed 19th-century Symiot room and bits and bobs going back to the 5th century AD. Up at the top, the **Kástro** is on the site of the ancient acropolis; its Byzantine and medieval walls top a temple of Athena; the coat of arms belongs to d'Aubusson. Within the fortifications the church of **Megáli Panagía** has good frescoes and post-Byzantine icons. The orginal church was blown up by the Germans when they discovered an arms cache. As a memorial, one of the church bells is made from the nose-cone of a bomb.

Around Sými

From Chorió it's a half-hour walk downhill to **Pédi** (ΠΕΔΙ) along a shady avenue of eucalyptus trees. The most fertile area of the island, there are smallholdings along the way, herds of goats, a few donkeys and fig trees in the fields. A small sandy beach and boatyard plus excellent taverna await to the left where the road forks, while to the right past the church you'll find rooms to let and a more developed beach with cafés and the Pedi Beach Hotel. Pédi is pretty, with typical fishermen's cottages edging the bay. From here you can follow the left-hand path up over the headland to **Ag. Marína** with a chapel-topped islet within swimming distance, site of a famous secret school before the War of Independence broke out. Water taxis from Pédi buzz to the 18th-century church of **Ag. Nikólaos** with its shingly tree-fringed beach and cantina. Otherwise follow the goat-track, marked with red paint, which begins to the far right of the bay, up and over the headland.

A road from Chorió goes to the southern tip of the island and Sými's main attraction, the vast 18th-century **Monastery of Taxiárchis Michael Panormítis**, set against a backdrop of cypresses and pine. In summer tourist boats from Rhodes descend on it for an hour at 11am, making for massive crowds. Archangel Michael of Panormítis Bay is Sými's patron, favourite of Greek sailors and goal of pilgrimages throughout summer—hence the seaside guest rooms, where the underwear of Greek families flaps by signs demanding modest dress. The monastery's landmark neoclassical bell-tower was built in 1905; its *choklákia* courtyard is strewn with flags; the church, coated with smoke-blackened frescoes, has, on a remarkable **iconostasis**, the stern, larger-than-life silver-plated icon of St Michael, painted by Ioánnis of the Peloponnese in 1724. Taxiárchis Michael is a busy archangel: at once heaven's generalissimo, slayer of the satanic dragon, weigher of souls (one of his names on Sými is *Kailiótis* because of the pain he brings mortal hearts) and patron saint of the Greek Air Force, he can also be called upon in storms and induces fertility. You can hardly miss the gold and silver ship ex votos and the wax babies left behind by the grateful faithful.

There are two small **museums,** one filled with more rich gifts from sailors: model ships and prayers in bottles which miraculously found their way to Panormítis bearing money for the monastery; Chinese plates and ivories donated by Symiots living in Africa; stuffed crocodiles, a weasel and mongoose. The second contains household furnishings, and the radio for British commandos operated by the abbot and two members of the Resistance, who were executed by the Germans in 1944. Outside, there's a small shop/*kafeneíon* with miserable service, a bakery selling white and 'brawn' bread, a decent taverna with wonderful sunset views (with a memorial to the abbot), a small sandy beach and an army barracks. You can walk in the woods surrounding the monastery, or follow the forest trail to the pebbly beach at **Marathoúnda** with resident goats.

Sesklí, the islet facing Panormítis, also belongs to the monastery. Its ancient name was Teutlousa, and Thucydides writes that it was here that the Athenians took refuge after their defeat by the Spartan navy during the Peloponnesian War. A few Pelasgian walls remain, and there are also a few ruins on the nearby islet **Strongilós**. There are regular barbecue trips from Gialos to Sesklí, which has a long pebbly beach shaded with tamarisk trees, and crystal waters. There are also trips to the islet of **Nímos**, a stone's throw from the Turkish coast.

The energetic can join organized walks overland while the more laid-back can sample ouzo or retsina on board lovely old caiques like the *Tríton* on round-island trips. Sými has 77 churches, many dedicated to Archangel Michael. One of the most interesting is **Michael Roukouniótis**, an hour's walk from Gialós. Built in the 18th century, it is a curious combination of Gothic and folk architecture, and holds its feast day beneath an old umbrella-shaped cypress. **Ag. Emiliános** is on an islet in the bay of the same name, connected to the shore by a causeway with a pleasant pebbly beach nearby. On the east coast, best reached by caique, **Ag. Giórgios** has a tree-shaded sandy beach and **Nánou Bay** has an excellent shingly one, fringed by trees, another favourite barbecue spot. There's a small chapel and masses of wild herbs. Other beaches include **Faneroméni** opposite Panormítis and the scenic bay of **Ag. Vassílis**, a two-hour-plus walk across the island.

Arnáki se Filo (Lamb in Filo Parcels)

Some of the smarter restaurants on Sými and the other Dodecanese prepare lamb in this delicious way. Serves four with a green vegetable or salad.

> *4 boneless lamb leg steaks, about ¾ inch thick (or 8 medallions of lamb cut from a loin), trimmed and shaped neatly and seasoned with pepper*
>
> *2 tbs butter or oil*
>
> *2 small onions, sliced thinly*
>
> *1 clove garlic, crushed*
>
> *8 sheets filo pastry*
>
> *$^1/_3$ cup melted butter*
>
> *2 tomatoes, medium sized, peeled and sliced*
>
> *1 tsp oregano*
>
> *100g feta cheese, cut in 4 slices*
>
> *parsley for garnish*

Heat butter or oil in a frying pan and brown steaks quickly on each side without cooking through. Set aside on a dish. Add onions to pan and fry on low heat until transparent, add garlic, and set aside.

Preheat oven to 200°C (400°F). Brush a sheet of filo pastry with melted butter, place another sheet on top and brush again with butter. Fold in half to make a filo square. Cover with a dry tea towel, then one dampened with warm water. Repeat with remaining filo so you have four squares (keep them covered while you work, to prevent the pastry from drying). Take one square and brush top with butter. Place a lamb steak (or two medallions) in the centre and lightly season with salt. Top with onion-garlic mixture, two slices of tomato, oregano, salt and pepper and a slice of feta. Bring up sides of filo pastry and double-fold over top. Fold in ends as you would a package then tuck ends underneath and place on a buttered baking tray. Repeat with remaining ingredients. Brush tops and sides of packages with melted butter and bake for 15 minutes. Garnish with parsley and serve immediately.

Sými ✉ *85600,* ✆ *(0241–)*   **Where to Stay and Eating Out**

Most of the island's accommodation is in Gialós but there are rooms to let in Chorió and Pédi. Kalodoukas Holidays, ✆ 71 077, ☎ 71 491, at the foot of the Kalí Stráta has character property to let, an excursion programme and a book exchange; Sými Tours, ✆ 71 307/689, ☎ 72 292, has villas and rooms to rent. Sými is very expensive in July and August. Cheaper rooms are often let on condition that you stay three nights or more to economize on sheet-washing. Beware cockroaches in high season. There's no campsite on Sými but unofficial camping is tolerated on remote beaches.

Gialós

The old municipal **Nereus**, ✆ 72 400, ☎ 72 404 (*C; exp–mod*) has been sympathetically restored and wonderfully painted in traditional colours; a few doors along, the elegant **Aliki**, ✆/☎ 71 665 (*A; lux–exp*) and **Dorian**, ✆ 71 181, ☎ 72 292 (*A; lux–exp*) up the steps just behind are two of the most stylish places to stay, both old sea captains' mansions, lovingly restored with fine wood interiors. The Aliki has a roof garden, and air-conditioning in some rooms; the Dorian has self-catering studios. **Grace**, ✆ 71 415 (*B; exp–mod*) is in another traditional house and has recently added smart studios; the **Opera House**, ✆ 71 856, ☎ 72 035 (*A; exp–mod*) has lovely family suites with air-conditioning set back from the harbour.

There are several small pensions and rooms to let in the quiet backwater beyond the town hall. Other options are the tatty but cheap and cheerful old **Glafkos**, ✆ 71 358, ☎ 76 800 (*inexp*); the **Egli**, ✆ 71 392 usually just open in high season; **Kokona** and next door **Maria**, ✆ 71 549 (*C; inexp*) are nicer. For stunning views over the harbour, especially at night, **Les Katerinettes** takes some beating, ✆ 71 676/413, or try the scenic **Katerina's Rooms**, with kitchen facilities ✆ 71 813. On the other side of Gialós **Albatross**, ✆ 71 707, ☎ 72 257 (*C; mod*), is a good choice.

The eateries in Sými fall into two categories: really good and genuine, and tourist traps along the harbour. In the back streets beyond the bank, **Meraklis** is one of the island's most authentic tavernas with excellent Greek home cooking and reasonable prices. The **Neraida** has delicious untouristy food at budget prices; next door, **Milopetra** offers a four-course

6000dr menu with a French touch (*evenings only*). **Hellenikon**, just back from the bridge, serves unusual *mezédes* and 140 kinds of Greek wine.

Over the bridge, **Taverna Yiannis** is another good place where you might hear impromptu Greek music, near the town hall and a few doors along. Out on the headland, restaurant **O Tholos** has an impressive menu in a romantic setting and great fresh grills. Old favourite **Les Katerinettes** is back under original management: don't miss the octopus and *pikilía* or selection of *mezédes*. You can send an e-mail home, or read the quality UK newspapers and magazines over baked potatoes or home-made chocolate cake at the **Vapori Bar** near the square.

Chorió

Horio, ✆ 71 800, ✉ 71 802 (*B; exp–mod, inc breakfast*) has been built in the traditional style with smart air-conditioned rooms and stunning views; surrounded by fields plus goats and donkeys, **Taxiarchis**, ✆ 72 012, ✉ 72 013 (*C; mod*) is an elegant neoclassical development, family-run apartments with a small bar, breakfast terrace, and breathtaking panorama of Pédi.

In upper Chorió the **Metapontis**, ✆ 71 491 (*B; exp–mod*) is in a very old Sými house cleverly converted to keep many of the traditional features like the *moussandra* sleeping gallery. Lower down the village **Fiona**, ✆ 72 088, is a comfortable bed and breakfast, and the owner plays the *sandouri*. Inexpensive rooms can also be arranged through the affable **Jean and Tonic** bar, ✆ 71 819. **Georgio's Taverna** is an institution at night, famous for exquisite Sými shrimps and the man himself on the accordion.

Pédi

A few rooms to let plus the **Pedi Beach**, ✆ 71 870, ✉ 71 982 (*exp–mod*), usually booked solid. There are several eateries but **Taverna Tolis** on the beach next to the boat yard is best for food and atmosphere.

Nimborió

If you really want to get away from it all, **Taverna Metapontis**, ✆ 71 820, at Nimborió has rooms to let, besides being a pretty spot for lunch; their taxi boat *Panagióta* will take you back to Gialós.

Entertainment and Nightlife

Sými buzzes at night, the lights from the houses and the bars reflecting their colours in the harbour like stained glass. The island's old *ouzerie* **Paco's** is still an institution but has a rival in smart new **Elpida**, doing traditional *mezédes* across the water in Mouragio. Nightlife revolves around three bars off the square, popular with locals and tourists alike. **Mina's** and rival **Vapori** next door, popular with yachties and up-market Brits, are both good bars but seem to be fighting an endless duel to haul in clientèle. For less conspicuous rivalry and conflicting sounds head for laid-back **Meltemi Bar**, the excellent Τεμβελα Σκαλα ('Lazy Steps') along the harbour where locals sometimes play traditional Greek music if the mood takes them.

The yachting crowd and sophisticated night owls head for the **Roof Garden**, which also does snacks, for mellow sounds and romantic views. You can bop at **The Club**, the new dancing bar in Gialós, or go to real bouzouki nights with traditional music and dance at the **Alethini Taverna** on the road to Pédi. Futher along, the **Valanidia** also has bouzouki with top singing stars in high season. There are a few bars in Chorió but friendly **Jean and Tonic** caters for locals as well as tourists and still reigns supreme for early outdoors happy hour and late nightcaps.

A Day Trip to Datça

One time Dorian capital and now small time Turkish resort, Datça is built around a horseshoe bay. It has beaches, but there are better ones further west along its peninsula, and local tour operators will happily sail you to them. They will also take you to ancient Cnidus.

Cnidus, at the very tip of the peninsula, was the headquarters of the Dorian Hexapolis. In ancient times, it was famous for a statue of Aphrodite by the great Praxiteles, modelled on the renowned courtesan Phryne (whose name means 'toad', although she once won a court case by baring her breasts before the judges). This first 3-D female nude was originally commissioned by Kos, but the islanders were too prudish to keep such a bombshell, and Cnidus picked it up. The city made the 'Aphrodite of Cnidus' the main tourist attraction along the coast, set in a special temple so the statue could be easily viewed from all angles, while a lusty crew of prostitute priestesses cared for every need of the devotees. The base of the statue has recently been discovered in the circular foundations of a Corinthian temple. The streets of Cnidus were laid out in a grid over a number of terraces; the walls and Hellenistic theatre are the best preserved of the remains. The lovely statue of Demeter in the British Museum came from here, and although excavations are still under way no one has yet located the observatory of Eudoxos, a native of the city, student of Plato and pioneer in astronomy and geometry.

Tílos (ΤΗΛΟΣ)

Remote Tílos has been one of the best-kept secrets in the Dodecanese for some time, with good unspoiled beaches, friendly people and wonderful walking country, a tranquil and authentic antidote to Kos and Rhodes. Although at first

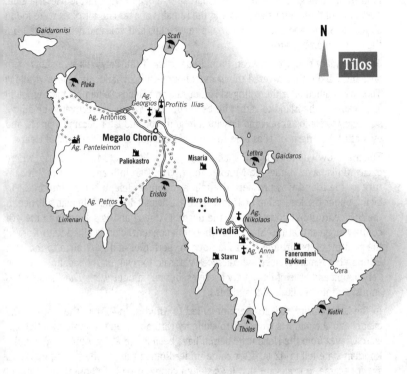

glance the island looks rugged and barren, inland it shelters groves of fig trees, almonds, walnuts, pomegranates and olives, and small farms growing all kinds of vegetables and tobacco, watered by fresh springs. It's even a lot cheaper than neighbouring islands like Sými. The harbour, Livádia, isn't the prettiest you'll ever find but it has a certain charm that soon grows on you. Village life goes on with few concessions to tourism, although it's beginning to trickle in: a package holiday programme, a few day trips and hydrofoil links with other islands have inspired a bit of new holiday development. But so far there's nothing overwhelming. It's as fine a place as any to do nothing; a dreaminess surrounds all practical activities and the visitor who neglects to wind his watch is in danger of losing all track of time.

History

Tílos was joined to Asia Minor six million years ago. When it broke away *c.* 10,000 years ago elephants were trapped on the island and adapted to the limited supply of food by shrinking. In the Grotto of Charcadio, a deep ravine in the Mesaria area, the bones of these mini-elephants and the remains of deer and tortoises were found alongside Stone Age pottery. Nearby, pumice cliffs and volcanic debris came from the eruption on Níssyros.

The legendary struggle between Poseidon and the Titan Polyvotis sent showers of lava and fall-out that covered the island's now fertile lowlands. In later mythology Tílos was named after the youngest son of Alia and Helios. When his mother fell ill Tílos came to the island to gather herbs to cure her. When she recovered he built a sanctuary to Helios Apollo and Poseidon in gratitude and later became a priest, and ever after the priests of Tílos bore the title of Hierapoli or Holy Servants of Helios.

The main town up to early Christian times was the Kástro at Megálo Chorió, where excavations have discovered Minoan and Mycenaean influences. In the 7th century BC the island was prosperous enough to found Gela, a colony important to Sicily, under the leadership of Tilinis. Tílos participated in the Athenian alliance in the 5th century but coins bearing the head of Athena and Poseidon from the 4th century suggest that the island was then independent, closely allied with Kos. At the summit of its fortunes it was famous for perfumes and gave birth to the poet Erinna, 'the female Homer' whose work was said to rival that of Sappho. She died very young and little of her poetry survives, but her famous work *The Distaff* gives an insight into her life and friendships.

In the 3rd century BC Tílos became allied to Rhodes. In 226 BC the walls of the citadel and the temples were destroyed in an earthquake and restored by a rich citizen. Graves from the Hellenistic period have been found at Ag. Antónis. When the Rhodian state fell in 42 BC Tílos came under Roman rule; in the subsequent dark age it became so irrelevant that it was often confused with Teftlousa, the island of Sesklí near Sými.

History returns to Tílos when the Knights of St John took over in 1309. They strung seven castles across the island and withstood a number of Turkish attacks from 1320 until 1522. In the 17th century Venetian admirals and Christian pirates raided the island to get back at the Turks; what bits survived these attackers fell prey to raiders from Mýkonos and Spétses from 1821 onwards in the name of the Greek Revolution. Tílos was taken by the Italians in 1912, by the Germans in 1943, when all the island's livestock was destroyed, and finally became part of Greece in March 1948.

Tílos in the 1990s is *the* Green island of the Dodecanese. The mayor of Tílos, a member of Greenpeace, has just banned hunting on the island, declaring it a wildlife refuge in violent opposition to local hunters. In 1997 it hosted a major Mediterranean environmental conference (not bad at all for an island with a permanent population of 300), attracting the likes of Gina Lollobrigida but forced to make do without its expected guest of honour, the late Jacques Cousteau.

By sea: once or twice a week to Níssyros, Kos, Kálymnos, Astypálaia, Páros, Piraeus, Léros, Lipsí, Pátmos, Náxos, Sýros, Kastellórizo, Sými and Rhodes. **By hydrofoil**: regular links with Rhodes, Níssyros, Kos, Kálymnos, Sými and Chálki. **Port authority**: ✆ 44 350.

By road: there's a regular **bus** service from Livádia to Megálo Chorió, Ag. Antónis and Éristos. You can also hire **mopeds** and **motorbikes**. If you see a yellow taxi in high season it'll be an Athens cabbie on holiday. You could try and flag him down. Otherwise you're on foot, but Tílos is good for walkers, with plenty of tracks.

Stefanákis Travel, ✆ 43 310/44 360, ✉ 44 315, on the steps to the left of the quay, are helpful with information on ferries, hydrofoils and accommodation; they also sell Tílos' traditional music on cassette. **Tílos Travel**, ✆ 53 259, also has information and rents out motorbikes and motorboats.

Festivals

Tílos is known for its ancient music played on the **sandoúri** and violin, dances and elaborate costumes. **17 January**, Ag. Antónis at Megálo Chorió; **28 June**, Ag. Pávlos; **25–27 July**, huge three-day festival or *panegýri*, Ag. Panteleímon at monastery; **28 July and 8 November**, Taxiárchis at Megálo Chorió, dance of the Koúpa; **15 August**, Panagías, Mikró Chorió.

Livádia and Megálo Chorió

There used to be nine villages on the island, but only the port **Livádia** (ΛΙΒΑΔΙΑ) and the capital Megálo Chorió are inhabited, and Livádia only since the 1930s. Popular with Greek families in high season, it has a tree-fringed pebble beach and water clear as gin. Village life revolves around the little central square, near a couple of embryonic supermarkets and an excellent bakery selling wonderful pastries. Spirits are fed by the pretty blue and white church of **Ag. Nikólaos** right on the waterfront. Further along the beach road the tiny early Christian basilica of **Ag. Panteleímon and Polýkarpos** is worth a visit for its mosaic floor. **Ag. Anna**, further back on the hillside, has 13th-century frescoes. At the far side of the bay the little sheltered harbour of **Ag. Stéfanos** is popular with yachts. The track from the harbour leads over the headland to the pebbly beach at **Lethrá**, about an hour's walk away, quiet even in August. Fishermen may take you out to the other beaches: two red sandy coves opposite Gaidaros islet, and Ag. Nikólas Bay to the north.

Megálo Chorió (ΜΕΓΑΛΟ ΧΩΡΙΟ), 8km uphill from Livádia, stands on the site of ancient Tílos and near the castle you can see Pelasgian walls built by the earliest known residents (if you discount the elephants) dating back to 1000 BC. The castle or Kástro was built by the Venetians, who incorporated a Classical gateway and stone from the ancient acropolis, once crowned by a temple to Pythian Apollo and Polias Athena. The pretty whitewashed village has a maze of alleys and flower-filled gardens and looks over a fertile plain, once famous for its almond trees. The town hall has the key to the church of **Archangel Michael** (1826) with a little double Arabic arch and other bits built into the walls and a 16ft Hellenistic wall just behind; its fine iconostasis has the silver icon from the original Taxiárchis church in the Kástro. Festivals are held in the courtyard on 8 November and 28 July when women dance the ancient dance of the *koúpa* or cup. The small **museum** contains elephant bones and a video about the island, accompanied by an ancient song by Erinna. Houses going back to the 7th century BC have been found above in the **Kastro**, currently the subject of state-financed restorations.

The road meanders down to the long sandy beach at **Éristos** (ΕΡΥΣΤΟΣ). At the far end you can go for an all-over tan. Further north is the deserted village of **Mikró Chorió** and the cave by a river gully where the bones of pygmy elephants, just 4ft high, were discovered in 1971. They coexisted with stone age dwellers, but it seems that the humans eventually killed them off some time around 4000 BC—the last elephants in Europe. With its amphitheatre of ruined houses the village looks sad—the owners took their roofs with them when they moved down to Livádia in the 1950s.

The old church of **Timía Zóni** has charming 18th-century frescoes and the newer church, a pink confection, is the hub of celebration on August 15 when the village comes alive again for the Assumption of the Virgin Mary. There are stunning views from the ghost town and the churches of **Sotíras**, **Ag. Elesas** and **Prodrómos** have 15th-century frescoes. The area is local famous for a plant called *rouvia* used to dye Easter candles red; its gathering is the subject of an ancient ritual, in which children play the part of Lazarus and hide under twigs until told to rise from the dead; the game is to hop up before before hopped on.

From Megálo Chorió the road runs to windswept **Ag. Antónios** which has a grotty beach, the island's one gas pump (*open afternoons only, 3–5*), a small chapel and an enormous tamarisk tree in the square. The main attraction along the beach is Tílos' other fossils—the petrified remains of human skeletons 'baked' into the rock, thought to belong to sailors caught in the lava when when Níssyros erupted in 600 BC. A rough track leads to the isolated beach at **Pláka**, while another winds its way up into the mountains to the lovely Byzantine **Monastery of Ag. Panteleímon**, founded in 1407, with red pantiled roof, set in a lush oasis of shady trees and gushing water. The fortified monastery, defended by a tall stone tower and even taller cypresses, is perched more than 660ft above the west coast with a breathtaking panorama. It has fine 15th-century frescoes, including one of the founder holding the monastery in his hand and others of Paradise, and a beautiful old marble drinking-fountain fringed by pots of basil. The bus driver arranges trips up on Sundays; the sunsets are superb.

Tílos ✉ *85002, ☎ (0241–)*   **Where to Stay and Eating Out**

An accommodation booth by the quay opens when the ferries and hydrofoils arrive. Everyone on Tílos seems to own at least a hundred goats, which provide the main ingredient of the local speciality, kid stuffed with rice, herbs, tomatoes and chopped liver and baked in the oven.

Livádia

There are plenty of small pensions and rooms in Livádia plus a few hotels, some newly built. **Irini**, ☎ 44 293, ✆ 44 238 (*C; mod*) has been tastefully tricked out in ethnic style and is set back from the beach in lovely gardens. Pleasant **Eleni**, ☎ 44 062, ✆ 44 063 (*mod*) is new blue and white and right on the beach, with minibus service. **Marina Beach**, a 20-minute walk around the bay at Ag. Stéfanos, ☎ 44 064, is another excellent bet, if a bit far-flung, but does good food. The smart **Panorama Studios**, ☎/✆ 44 365 (*mod*), perched on the hillside above the village, have great views from the flower-filled terrace. The same management also runs the **Olympus Apartments** near the beach.

The family-run **Castellos Beach**, ☎ 44 267 (*mod*) has luxurious, modern rooms with fridges and fans overlooking the sea; in the village **George's Apartments**, ☎ 44 243, are also comfortable with kitchen facilities. **Livadia**, ☎ 52 202 (*E; inexp*), has ceiling fans and is just behind the square; **Stefanakis Apartments**, ☎ 44 310/360, ✆ 44 315, behind the bakery, are also a comfortable option with daily maid service. Other budget pensions and rooms worth trying include **Stamatia**, ☎ 53 255, on the beach, **Rena**, ☎ 44 274, and **Pension Perigiali**, ☎ 53 398.

On the row of rooms to let at the western end of the beach **Spiros**, ☎ 53 339, has private bathrooms; **Paraskevi**, ☎ 53 280, and **Stamatis**, ☎ 53 334, have shared facilities. The food is better than average in Livádia. For fish and seafood the **Trata** in the village is first choice, but a bit pricier than most. The **Blue Sky Taverna** above the jetty has wonderful harbour views; for good Greek home cooking head for **Irina** right on the beach, popular with the locals, which has a wide choice of dishes and cheap beer. Great for lunch with tables on the sand shaded by trees; or follow the Brits to roadside **Sophia** which also has excellent food and friendly service.

Other good eateries include **Kostas**, beneath Stefanákis Travel; **Michaelis** which specializes in spit roasts; **Meraklis** for chicken, *souvláki*, etc. next door to the supermarket. **Kafeneion Omonia** is very Greek and good for cheap breakfast and snacks, although food can be scarce at night; it's also the place for a pre-dinner ouzo.

Megálo Chorió

In Megálo Chorió, **Sevasti**, ✆ 53 237 (*inexp*) has budget rooms next door to the Kali Kardia Taverna; or **Miliou Apartments**, ✆ 21 002, ✉ 44 204, in the village centre has pleasant rooms with a traditional touch set in a lush garden. There's even an aviary full of budgies for company. All the tavernas are good; from friendly **Konstantina's** terrace you can watch the hawks floating over the valley below.

Éristos

Eristos Beach Apartments, ✆ 44 336, ✉ 44 024 (*inexp*) are simple, but all have fans and verandas. Set back from the beach, the **Nausika Taverna** also has inexpensive but comfortable rooms, while at the roadside the **Tropicana Restaurant**, ✆ 53 242, is a peaceful haven in a tropical garden with chalet-type rooms. It is good for fresh seafood and local vegetable dishes served in a rose-covered arbour. There is no official campsite on Tílos, but most people camp here.

Ag. Antónis

The **Hotel Australia**, ✆ 53 296 (*D; inexp*), is immaculate and run by Greek-Australian brothers who meet guests from the ferry. The **Delfini Fish Restaurant** is owned by fishermen; they also do stuffed kid.

Entertainment and Nightlife

Nightlife in Tílos centres on the tavernas and bars. People sit in the square at **Yiorgo's** or the **Omonia** for an after-dinner coffee or nightcap. **La Luna Bar** on the quay plays music and attracts the young.

Night owls can head for deserted **Mikró Chorió** where a group of friends have set up a unique dancing bar in an old restored house. They have put lights in the ruins to give the impression that the village has come alive. Action begins at midnight, with rock until 1.30 am and afterwards Greek, and the dancing often goes on until dawn. Daybreak views over Livádia take some beating—and there are no neighbours to complain about the noise.

Greek holds a special place as the oldest spoken language in Europe, going back at least 4000 years. From the ancient language Modern Greek, or Romaíka, developed into two forms: the purist or *katharévousa*, literally 'clean language', and the popular, or Demotic *demotikí*, the language of the people. But while the purist is consciously Classical, the popular is as close to its ancient origins as say, Chaucerian English is to modern English. These days few purist words are spoken but you will see the old *katharévousa* on shop signs and official forms. Even though the bakery is called the *foúrnos* the sign over the door will read ΑΡΤΟΠΟΛΕΙΟΝ, bread-seller, while the general store will be the ΠΑΝΤΟΠΟΛΕΙΟΝ, seller of all. You'll still see the pure form on wine labels as well.

At the end of the 18th century, in the wakening swell of national pride, writers felt the common language wasn't good enough; archaic forms were brought back and foreign ones replaced. Upon independence, this artificial construction called *katharévousa* became the official language of books and even newspapers. The more vigorous Demotic soon began to creep back; in 1901 Athens was shaken by riots and the government fell when the New Testament appeared in *demotikí*; in 1903 several students were killed in a fight with the police during a *demotikí* performance of Aeschylus. When the fury subsided, it looked as if the Demotic would win out by popular demand till the Papadópoulos government (1967–74) made it part of its 'moral cleansing' of Greece to revive the purist. *Katharévousa* was the only language allowed in schools and everything had to be written in the pure form. The great debate was settled in 1978 when Demotic was made the official tongue.

Greeks travel so far and wide that even in the most remote places there's usually someone who speaks English, more likely than not

Language

with an American, Australian or even South African drawl. On the other hand, learning a bit of Greek can make your travels more enjoyable. Usually spoken with great velocity, Greek isn't a particularly easy language to pick up by ear. But even if you have no desire to learn Greek, it is helpful to know at least the alphabet—so that you can find your way around—and a few basic words and phrases.

Greekspeak

Sign language is an essential part of Greek life and it helps to know what it all means. Greekspeak for 'no' is usually a click of the tongue, accompanied by raised eyebrows and a tilt of the head backwards. It could be all three or a permutation. 'Yes' is usually indicated by a forward nod, head tilted to the side. If someone doesn't hear you or understand you properly they will often shake their heads from side to side quizzically and say '*Oríste?*' Hands whirl like windmills in conversations and beware the emphatic open hand brought sharply down in anger. A circular movement of the right hand usually implies something very good or in great quantities. Women walking alone might hear hissing like a demented snake emanating from pavement cafés. This will be the local Romeos or *kamákis* trying to attract your attention.

Greeks also use exclamations which sound odd but mean a lot, like *po, po, po!* an expression of disapproval or derision; *brávo* comes in handy for praise while *ópa!* is useful for whoops! look out! or watch it!; *sigá sigá* means slowly, slowly; *éla!*, come or get on with you, *kíta!* look. Other phrases you'll hear all the time but won't find in your dictionary include:

paréa	gang, close friends	*listía*	rip-off
pedhiá	guys, the lads	*alítis*	bum, no-good person
ré, bré	mate, chum, slang for friends	*palikári*	good guy, brave, honourable
endáxi	OK	*pedhí mou/*	my boy/my girl
malákka	rude, lit. masturbator, used	*korítsi mou*	
	between men as term of endearment	*yasoo koúkla/os*	Hi doll, hello gorgeous
kéfi	high spirits, well-being	*etsi íne ee zoí*	that's life!
kaïmós	the opposite, suffering, sad	*ti na kánoume*	what can we do!
lipón	well, now then	*kaló taxídhi*	good trip, Bon Voyage!
hérete	formal greeting	*kalí órexi*	Bon appetit!
sto kaló	go with God, formal parting		

The Greek Alphabet

Pronunciation			English Equivalent	Pronunciation			English Equivalent
A	α	*álfa*	short 'a' as in 'father'	N	ν	*ni*	n
B	β	*víta*	v	Ξ	ξ	*ksi*	'x' as in 'ox'
Γ	γ	*gámma*	guttural g or y sound	O	o	*ómicron*	'o' as in 'cot'
Δ	δ	*délta*	hard th as in 'though'	Π	π	*pi*	p
E	ε	*épsilon*	short 'e' as in 'bet'	P	ρ	*ro*	r
Z	ζ	*zíta*	z	Σ	σ	*sigma*	s
H	η	*íta*	long 'e' as in 'bee'	T	τ	*taf*	t
Θ	θ	*thíta*	soft th as in 'thin'	Υ	υ	*ípsilon*	long 'e' as in 'bee'
I	ι	*yóta*	long 'e' as in 'bee'; sometimes like 'y' in 'yet'	Φ	φ	*fi*	f
K	κ	*káppa*	k	X	χ	*chi*	German ch as in 'doch'
Λ	λ	*lámtha*	l	Ψ	ψ	*psi*	ps as in 'stops'
M	μ	*mi*	m	Ω	ω	*oméga*	'o' as in 'cot'

Dipthongs and Consonant Combinations

AI	αι	short 'e' as in 'bet'
EI	ει, OI οι	'i' as in 'machine'
OY	ου	*oo* as in 'too'
AY	αυ	*av* or *af*
EY	ευ	*ev* or *ef*
HY	ηυ	*iv* or *if*
ΓΓ	γγ	*ng* as in 'angry'
ΓΚ	γκ	hard 'g'; *ng* within word
NT	ντ	'd'; *nd* within word
ΜΠ	μπ	'b'; *mp* within word

Useful Phrases

Yes	*né/málista* (formal)	Ναί /Μάλιστα
No	*óchi*	Οχι
I don't know	*then xéro*	Δέν ξέρω
I don't understand... (Greek)	*then katalavéno... (elliniká)*	Δέν καταλαβαίνω...(Ελληνικά)
Does someone speak English?	*milái kanis angliká?*	Μιλάει κανείς αγγλικά?
Go away	*fíyete*	Φύγετε
Help!	*voíthia!*	Βοήθεια!
My friend	*o fílos moo* (*m*)	Ο φίλος μου
	ee fíli moo (*f*)	Η φίλη μου
Please	*parakaló*	Παρακαλώ
Thank you (very much)	*evcharistó (pára polí)*	Ευχαριστώ (πάρα πολύ)
You're welcome	*parakaló*	Παρακαλώ
It doesn't matter	*thén pirázi*	Δέν πειράζει
OK, alright	*endaxi*	Εντάξι
Of course	*vevéos*	Βεβαίος
Excuse me, sorry	*signómi*	Συγγνώμη
Pardon? Or, from waiters, what do you want?	*oríste?*	Ορίστε ?
Be careful!	*proséchete!*	Προσέχεται!
Nothing	*típota*	Τίποτα
What is your name?	*pos sas léne?* (*formal*)	Πώς σάς λένε?
	pos se léne?	Πώς σέ λένε?
How are you?	*ti kánete?* (*formal/pl*)	Τί κάνεται?
	ti kanis?	Τί κάνεις?
Hello	*yásas, hérete* (*formal/pl*)	Γειάσας, Χέρεται
	yásou	Γειάσου
Goodbye	*yásas, hérete* (*formal/pl*)	Γειάσας, Χέρεται
	yásou, adío	Γειάσου, Αντίο
Good morning	*kaliméra*	Καλημέρα
Good evening/good night	*kalispéra/kaliníchta*	Καλησπέρα /Καληνύχτα
What is that?	*ti íne aftó?*	Τί είναι αυτό?

What?	tí?	Τί;
Who?	piós? (m), piá? (f)	Ποιός; Ποιά;
Where?	poo?	Ποιός;
When?	póte?	Πότε;
Why?	yiatí?	Γιατί;
How?	pos?	Πώς;
I am/ You are/He, she, it is	íme/íse/íne	Είμαι /Είσε /Είναι
We are/ You are/They are	ímaste/ísaste/íne	Είμαστε /Είσαστε /Είναι
I am lost	échasa to thrómo	Εχασα το δρόμο
I am hungry/I am thirsty	pinó/thipsó	Πεινώ /Διψώ
I am tired/ill	íme kourasménos/arostos	Είμαι κουρασμένος /άρρωστος
I am poor	íme ftochós	Είμαι φτωχός
I love you	s'agapó	Σ΄αγαπώ
good/bad/so-so	kaló/kakó/étsi kétsi	καλό /κακό /έτσι κ΄έτσι
slowly/fast	sigá sigá/grígora	σιγά σιγά / γρήγορα
big/small	megálo/mikró	μεγάλο /μικρό
hot/cold	zestó/crío	ζεστό /κρίο

Shops, Services, Sightseeing

I would like...	tha íthela...	Θά ήθελα...
where is...?	poo íne...?	Πού είναι...?
how much is it?	póso káni?	Πόσο κάνει?
bakery	foúrnos/artopoleion	φούρνος /Αρτοπολείον
bank	trápeza	τράπεζα
beach	paralía	παραλία
church	eklisía	εκκλησία
cinema	kinimatográfos	κινηματογράφος
hospital	nosokomío	νοσοκομείο
hotel	xenodochío	ξενοδοχείο
hot water	zestó neró	ζεστό νερό
kiosk	períptero	περίπτερο
money	leftá	λεφτά
museum	moosío	μουσείο
newspaper (foreign)	efimerítha (xéni)	εφημερίδα (ξένη)
pharmacy	farmakío	φαρμακείο
police station	astinomía	αστυνομία
policeman	astifílakas	αστιφύλακας
post office	tachithromío	ταχυδρομείο
plug, electrical	príza	πρίζα
plug, bath	tápa	τάπα
restaurant	estiatório	εστιατόριο
sea	thálassa	θάλασσα
shower	doush	ντούς
student	fititís	φοιτητής
telephone office	Oté	ΟΤΕ
theatre	théatro	θέατρο
toilet	tooaléta	τουαλέττα

Time

What time is it?	*ti óra íne?*	Τί ώρα είναι
month/week/day	*mína/evthomáda/méra*	μήνα /εβδομάδα /μέρα
morning/afternoon/evening	*proí/apóyevma/vráthi*	πρωί /απόγευμα /βράδυ
yesterday/today/tomorrow	*chthés/símera/ávrio*	χθές /σήμερα /αύριο
now/later	*tóra/metá*	τώρα /μετά
it is early/late	*íne norís/argá*	είναι νωρίς/αργά

Travel Directions

I want to go to …	*thélo na páo sto (m), sti (f)…*	Θέλω νά πάω στό, στη…
How can I get to…?	*pós boró na páo sto (m), sti (f)…?*	Πώς μπορώ νά πάω στό, στη…?
Where is…?	*poo íne …?*	Πού είναι…?
How far is it?	*póso makriá íne?*	Πόσο μακριά είναι
When will the… come?	*póte tha érthi to (n), ee (f), o (m)…?*	Πότε θά έρθη τό, ή, ό…?
When will the… leave?	*póte tha fíyí to (n), ee (f), o (m)…?*	Πότε θά φύγη τό, ή, ό…?
From where do I catch…?	*apó poo pérno…?*	Από πού πέρνω…?
How long does the trip take?	*póso keró pérni to taxíthi?*	Πόσο καιρό πέρνει τό ταξίδι?
Please show me	*parakaló thíkste moo*	Παρακαλώ δείξτε μου
the (nearest) town	*to horió (to pió kondinó)*	Το χωριό (το πιό κοντινό)
here/there/near/far	*ethó/ekí/kondá/makriá*	εδώ /εκεί /κοντά /μακριά
left/right	*aristerá/thexiá*	αριστερά /δεξιά
north/south	*vória/nótia/anatoliká/thitiká*	βόρεια /νότια /ανατολικά /δυτικά

Driving

where can I rent …?	*poo boró na nikiáso …?*	Πού μποπώ νά νοικιάσω …?
a car	*éna aftokínito*	ένα αυτοκινητο
a motorbike	*éna michanáki*	ένα μηχανάκι
a bicycle	*éna pothílato*	ένα ποδήλατο
where can I buy petrol?	*poo boró nagorásso venzíni?*	Πού μπορώ ν'αγοράσω βενζίνη?
where is a garage?	*poo íne éna garáz?*	Πού είναι ένα γκαράζ?
a mechanic	*énan mihanikó*	έναν μηχανικό
a map	*énan chárti*	έναν χάρτη
where is the road to…?	*poo íne o thrómos yiá…?*	Πού είναι ο δρόμος γιά…?
where does this road lead?	*poo pái aftós o thrómos?*	Πού πάει αυτός ο δρόμος?
is the road good?	*íne kalós o thrómos?*	Είναι καλός ο δρόμος?
EXIT	*éxothos*	ΕΞΟΔΟΣ
ENTRANCE	*ísothos*	ΕΙΣΟΔΟΣ
DANGER	*kínthinos*	ΚΙΝΔΥΝΟΣ
SLOW	*argá*	ΑΡΓΑ
NO PARKING	*apagorévete ee státhmevsis*	ΑΠΑΓΟΡΕΥΕΤΑΙ Η ΣΤΑΘΜΕΥΣΙΣ
KEEP OUT	*apagorévete ee ísothos*	ΑΠΑΓΟΡΕΥΕΤΑΙ Η ΕΙΣΟΔΟΣ

Numbers

one	*énas* (m), *mía* (f), *éna* (n)	ένας, μία, ένα
two	*thío*	δύο
three	*tris* (m, f), *tría* (n)	τρείς, τρία
four	*téseris* (m, f), *téssera* (n)	τέσσερεις, τέσσερα
five	*pénde*	πέντε
six	*éxi*	έξι
seven/eight/nine/ten	*eptá/ októ/ ennéa/ théka*	επτά/οκτώ/εννέα/δέκα
eleven/twelve/thirteen	*éntheka/ thótheka/ thekatría*	έντεκα/δώδεκα/δεκατρία
twenty	*íkosi*	είκοσι
twenty-one	*íkosi éna* (m, n) *mía* (f)	είκοσι ένα, μία
thirty/forty/fifty/sixty	*triánda/ saránda/ penínda/ exínda*	τριάντα/σαράντα/ πενήντα/εξήντα
seventy/eighty/ninety	*evthomínda/ ogthónda/ enenínda*	ευδομήντα/ ογδόντα/ ενενήντα
one hundred	*ekató*	εκατό
one thousand	*chília*	χίλια

Months/Days

January	*Ianooários*	Ιανουάριος
February	*Fevrooários*	Φεβρουάριος
March	*Mártios*	Μάρτιος
April	*Aprílios*	Απρίλιος
May	*Máios*	Μάιος
June	*Ioónios*	Ιούνιος
July	*Ioólios*	Ιούλιος
August	*Avgoostos*	Αύγουστος
September	*Septémvrios*	Σεπτέμβριος
October	*Októvrios*	Οκτώβριος
November	*Noémvrios*	Νοέμβριος
December	*Thekémvrios*	Δεκέμβριος
Sunday	*Kiriakí*	Κυριακή
Monday	*Theftéra*	Δευτέρα
Tuesday	*Tríti*	Τρίτη
Wednesday	*Tetárti*	Τετάρτη
Thursday	*Pémpti*	Πέμπτη
Friday	*Paraskeví*	Παρασκευή
Saturday	*Sávato*	Σάββατο

Transport

the airport/aeroplane	*to arothrómio/ aropláno*	τό αεροδρόμιο /αεροπλάνο
the bus station/bus	*ee stási leoforíou/ leoforío*	ή στάση λεωφορείου /λεωφορείο
the railway station/the train	*o stathmós too trénou/to tréno*	ό σταθμός τού τραίνου/τό τραίνο
the port/port authority	*to limáni/ limenarchío*	τό λιμάνι/λιμεναρχείο
the ship	*to plío, to karávi*	τό πλοίο, τό καράβι
the steamship	*to vapóri*	τό βαπόρι
the car	*to aftokínito*	τό αυτοκίνητο
a ticket	*éna isitírio*	ένα εισιτήριο

The Menu (ΚΑΤΑΛΟΓΟΣ)

Finding your way round a Greek menu, *katálogos*, takes some doing, but there's a basic layout with prices before and after local tax. You begin with Orektiká, ΟΡΕΚΤΙΚΑ; dishes cooked in olive oil are known as Laderá, ΛΑΔΕΡΑ; main courses are Entrádes, ΕΝΤΡΑΔΕΣ; Fish are Psária, ΨΑΡΙΑ; dishes with minced meat, Kimádhes, ΚΥΜΑΔΕΣ and things grilled or barbecued to order are either Psitá, ΨΗΤΑ or Tis Oras, ΤΗΣ ΩΡΑΣ.

Ορεκτικά (Μεζέδες)	Orektiká (Mezédes)	Appetisers
ελη̈́ες	eliés	olives
κοπανιστι (τυροσαλατα)	kopanistí (tirosaláta)	cheese purée, often spicy
ντολμάδες	dolmádes	stuffed vine leaves
μελιτζανοσαλατα	melitzanosaláta	aubergine/eggplant dip
ποικιλια	pikilía	mixed hors-d'œuvre
μπουρεκι	bouréki	cheese and vegetable pie
τυροπιττα	tirópitta	cheese pie
αξινι	eahíni	sea urchin roe (quite salty)
Σούπες	**Soópes**	**Soups**
αυγολέμονο	avgolémono	egg and lemon soup
χορτόσουπα	chortósoupa	vegetable soup
ψαρόσουπα	psarósoupa	fish soup
φασολαδα	fasolada	bean soup
πατσας	patsás	tripe and pig's foot soup (for late nights and hangovers)
Λαδερά	**Laderá**	**Cooked in Oil**
μπαμιες	bámies	okra, ladies' fingers
γιγαντες	yígantes	butter beans in tomato sauce
μπριαμ	briám	aubergines and mixed veg
φασόλακια	fasólakia	fresh green beans
φακή	fakí	lentils
Ζυμαρικά	**Zimariká**	**Pasta and Rice**
πιλάφι, ρυζι	piláfi/rizi	pilaf/rice
σπαγκέτι	spagéti	spaghetti
μακαρόνια	macarónia	macaroni
Ψάρια	**Psária**	**Fish**
αστακός	astakós	lobster
καλαμαρια	kalamaria	squid
χτάπόδι	chtapóthi	octopus
γαρίδες	garíthes	prawns (shrimps)
ξιφιας	ksifías	swordfish
μαρίδες	maríthes	whitebait
συναγρίδα	sinagrítha	sea bream
φαγρι	fangri	bream
σαρδέλλα	sardélla	sardines
σκουμβρι	skoumbri	mackerel
στρείδια	stríthia	oysters
λιθρίνια	lithrínia	bass
μιδια	mídia	mussels

Αυγά	Avgá	Eggs
ομελέττα μέ ζαμπόν	omeléta me zambón	ham omelette
ομελέττα μέ τυρί	omeléta me tirí	cheese omelette
αυγά τηγανιτά (μπρουγέ)	avgá tiganitá (brouyé)	fried (scrambled) eggs
άυγά και μπεικον	avgá kai bakón	egg and bacon

Εντραδεσ	Entrádes	Main Courses
κουνέλι	kounéli	rabbit
συκώτι	seekóti	liver
μοσχάρι	moschári	veal
αρνι	arní	lamb
λουκάνικο	lukániko	sausage
κατσυκι	katsíki	kid
κοτόπουλο	kotópoulo	(roast) chicken
χοιρινό	chirinó	pork

Κυμάδεσ	Kymadhes	Minced Meat
παστίτσιο	pastítsio	mince and macaroni pie
μακαρόνια με κυμά	makarónia me kymá	spaghetti Bolognese
μπιφτεκι	biftéki	hamburger, usually bunless
σουτζουκάκια	soutzoukákia	meatballs in sauce
μελιτζάνες γεμιστές	melitzánes yemistés	stuffed aubergines/eggplants
πιπεριές γεμιστές	piperíes yemistés	stuffed peppers

Της Ωρας	Tis Oras	Grills to Order
μπρισολα	brisóla	beefsteak with bone
μπριζόλες χοιρινές	brizólas chirinés	pork chops
σουβλάκι	souvláki	meat or fish kebabs on a skewer
παιδακια	paidakia	lamb chops
κεφτέδες	keftéthes	meat balls

Σαλάτες	Salátes	Salads and Vegetables
ντομάτες	domátes	tomatoes
αγγούρι	angoúri	cucumber
ρώσσικη σαλάτα	róssiki saláta	Russian salad
σπανακι	spanáki	spinach
χοριάτικη	choriátiki	salad with feta cheese and olives
κολοκυθάκια	kolokithákia	courgettes/zucchini
πιπεριεσ	piperiés	peppers
κρεμιδι	kremídi	onions
πατάτες	patátes	potatoes
μαρούλι	maroúli	lettuce
αγκιναρες	angináres	artichokes

Τυρια	Tiriá	Cheeses
φέτα	féta	goat's cheese
κασέρι	kasséri	hard buttery cheese
γραβιέρα	graviéra	Greek 'Gruyère'
μυζήθρα	mizíthra	soft white cheese
προβιο	próvio	sheeps' cheese

Γλυκά	Glyká	Sweets
παγωτό	pagotó	ice cream
μπακλαβά	baklavá	nuts and honey in filo pastry
γιαούρτι (με μελι)	yiaoúrti (me méli)	yoghurt (with honey)

| ρυζόγαλο | *rizógalo* | rice pudding |
| μπουγάτσα | *bougátsa* | custard tart |

Φρούτα — **Fróóta** — Fruit

πορτοκάλι	*portokáli*	orange
ροδι	*ródi*	pomegranate
μήλο	*mílo*	apple
κερασι	*kerási*	cherry
ροδάκινο	*rothákino*	peach
πεπόνι	*pepóni*	melon
καρπούζι	*karpoúzi*	watermelon
ακτινιδι	*aktinídi*	kiwi
σύκα	*síka*	figs
σταφύλια	*stafília*	grapes
μπανάνα	*banána*	banana
βερύκοκο	*veríkoko*	apricot
φραουλεs	*fráoules*	strawberries

Miscellaneous

ψωμί	*psomí*	bread
βούτυρο	*voútiro*	butter
μέλι	*méli*	honey
μαρμελάδα	*marmelátha*	jam
αλάτι	*aláti*	salt
πιπέρι	*pipéri*	pepper
ζάχαρη	*záchari*	sugar
λάδι	*láthi*	oil
λεμόνι	*lemóni*	lemon
πιάτο	*piáto*	plate
μαχαίρι	*mahéri*	knife
πηρούνι	*piroóni*	fork
κουτάλι	*koutáli*	spoon
λογαριασμό	*logariasmó*	the bill/check

Drinks

άσπρο κρασί	*áspro krasí*	wine, white
ασπρο/κοκκινο/κοκκινελι	*áspro/kókkino/kokkinéli*	white/red/rosé
ρετσίνα	*retsína*	wine, resinated
νερό (βραστο/μεταλικο)	*neró (vrastó /metalikó)*	water (boiled/mineral)
μπύρα	*bíra*	beer
χυμόs πορτοκάλι	*chimós portokáli*	orange juice
γάλα	*gála*	milk
τσάί	*tsái*	tea
σοκολάτα	*sokoláta*	chocolate
καφε	*kafé*	coffee
φραππε	*frappé*	iced coffee
παγοs	*págos*	ice
ποτίρι	*potíri*	glass
μπουκαλι	*boukáli*	bottle
καραφα	*karáfa*	carafe
στήν γειά σαs!	*stín yásas (formal, pl)*	to your health! Cheers!
στήν γειά σου!	*stín yásou (sing)*	

Glossary of Terms

acropolis — fortified height, usually the site of a city's chief temples

agíos, agía, agii — saint or saints, or holy abbreviated **Ag.**

ágora — market and public area in a city centre

amphora — tall jar for wine or oil, designed to be shipped (the conical end would be embedded in sand)

áno/apáno — upper

caique — a small wooden boat, pronounced '*kaEEki*' now mostly used for tourist excursions

cella — innermost holy room of a temple

choklakía (or **hokalaía**) — black and white pebble mosaic

chóra — simply, 'place'; often what islanders call their 'capital' town, although it usually also has the same name as the island itself

chorió — village

dimarchíon — town hall

EOT — Greek National Tourist Office

epachía — Orthodox diocese; also a political county

exonarthex — outer porch of a church

heroön — a shrine to a hero or demigod, often built over the tomb

iconostasis — in an Orthodox church, the decorated screen between the nave and altar

kalderími — stone-paved pathways

kástro — castle or fort

katholikón — monastery chapel

káto — lower

kore — Archaic statue of a maiden

kouros — Archaic statue of a naked youth

larnax — a Minoan clay sarcophagus resembling a bathtub

límani — port

limenarchíon — port authority

loutrá — hot spring, spa

megaron — Mycenaean palace

metope — sculpted panel on a frieze

meltémi — north wind off the Russian steppe that plagues the Aegean in the summer

moní — monastery or convent

monopáti — footpath

narthex — entrance porch of a church

néa — new

néfos — smog

nísos/nísi — island/islands

nomós — Greek province

OTE — Greek national telephone company

paleó — old

panagía — Virgin Mary

panegýri — Saint's feast day

pantocrátor — the 'Almighty'—a figure of the triumphant Christ in Byzantine domes

paralía — waterfront or beach

períptero — street kiosk selling just about everything

pírgos — tower, or residential mansion

pithos (pithoi) — large ceramic storage jar

plateía — square

skála — port

spílio — cave or grotto

stoa — covered walkway, often lined with shops, in an *ágora*

temenos — sacred precinct of a temple

tholos — conical Mycenaean temple

Note: Page numbers in *italics* refer to maps.

Index

Also Available from Cadogan Guides...

Country Guides

Antarctica
Belize
The Caribbean and Bahamas
Central Asia
China: The Silk Routes
Egypt
France: Southwest France;
    Dordogne, Lot & Bordeaux
France: Southwest France;
    Gascony & the Pyrenees
France: Brittany
France: The South of France
France: The Loire
Germany
Germany: Bavaria
Greece: The Greek Islands
Guatemala
India
India: South India
India: Goa
Ireland
Ireland: Southwest Ireland
Ireland: Northern Ireland
Italy
Italy: The Bay of Naples and Southern Italy
Italy: Lombardy, Milan and the Italian Lakes
Italy: Tuscany and Umbria
Italy: Three Cities—Rome, Florence and Venice
Japan
The Yucatán and Southern Mexico
Morocco
Portugal
Portugal: The Algarve
Scotland
Scotland's Highlands and Islands
South Africa
Spain
Spain: Southern Spain
Spain: Northern Spain
Syria & Lebanon
Tunisia
Turkey
Zimbabwe, Botswana and Namibia

City Guides

Amsterdam
Brussels, Bruges, Ghent & Antwerp
Florence, Siena, Pisa & Lucca
London
Manhattan
Moscow & St Petersburg
Paris
Prague
Rome
Venice

Island Guides

NE Caribbean; The Leeward Is.
SE Caribbean; The Windward Is.
The Caribbean: Jamaica
Crete
Cyprus
Mykonos, Santorini & the Cyclades
Corfu & the Ionians
Madeira & Porto Santo
Malta
Sicily

Lazy Days

Lazy Days Out across the Channel
Lazy Days Out in Tuscany
Lazy Days Out in Provence
Lazy Days Out in Andalucía
Lazy Days Out in the Loire
Lazy Days Out in the Dordogne & Lo

Plus...

Southern Africa on the Wild Side
Healthy Travel: Bugs, Bites & Bowe
Travel by Cargo Ship
Henry Kelly in the West of Ireland
London Markets
Mars
Hell